RECOLLECTIONS OF THE
EARLY REPUBLIC

Selected Autobiographies

RECOLLECTIONS OF THE EARLY REPUBLIC

Selected Autobiographies

Edited by
Joyce Appleby

Northeastern University Press
Boston

Northeastern University Press

Library of Congress Cataloging-in-Publication Data
Recollections of the early republic : selected
autobiographies / edited by Joyce Appleby.
p.   cm.
Includes bibliographical references (p.   ).
Contents: John Ball, 1794–1884—Daniel Drake,
1785–1852—Julia Anne Hieronymus Tevis,
1799–1879—Charles Ball, 1785[?]–1837—Chester Harding,
1792–1866—Lucy Fletcher Kellogg, 1793–1878—Chauncey
Jerome, 1793–1868—Allen Trimble, 1783–1870—Harriet B.
Cooke, 1786–post-1858—Alfred M. Lorrain, 1790–1860.
ISBN 1-55553-301-9 (pb : alk. paper). —
ISBN 1-55553-302-7 (cloth : alk. paper)
1. United States—History—1783–1865—Biography.
2. Autobiographies—United States.
I. Appleby, Joyce Oldham.
E339.R35   1997
920.073—dc21
[B]   96-48086

Designed by Joyce C. Weston

Composed in Slimbach by Coghill Composition, Richmond,
Virginia. Printed and bound by Maple Press, York,
Pennsylvania. The paper is Sebago Antique, an acid-free stock.

MANUFACTURED IN THE UNITED STATES OF AMERICA
01   00   5   4   3   2

$\mathcal{A}$CKNOWLEDGMENTS

I would like to thank the John Simon Guggenheim Memorial Foundation as well as the American Antiquarian Society and the Society for Eighteenth Century Studies for the support that made possible this study of autobiographies in the early Republic.

CONTENTS

CONTENTS

INTRODUCTION

~ ℸ ~

*T*H E men and women whose autobiographies are featured in this collection were part of a very special generation. Born between 1783 and 1800, they grew up with the newly united states. Too late to participate in the War for Independence or in the ratification of the Constitution, their lives paralleled the initial years of the country created by the Revolution and the Constitution. As a cohort—men and women living in the same span of time—they shared the experience of being the firstborn Americans.

Although they did not know each other, the autobiographers had much in common. Had they met one another in old age, they could have reminisced about the same things: the fervor aroused by the French Revolution, which split their leaders into antagonistic Federalist and Republican camps; General Anthony Wayne's victory over the confederated Indian tribes at Fallen Timbers, which opened up the upper Ohio River valley for American settlers; the outpouring of grief at the death of George Washington; the Haitian revolt that created the first black republic; the Richmond theater fire of 1811 with its seventy-one fatalities; and Lafayette's triumphal tour through the states in 1825–26. They could have marveled again at the Hudson River voyage of the *Clermont*, the first successful steamboat; the Cain Ridge revival meeting, which drew upwards of 20,000 persons; or the solar eclipse in 1806, when the total darkness of a June morning sent birds flying back to their roosts.

Although this cohort arrived on the American scene after the successful conclusion of the War for Independence, its legacy affected their lives profoundly. The Revolution had launched a new nation; or rather, as one contemporary said of the Constitution, Americans now had a "roof for a new united states." It remained for this generation to fill in the walls and furnish the rooms. Interestingly, the men and women born after Independence felt a peculiar urgency to discuss what the nation stood for. Unlike their parents, never being forced to revoke an earlier loyalty to Great Britain, they were much freer to imagine what the United States might become. They were also conscious of not having participated in those revolutionary events whose celebration marked their childhoods. All around them were men and women who had fought in the war or had run the farm for an absent spouse or parent or had committed to a boycott or had hidden farm produce from marauding British troops. Every Fourth of July, aging veterans retold their stories of the hardship winter at Valley Forge, of the devastation at the siege of Charleston, and of the glorious victory at Yorktown. There was no escaping the Revolutionary heritage.

Psychologically, experiencing a major event is different from learning about it from others. The cohort born after 1783 had to deal with the American assertion of independence as an earthshaking success, which created for them both a noble past and a great public responsibility. Their youth was suffused with politics because the 1790s ushered in a decade of fierce, partisan disputes as the country's leaders—the old Revolutionary elite—began to argue over the meaning of the American Revolution. Heirs to a national tradition that was longer on rhetoric than years, the first American generation grew up amidst intense curiosity and worried concern about democratic governance in a world still filled with monarchies.

Perhaps the most enduring legacy of the Revolution for this generation was the affirmation "We hold these truths to be self-evident, that all men are created equal, that they are endowed by their Creator with certain unalienable rights, that among these are Life, Liberty, and the pursuit of Happiness." Enslaved Americans—a significant twenty-four percent of the population in 1790, according to the first census—recognized in these philosophical propositions the basis of their own claims for inclusion in the new nation and began to agitate for recognition. Many free Americans felt troubled by the contradiction between slavery and the lofty principles of liberty and equality that shored up the nation's legitimacy. This widely felt contradiction found a focus, north and south, in political campaigns against slavery. The system of coerced labor that had been introduced into the British colonies with scarcely a murmur from moralists in the seventeenth century suddenly appeared a stain to be removed.

Because so many Americans took natural rights literally, they responded to the chance to end slavery by repealing the state laws in the North which created property in human beings. This success in replacing slave codes with statutes providing for the gradual emancipation of enslaved men and women marked a democratic triumph. Starting with Pennsylvania in 1780 and ending twenty years later with New Jersey, the northern states, one by one, removed the legal support for slavery. These legislative actions also institutionalized a deep division in the country at the very moment when the states had agreed to form "a more perfect union" by ratifying the Constitution. The old surveyors' boundary between Maryland and Pennsylvania, the Mason-Dixon line, became a potent symbol of the divide between the realms of freedom and of slavery.

For many Americans, the contradiction between slavery and freedom had a political parallel in the efforts of the Federalist elite to establish an energetic national government removed from popular politics. While many northern Federalists took the lead in antislavery activities, they rejected the idea that ordinary men—the shopkeepers, carpenters, teamsters, and sailors in their midst—should play any part in governing. Finding this reassertion of upper-class control repellent, many ordinary Americans drew inspiration from the French Revolution, whose leaders called for "liberty, equality, and fraternity." The French Revolutionaries' embrace of newness suggested that the American novelty of democratic society, rather than being proof of provincial oddity, was a harbinger of things to come. The lowering of property qualifications brought many poorer white men into the realm of citizenship. As the partisan turmoil of the 1790s demonstrated, these men did not just want to vote; they wanted to experience full political participation—gathering in public meetings, debating matters of policy, and forming parties to mobilize fellow citizens. In 1800 when they succeeded in electing their champion, Thomas Jefferson, as president, the white men of the country's voting population changed American politics forever.

Jefferson more than fulfilled the Republicans' expectations when he decreased the size of government, reduced taxes, and established land offices in the West. The westward movement of families away from eastern centers of authority and refinement—which Federalists had so feared—began in earnest. Land sales soared, going from 67,751 acres in 1800 to 497,939 in 1801 and totaling over 500,000 in both 1805 and 1806. The trickle of families that followed Daniel Boone through the Cumberland Gap to Tennessee and Kentucky in the 1790s grew to a stream, even though their move brought settlers into constant and violent interaction with Native Americans. New Englanders—the most mobile of all people—were more likely to go north to Vermont and Maine or west to the New York frontier, but some pushed on further to Pittsburgh, where they could buy a raft and float downriver to the settlements on the banks of the Ohio. Meanwhile Southerners, in parallel columns of migration, swept west to Alabama, Mississippi, and Louisiana, the last of which had just been bought for the nation in 1803.

Like the release of a tightly coiled wire, Americans sprang out of their settled states, moving in a variety of directions—into new communities, into new occupations, into new churches. At the end of Jefferson's years as president, a greater proportion of the American population lived on the frontier than at any other time in our history, before or since. In the decades that followed Jefferson's election, the meaning of a democratic political order became manifest.

Equally unexpected in these years was the growth of a free black population. Many African-American men had won their freedom by fighting in the Continental Army. Others were manumitted by Southern owners or else benefited from the gradual emancipation in the North. Self-liberation added to their numbers as more and more men and women learned how to make their way to the free states. Gathered in the cities for the most part, the black members of the first American generation created the churches, newspapers, and schools for a vibrant, if fragile, African-American society. They also aroused a new strain of racial prejudice, which found expression in violent attacks upon the homes and shops of African Americans who dared to assert their right to participate in American public life.

During George Washington's first administration under the Constitution, an upturn in the Atlantic economy brought an end to the long post-Revolutionary depression. With the pall of the depression lifted, the new government moved swiftly to address national needs. Continued population growth in Europe raised the price of all foodstuffs and created strong incentives for American farmers to plant for the market. More and more of them, even in frontier areas, were drawn into the international trade networks of the Atlantic. Simultaneously thousands of new manufacturing ventures provided domestic markets for the produce of American farms. In 1793 Eli Whitney's invention of the cotton gin made it profitable to grow short, staple cotton for the English textile industry, triggering a Southern expansion that paced the grain-farming frontier of the North. Meanwhile the outbreak of war in Europe brought American merchants and shipmasters a whole new trade as "neutral carriers" for the belligerent nations. So rewarding was this shipping that, for the first time, the wealth of the North surpassed that of the staple-producing South.

Equally impressive was the laying out of new towns and the growth of old cities, especially those in the mid-Atlantic states. Communities mushroomed on the frontier while older towns, with growth rates of over fifty percent per decade, were newly fashioned in terms of people, institutions, and construction. Commerce set the pace for development in the first three decades of the nineteenth century as merchants and shopkeepers scoured the rural hinterlands for food, fibers, and skins that could be sold to manufacturers for processing, then turned around and offered for sale as textiles, tools, printed works, and household goods issued from the new factories.

With commerce came an intensified flow of information as well as goods. Having fewer than 100 newspapers to choose from in 1790, by 1810 Americans were buying twenty-two million copies of 376 papers annually—even though the country had only eight million people, half below the age of sixteen and one-fifth enslaved and forbidden to read— the largest aggregate circulation of newspapers of any country in the world! Ten years later, the number of newspapers published in America had more than doubled, along with the size of the literate public. The French philosophe, Pierre Samuel Dupont, reported that a large portion of the American public reads the Bible, but all of the nation, he said, "assiduously peruses the newspapers. The fathers read them aloud to their children while the mothers are preparing the breakfast." Postal riders became the crucial link in the communication chain of rural America. While the population was doubling, the number of post offices increased 30-fold, from 75 to 2,300, and the number of miles of post roads grew 23-fold, from 1,875 to 44,000. Fifty years earlier there had been only private libraries, in the great houses of gentlemen. Now the wide diffusion of learning forced ordinary readers to evaluate the sources of information and opinion. As one dejected Federalist noted, "knowledge has induced the laity to think and act for themselves."

The profits from foreign trade and cotton spread rapidly throughout the American states, filling thousands of pockets with just enough money to finance a new venture—whether it was getting a teaching post, starting a store, investing in an invention, buying supplies for a frontier stake, venturing a cargo to the West Indies, buying a slave, or making a bid for personal freedom. The digest of patents that the first commissioner of patents put together reveals just how quickly American ingenuity began to change the rural landscape, with inventions in metallurgy, chemical processes, and civil engineering, and in the technologies for grinding mills, hydraulic implements, machine tools, and household conveniences. Never had so many people in one society entered the ranks of enterprise with such unabated zeal for the hard work of attaining a material goal. From an accountant's point of view, young Americans were poor, reckless, and debt-prone, but they were ready to risk their futures on change, and not all the prudence of the ages could have stopped them.

The European wars that brought great prosperity to American shippers and farmers also plunged the nation into a twenty-year diplomatic struggle. Because they were fighting France's archenemy, Great Britain, Americans had received substantial help from the French monarchy in their War for Independence. When the French Revolution provoked another general European war, the United States found itself caught between its alliance with France and its dependence upon British trade. As France and England became more and more tightly wound into all-out war, the new American republic found it harder and harder to avoid being dragged into the conflict, especially since its merchant ships were carrying the foodstuffs and supplies which each belligerent wished to deny its enemy. Attacked on the high seas at various times by each of the principal antagonists, the United States found its policy of neutrality difficult to maintain.

Jefferson applied an embargo to avoid war; his successor, President James Madison, tried playing one country off against the other, but to no avail. In 1812, the United States again went to war against Great Britain, this time to defend its scope of action, its citizens and their property, and its boundaries. The War of 1812 brought British fleets to bombard the Atlantic seaboard cities, British armies to burn down Washington, D.C., and long and costly campaigns on and around the Great Lakes. When peace came after eighteen months of fighting, few disputes had been settled, but the sons and grandsons of Revolutionary War veterans had been given a chance to show their military mettle in defense of American liberties. While the war created a whole new crop of heroes, its conclusion triggered another wave of settlement along the western frontier, pushing the frontier line eighty-three miles westward in just ten years.

Even more profound than the toppling of upper-class political leadership or the thickening of market connections in the United States was the transformaton of American religion. Protestant churches, established by law, had dominated spiritual and ceremonial life in the colonial period, but after the Revolution proponents of religious freedom began a long campaign to end state support for religion. At the same time, Baptists and Methodists, who had never enjoyed official standing, began proselytizing aggressively, particularly on the frontier, where people were living without any churches. Circuit riders reached out to new converts, sometimes gathering the "awakened" in great camp meetings like the one at Cain Ridge, Kentucky, in 1801 where some 20,000 people listened to gospel preaching for five days running. As if by spontaneous combustion, religious enthusiasm erupted across the land, with many fired up ministers creating entirely new Protestant denominations. Spurning the genteel religious routines of the learned clergy, the revivalists used innovative techniques to bring sinners to Christ and, once won, leave them with confidence in their own unaided ability to discover Christian doctrine. In their sermons, the radical preachers attacked hierarchical ecclesiastical structures as well as the Calvinists' preoccupation with damnation.

Like the popularization of national politics, this surge of vital religion led to the Christian conversion of hundreds of thousands of men and women, black and white, Northern and Southern. The "mushroom candidates" ridiculed by the Federalists had their analogues in the backwoods preachers who took religion to the unchurched. Hundreds of youthful, uneducated, revivalist ministers nurtured the people's spiritual longings while spreading lessons about individual empowerment that echoed the Republicans' political message. Here was another form of liberation for ordinary Americans, who responded by deserting the Congregational, Presbyterian, and Episcopal Churches and flocking to the evangelizers. The proportion of preachers to laymen rose from 1 in 1,500 at the time of the Revolution to 1 in 500 thirty years later. Within twenty years the Methodist and Baptist Churches had become the most popular in the North, the South, and the West, while other denominations in the United States did not escape the influence of the evangelical movement and its emphasis upon personal conversion.

The single most striking feature of social life in the years following Jefferson's election was the proliferation of voluntary associations, a phenomenon that gave the United States its lasting reputation as a nation of joiners. Societies formed in large cities and rural villages alike. The zeal for self-improvement found outlets in debating and study clubs, a particular favorite among young adults. Sometimes people cooperated to build circulating libraries. Fire societies, along with other mutual benefit associations, multiplied with the growth of cities. Likewise, almost all religious denominations had auxiliaries. Women were unusually active in this new associational life as the principal organizers for the provision of charity and relief from suffering. Every town had its Female Domestic Missionary Society and its Home for Friendless Women.

The formation of new voluntary associations was limited only by the reigning social imagination. There was even an Association of American Patriots for the Purpose of Forming a National Character, started in 1808. The most common impulse promoting voluntary clubs was an urge to reform society—often prompted by a religious revival. Of these reformist impulses, first and most enduringly there was the temperance movement. Then there was reform of prisons and hospitals and Sabbatarianism. Later there was nativism and, most productive of reforming zeal, the antislavery movement. There were literally hundreds of antislavery societies, many flourishing in the South. These multifarious voluntary associations revealed an efficiency in mobilizing recruits and in circulating information that far exceeded anything done by public authority.

Where the educated elite had wish to establish national identity upon the basis of America's distinctive contributions to great literature and art or achievements in science and diplomacy, the reformers and revivalists were expressing a different sense of nationhood. For them the United States represented a new kind of social existence, where personal fulfillment came through public reform. The activists' optimism about concerted efforts to eliminate slavery, correct the treatment of the insane and criminal, reorganize charity, and raise the tone of public morals became a part of American character.

To understand the quality of the lives of America's first generation, it is important to remember that the country was economically primitive by any modern standard. Until the end of the 1820s, only those living on the nation's rivers could be sure of transportation—and then only in one direction. Roads did not go very far inland and were impassable in rainy months. In 1790, ninety percent of the population was engaged in farming, much of it of the most basic kind. Most people lived in very simple homes. Enslaved families were often crowded into barracks-like structures. Life expectancy was forty-five years for those white women and men who successfully made it to the age of twenty. For African Americans the picture was much bleaker, with life expectancy dropping as low as thirty-five. The American mortality rates of the eighteenth century, remarkably low, had taken a turn for the worse in the 1790s and continued high for the next hundred years while the new killers— tuberculosis, yellow fever, and cholera—took their terrible toll. Women in 1800 bore an average of seven children, with each delivery a threat to their health. Such high fertility made for a youthful nation; fifty-eight percent of America's population was under twenty in 1820, compared to forty-four percent in 1899 and thirty-two percent in 1950.

The amount that people worked also made life hard by current standards. As late as 1870, the average workday in a six-day week was slightly under ten hours. Wages, good by European standards, were far from generous when the cost of food, clothing, and shelter took eighty percent or more of a worker's wages. Average, unskilled laborers got seventy-five cents a day in the early part of the century, while frontier farm workers received even less for the backbreaking work of clearing the land. Hired-out slaves got comparable wages. It has been estimated that in New York City as late as the middle of the century not even one percent of the population annually earned the equivalent of $7,000 in 1980 dollars; but people take their bearings from what has gone before them, not from unimaginable, future attainments.

Although the country's total population tripled from just under four million in 1790 to almost thirteen million in 1830, only four percent of that total increase came from immigration. In 1820, the first year when such figures were gathered, just 8,385 immigrants entered the country, and only three percent of the population of ten million had been born outside the United States. Of the foreign-born increase that did occur, the greatest part resulted from enslaved Africans being brought to South Carolina, the center for the foreign slave trade until 1808 when the constitutional prohibition took effect.

Having been born into the rural simplicity that marked the lives of ninety percent of the people, the first generation of Americans grew up during a period of economic development that created a sizable urban population. The sharp pace of American economic development was set in large part by the number of people willing to connect with market enterprises. While some left the hamlets of their birth to secure a farm for themselves in the West, others gave up farming altogether and became drovers, storekeepers, peddlers, mechanics, schoolteachers, or professional men. Still others invented new products or new trades.

Writing an autobiography was one of the many novel activities of this period, and over 300 men and women in this cohort wrote one. By no means typical, these autobiographers are nonetheless representative of those Americans who left the place of their birth to try their hand at something new. Four characteristics mark those who wrote retrospective accounts. First, they had lived long enough to reach the stage of life when one looks back and ruminates about the past. Second, in their own eyes, they had achieved something of value. Third, they had witnessed great changes in the course of their lives. And finally, they usually had families—both children and grandchildren—urging them to commit to paper their stories of the olden days. Invariably having responded in early life to opportunities that took them away from their place of birth, the autobiographers record a common experience of making one's way in an utterly new world. The rites of passage into adulthood involved the literal passage away from home. As prosperous old-timers, triumphing over humble beginnings and the biblical dispensation of "three score years and ten," they viewed their lives as successes and took from their success a vindication of the path they had followed.

All of these autobiographies have strong story lines where fresh starts, unexpected encounters, and solemn resolutions are most salient. One might schematize the narratives as follows: the unforeseen break with childhood expectations; the wonder of a new life prospect; the encounters that teach moral lessons; the outcomes and observations. Most of the writers expressed the belief that their lives were memorable because their departure from home signaled a break with tradition. They perceived their careers to have been fashioned by choice. As they recorded those choices, they groped for an understanding of how to conduct one's life.

Only in the United States did the the creation of a new political order accompany the dramatic changes of the early industrial revolution. Only here did the decisions that individuals made about their personal lives play so large a part in shaping the character of public institutions. In the absence of a presiding upper class, an established church, or a fully articulated government, personal undertakings did the work of authority. And if these autobiographers are typical, early Americans quite unself-consciously mingled their private ambitions with public engagements. They practiced law, sought out land investments, developed mercantile operations while simultaneously serving in their legislatures, participating in revivals, organizing reform movements, and keeping in touch with peers who were equally involved in getting things done.

Successful Americans wrote about their country as the locus for potent exchanges of talents and riches. This blueprint of a functional, mobile, future-oriented society replaced the older picture of communities unified by a stable but static social order. Within this image of an improving America, the personal qualities of intelligence, honesty, commitment, and enterprise came to represent the personal forces that animated the social whole. Accordingly, the autobiographers served as models of innovation for a society losing a desire to replicate past ways of doing things. We could call these autobiographies a kind of cultural capital that was accumulating in America alongside the savings from industry. In the division of ideological labor, they supplied the empirical evidence to validate American free enterprise. Those Americans who entered the churning world of novelty left behind a settled way of life marked by limited horizons and prescribed rules. That these writings about successful breaks with the past were published in the years when vast numbers of young people were leaving the farm and the shop to move into factory employment may have helped mask the divestiture of hope in these later generations. The easy access to opportunity, the just reward of virtue, the irrepressible pluck in the face of adversity—so simply depicted in these first-person accounts from America's charter cohort—sank deep into public consciousness to become the qualities that defined America. The memories of the first generation of Americans outlasted the world in which they left their mark.

$\mathcal{F}$URTHER $\mathcal{R}$EADING

$\sim \tilde{\ell} \sim$

$\mathcal{F}$ O R material on American political developments in this period, see Richard Beeman et al., eds., *Beyond Confederation: Origins of the Constitution and American National Identity*, Chapel Hill, 1987; Joyce Appleby, *Capitalism and a New Social Order: The Republican Vision of the 1790s*, New York, 1984; Arthur Zilversmit, *The First Emancipation*, Chicago, 1967; Stanley Elkins and Eric McKittrick, *The Age of Federalism: The Early American Republic, 1789–1800*, New York, 1993; Noble Cunningham, *The Process of Government under Jefferson*, Princeton, 1978; and Norman K. Risjord, *Jefferson's America, 1760–1815*, Madison, 1991.

The impact of the Revolution upon African Americans can be followed in Ira Berlin, "The Revolution in Afro-American Life," in Alfred F. Young, ed., *The American Revolution: Explorations in American Radicalism*, De Kalb, 1976; Sylvia R. Frey, *Water from the Rock: Black Resistance in a Revolutionary Age*, Princeton, 1991; Sterling Stuckey, *Slave Culture: Nationalist Theory and the Foundations of Black America*, New York, 1987; and Gary B. Nash, *Forging Freedom: The Formation of Philadelphia's Black Community, 1720–1840*, Cambridge, 1988.

Information about the standard of living and life expectancy is presented in Andrew R. L. Cayton, "The Early National Period," in *Encyclopedia of American Social History*, vol. I, ed. Mary Kupiec Cayton, Elliott J. Gorn, and Peter W. Williams, New York, 1993; Clayne L. Pope, "The Changing View of the Standard-of-Living Question in the United States," in *American Economic Association Papers and Proceedings,* 83 (May 1993); Bureau of the Census, *Statistical Abstract of the United States,* Washington, D.C., 1992; and Warren S. Thompson, "The Demographic Revolution in the United States," in *Annals of the American Academy of Political and Social Sciences,* no. 262 (1949).

Economic and social change can be studied in Sean Wilentz, *Chants Democratic: New York City and the Rise of the American Working Class, 1788–1850,* New York, 1984; Howard B. Rock, *Artisans of the New Republic: The Tradesmen of New York City in the Age of Jefferson,* New York, 1979; William J. Baumol et al., *Productivity and American Leadership,* Boston, 1989; Henry L. Ellsworth, *A Digest of Patents Issued by the United States, from 1790 to January 1, 1839,* Washington, D.C., 1840; Kenneth Sokoloff, "Inventive Activity in Early Industrial America: Evidence from Patent Records, 1790–1846," in *Journal of Economic History,* 48 (1988); Malcolm Rohrbough, *The Land Office Business: The Settlement and Administration of American Public Lands, 1789–1837,* New York, 1968, and *The Trans-Appalachian Frontier,* New York, 1978; Robert E. Gallman and John Joseph Wallis, eds., *American Economic Growth and Standard of Living Before the Civil War,* Chicago, 1993; Nancy F. Cott, *The Bonds of Womanhood: "Women's Sphere" in New England, 1780–1835,* New Haven, 1977; Joan M. Jensen, *Loosening the Bonds: Mid-Atlantic Farm Women, 1750–1850,* New Haven, 1986; Mary P. Ryan, *Cradle of the Middle Class: The Family in Oneida County, New York, 1790–1861,* New York, 1981; Michael Grossberg, *Governing the Hearth,* Chapel Hill, 1985; Michael Tadman, *Speculators and Slaves: Masters, Traders, and Slaves in the Old South,* Madison, 1989; Stuart W. Bruchey, ed., *Small Business and American Life,* New York, 1980; Otto Mayr and Robert C. Post, eds., *Yankee Enterprise: The Rise of the American System of Manufactures,* Washington, D.C., 1981; Richard L. Bushman, *The Refinement of America: Persons, Houses, Cities,* New York, 1992; and Gavin Wright, *The Political Economy of the Slave South: Households, Markets, and Wealth in the Nineteenth Century,* New York, 1978.

The impact of printing, publishing, and literacy upon American society in this period is traced in William J. Gilmore-Lehne, *Reading Becomes a Necessity of Life,* Nashville and Knoxville, 1989; Frank Luther Mott, *American Journalism: A History of Newspapers in the United States through 250 Years, 1690–1940,* New York, 1947; Rosalind Remer, *Printers and Men of Capital: Philadelphia Book Publishers in the New Republic,* Philadelphia, 1996; Richard John, *Spreading the News: The American Postal System from Franklin to Morse,* Cambridge, 1995; Allen R. Pred, *Urban Growth and the Circulation of Information: The United States System of Cities, 1790–1840,* Cambridge, 1973; Mary Kelley, *Private Woman, Public Stage: Literary Domesticity in Nineteenth Century America,* New York, 1984; and Richard D. Brown, *Knowledge Is Power: The Diffusion of Information in Early America,* New York, 1989.

American religious developments are treated in Jon Butler, *Awash in a Sea of Faith: Christianizing the American People,* Cambridge, 1990; Edwin Gaustad, *Historical Atlas of America,* New York, 1962, and *A Religious History of America,* rev. ed., New York, 1974; Nathan Hatch, *The Democratization of American Christianity,* New Haven, 1989; Barbara Leslie Epstein, *The Politics of Domesticity: Women, Evangelism, and Temperance in the Nineteenth Century,* Middletown, 1981; Donald G. Matthews, *Religion in the Old South,* Chicago, 1977; and John B. Boles, *The Great Revival, 1787–1805,* Lexington, Ky., 1972.

The preponderance of autobiographies written in this period come from white, male New England ministers, most of them Methodists or Baptists. Women represent six percent of the total. Slightly less than eight percent were written by African-American men and women. All of the autobiographies listed in Louis Kaplan, ed., *A Bibliography of American Autobiographies,* Madison, 1961, are available on microfilm.

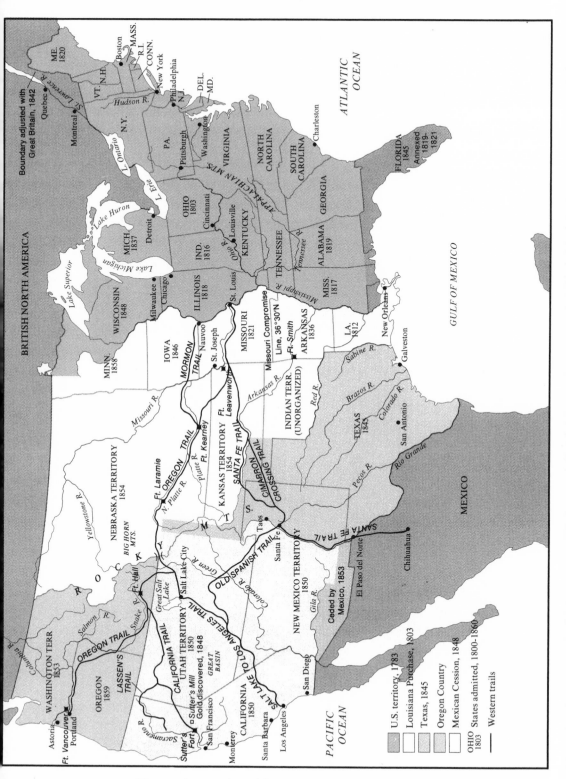

Westward expansion of the United States, 1800–1860.

JOHN BALL

1794–1884

*T*HE adventures of John Ball and his sister, Deborah, tell a lot about the kind of society America was becoming. Ball's father had been a part of an exodus of New Englanders who pushed into the hill country around Hebron, Vermont, during the last years of the Revolutionary War. Once a year, the senior Ball went to Boston to exchange his butter and cheese for manufactured items; otherwise, the family was entirely self-sufficient. The tenth of ten children, John Ball formed the intention of leaving home when he was a teenager, but he accepted without challenge his father's claim to his working time until age twenty-one. In his autobiography, Ball describes how he struggled with his father to gain more schooling until he was allowed to go to Groton where a clergyman kept "a kind of private school." His teacher then made the crucial decision to teach this frontier lad Latin, an intellectual attainment that enabled Ball to go on to Dartmouth. Mindful of the obligations he was born into, Ball struck a deal with an older brother to the effect that "if he would stay and provide well for our parents I would set up no claim from that source."[1]

John Ball's father lent him a bit of money during his college years, but remained unsympathetic to Ball's desire for more schooling, his own education having been limited to reading, writing, and ciphering. The

---

1. John Ball, *Autobiography of John Ball, 1794–1994*, compiled by his daughters: Kate Ball Powers, Flora Ball Hopkins, Lucy Ball (Grand Rapids, Michigan, 1925), pp. 12–14.

books at home included the Bible, Isaac Watts's *Hymns,* Noah Webster's *Spelling Book* "with its fables and accompanying pictures," Jedidiah Morse's *Geography,* and Daniel Adams's *Arithmetic*—not much as a library, but a telling testimony to the reach of New England literacy. More attractive a person in Ball's retrospective view is his mother. "My mother had never been to school at all," he explains, "but she . . . was very fond of reading, when she could obtain a book and had the time. She had naturally a fine mind, and was ever curious to learn all that could be, within her very limited means." The language of her family prayers, he recalled, was as "beautiful as was ever uttered by the most highly educated person."[2]

Ball's youthful encounters demonstrate that the early Republic was a "small world." His Dartmouth days coincided with the struggle over the institution's charter, which was resolved in the Supreme Court. When Ball himself went to Utica to be admitted to the New York bar, an eighty-year-old Aaron Burr was creating a stir by his appearance as one of the session's litigators. When Ball visited Washington, D.C., a few years later, he called on General Jackson at the White House. Although Ball had no introduction, Jackson "received me kindly," Ball remembers. He also details his visit of the same day to the Supreme Court, where Justice John Marshall was delivering his celebrated decision in the Cherokee case.[3]

Even more remarkable for the era, John's sister also formed a plan for escaping the rural penury of Hebron. Ball explains in his memoirs that Deborah possessed "a vigorous body and mind" and was quite self-reliant, learning the tailor's trade in order to get out on her own. She later moved to Lansingburgh, New York, after marrying William Powers, who started one of the country's first "floor oilcloth" manufacturing establishments. Crowned with quick success, William Powers built a five-story brick factory, only to perish the next year in a fire that destroyed it all. Saddled with an $8,000 debt, Deborah Ball Powers offered

---

2. Ball, *Autobiography,* p. 8.
3. Ball, *Autobiography,* pp. 20, 29, 46, 52.

her creditors the remains of the factory if they would extinguish the debt; but they refused, so she hired a housekeeper and took over the operation, doing all the designing and ornamenting herself. Ball, recently returned from a stint running a small, private school in Georgia, helped his sister run the business, traveling a circuit from Troy to New York to Philadelphia and Baltimore taking orders from linoleum samples. Reflecting on his sister's surprising competence, Ball recalls that "at first she seemed much to rely on me in all matters of business, but after a time she showed a readiness in taking a part in all the concerns of the establishment." Relieved of this responsibility, he was free to leave again.[4]

Ball continued to play the rolling stone. In early 1832 he joined Nathaniel Wyeth, an entrepreneur who had proved his mettle in the ice exporting business that flourished around Walden Pond, and who was organizing an expedition to Oregon. Wyeth had been inspired by the Pacific dreams of Hall Jackson Kelley, a New Hampshire schoolteacher and surveyor, who had become obsessed with the idea of colonizing in the far northwest even though, or perhaps because, that pristine area between the Mississippi and the Pacific had changed little since the days of Columbus.

Joining the Wyeth party in Baltimore, Ball got to ride on the longest stretch of railroad in the United States, from Baltimore to Frederick, Maryland. From Frederick the party followed the National Cumberland Road on foot to Pittsburgh, whence they took a boat to Cincinnati. Ever the fortunate traveler, Ball found himself in the company of Lyman Beecher, the most famous minister in the United States, who was just then en route to his rendezvous in the West to be the first president of Lane Theological Seminary.

From Cincinnati the Wyeth expedition passed on to a settlement of Mormons who had sought refuge the previous fall on the Illinois frontier. The last sight for the explorers, before plunging into the uncharted wil-

---

4. Ball, *Autobiography,* pp. 52–53, 55.

derness, was the progress of a steamboat carrying soldiers up the Mississippi to fight in the Black Hawk War. Two years later, Ball returned from Oregon by way of Cape Horn. With his typical luck, he managed to get a job on the American man-of-war *Boxer,* commanded by then-Lieutenant David Farragut, later to become a national hero in the Civil War when he inspired his men in the attack on Mobile Bay with the cry "Damn the torpedoes. Full speed ahead!"[5]

Ball's great financial opportunity came in 1836 when two physicians and his sister's partner in Troy, New York, pooled their money to invest in Michigan land and proposed that he, the intrepid wilderness traveler, go to the new territory and use his knowledge to make proper land selections for them. "It was the great year of speculation," Ball explains, "and I have always thought it strange that so sober men as those would have yielded to the mania that so pervaded the country."[6] He nonetheless took up their proposition and remained in Michigan to become a prosperous pioneer of Grand Rapids, a state legislator, and the architect of Michigan's public school system. At age fifty-six he married a Michigan schoolteacher from New England and had a family of five children.

～ᶜ～

*T*H I S twelfth day of November, 1874, is my birthday, and I enter my eightieth year, having been born in 1794.

Now going back to the time of my birth, let me look at the state and condition of the world in general, and my own country in particular.

It was only eighteen years from our Declaration of Independence and but five after the first inauguration of our government, the commencement of Washington's second term as President.

Franklin was dead, but most of the actors in our Revolution and the formation of our government were still living and acting their part in carrying out the provisions of the Government they had so patriotically achieved and put in operation.

---

5. Ball, *Autobiography,* pp. 61–65, 123.
6. Ball, *Autobiography,* p. 133–43.

Old blind George the Third was King of England still, and the French Revolution had just been achieved. The first Napoleon had lately been promoted from Colonel to Brigadier General for having driven the British out of Toulon. He was then twenty-five years old.

The United States then numbered fifteen, Vermont and Kentucky having been added to the original thirteen, and it was bounded south by Florida and Louisiana and west by the Mississippi River. And the vast country northwest of the Ohio River was not even organized into a territory. For in that same year, 1794, General Wayne fought his last battle with the Indians in what is now Ohio and Indiana.

There were then in the United States about 4,000,000 inhabitants, one-tenth of the present population, not probably more than 200,000 west of the Alleghanies, and Western New York and Pennsylvania but little settled. . . .

Of my immediate ancestors, they were honest and honorable but never acquired any special renown. My grandfather's name on my mother's side was Nevins, the only grandparent I ever saw. He was of Scotch descent and said to have been born on his mother's passage to this country. They called him Deacon. He was of the Scotch Presbyterian order, and I remember he chided us children severely for any levity on Sunday.

My father and a few neighbors were ordered out to join the Revolutionary army at Saratoga. But after a few days' march they were directed to return and guard their own back settlements against the Indians residing between them and Canada, and they, the Indians, did sack the little settlement at Royalton, Vermont. So my father did not become a hero of the Revolution. He first settled on the plain on the river that falls into Newfound pond, in Hebron, but soon moved two miles north onto a part called Tenney's Hill, on to the very top of the hill. The land on his farm of two hundred acres descending in every direction except to the north, which rose into forest and naked mountain rocks. On this hill, detached from all the rest of the world, having steep sides and rising up to 1,000 feet in height, there settled at first three or four families and it never exceeded eight or ten.

Here on this bleak, high hill was I born, the tenth child of my parents, the oldest, Sarah, nearly twenty years my senior. Then Hannah, Bridget Snow, named for a grandmother, Lucy, Nathaniel, Ebenezer, Willie, as he was always called who died in childhood, Deborah and William, all reared in comparative indigence but entire and absolute independence. My parents being quite as well off as their townsmen and neighbors, with their economy and indomitable industry, each and all sustained themselves on those granite hills in comfort and compe-tency—circumstances that have given the New Englander his character. Every child worked, doing what his age and capacity best fitted him to perform.

We were all born in log cabins. One cabin was burned, from which an infant child was saved. My earliest recollection, when about three years old, is the blasting of some big granite boulders for the building of the chimney of the new frame house my father was then building. I had gone out with the other children to be witness at a distance. Big stones formed each jamb and back of the fireplace, and a long mica slate piece from a quarry on the farm, made the mantle tree above. By some way was procured brick enough to make an oven, the oven in which my good mother baked that splendid rye and Indian bread, in big loaves; pork and beans, apples to eat with our bread and milk, and mince, pumpkin and apple pies.

She fed us well, but almost entirely from the products from the farm, the fields and the dairy. But we were taught by her and father, too, to eat what was prepared for us, asking no questions. For breakfast and dinner my father always had his mug of cider; mother and older children tea or coffee, sometimes, the latter often made from brown bread or peas, and for supper bread and milk was the almost universal dish for all.

Work of some kind was the business of my earliest years, to pick up chips, draw the cider, drive the cows to and from pasture, bring the water from the spring, a short distance off, those splendid springs of pure soft water, for it does not dissolve the granite as the lime rock. There were the upper and the lower springs near the house. Jobe's Spring, named from the man who once lived near it, and numerous others. And there were the West Brook and the East Brook, little rippling springs from the mountains north of the farm. In these we bathed in the warm summer days, but never learned to swim, to my after regret, for there was no water to float a boy nearer than the lake two miles away.

In the spring and summer I dropped the corn, rode the horse to plow it, shook out the hay or grain to dry as my older brothers mowed it, and raked after them as they pitched and loaded the hay, and when older played my due part with the scythe. At that I could beat my brother

William, though he was older and much stronger than myself. But at mowing I never saw the man who could mow with the ease and rapidity of my brother Nathaniel. Then I picked up the stones in the plow fields and assisted in drawing and laying stones into walls or fences. I took my due part in hoeing the corn and potatoes and gathering and digging the same. I now well recollect where I was hoeing corn in the east field with my brother when that celebrated eclipse of the sun of 1806 happened. It was not quite total there, but was, in the south part of the state. It was to us a very interesting sight, and then so dark the cocks crowed.

With me it was all work and no play. The only holidays of the year were the Fourth of July and Thanksgiving. Few amusements indoors or out. And Sunday, with its rigid requirement for its observances, was the dullest day of all. We usually went to a meeting, a walk of two miles down and up a steep hill, after a hard week's work. In winter there was little time to play and that was mostly occupied in sliding down the hills on the snow, on sleds made by ourselves. A bent sapling, or small ash tree split, small posts and slats, made a light, but strong vehicle. And there was the care of the cattle at the barns, the feeding and milking the cows; and in the spring the care of the calves and lambs.

Our opportunity for an education was very limited. New Hampshire had no public fund for that purpose, and their laws provided that each town should annually vote such an amount as should be needed for the purpose of schools, to be divided between the districts, according to the number of children in each, of a certain age. The number of children in our district was so small that our part of the money would support a school but six or seven weeks in the year. And there was no remedy, for as small as the number of scholars was, being only from ten to fifteen, we were so detached from any other inhabited territory we could not be attached to any other district.

My father's education being very limited, he did not seem to think any further education than an ability to read, write and cipher in the simple rules to be needful. And at home we had no book instruction, for we had no other than the Bible, Watts' Hymns and Psalms, an annual almanac, and a few school books, consisting of Webster's Spelling Book with its fables and accompanying pictures, Morse's Geography, the author, the father of the telegraph man; Adam's Arithmetic, and some school reading book.

My mother had never been to school at all, but she could read and was very fond of reading, when she could obtain a book and had the time. She had naturally a fine mind, and was ever curious to learn all that could be, within her very limited means. With her aspirations her life was truly hard. Our parents observed quite strictly, the then, more than now, universal custom of family prayers, morning and evening, and the asking a blessing and returning thanks at table. When my father was absent, whose prayers were rather formal, my mother performed the duty, and with wonderful ability. The petitions were varied and appropriate to the occasion, and the language correct and beautiful as was ever uttered by the most highly educated person. . . .

I have said that the family subsisted almost entirely on the products of the farm. Still once in the year, in winter, my father would take some butter, cheese and perhaps other products and go below, as it was called, to his old home, Hollis, and sometimes Boston, and exchange the same for the year's supply of groceries and other needed things. His return was a time of quite a sensation in the family.

But little was brought home in the way of clothing, for that was almost entirely made for the men, and women too, from the wool and flax produced on the farm, manufactured by my mother and sisters. There were the big spinning wheels for the wool and the little foot wheel for the linen, the twirling of which, by my industrious mother, I have often heard from my bed. And they, too, wove on the hand loom the yarn they spun. I remember when even the carding machines first came into use in that part of the country. For men's use the woolen cloth was dyed and dressed at the mill. This fulled and dressed cloth for men's garments was sometimes made up by professed tailors, men and women, who went from house to house to do such jobs. But the women made all of the thin clothes, and bleached the linen cloth after woven, and made the same into sheets, shirts, table-cloths and towels.

My parents were attached to the Congregational Church, as most of the people were, in my childhood, in that part of the country. They had erected a church in Hebron about the year 1800, and the minister was a Mr. Page, who was generally well liked and all he said, according to the times, was implicitly received, till at the time of the election of Jefferson for President, he preached a political sermon, and as a Mr. Bartlet said, "Mr. Page, we employ you to preach Jesus Christ and him crucified, but you preach Thomas Jefferson and him justified." His people, though agreed in their religion, were not in their politics; so, of course, it gave great offense to Mr. Jefferson's political opponents, and the church being about equally divided politically, they became so in their fellowship. Their differences and difficulties soon became unreconcilable, even so far as to seriously interfere with kind, neighborly feeling.

One reason for thus speaking of it is its sad effect upon my mother's happiness, and on my own mind, although so young, being but seven or eight years old, so young that my parents, not supposing I should notice it, carried on their sad conversation on the subject in my hearing. They were of the opposing side to the minister and were much dissatisfied with him and his adherents. Hard things were said on both sides. My father would say, "They lie," but my mother, out of her charity, would answer, "They do not mean to," and father would answer, "They do, they know they lie." Young as I was I better understood the purport of all this than they or anyone would think. In spite of my prior instruction, the thought would arise in my mind, as to the utility of churches, ministers and all those things, and it probably has had its influence on my life.

A few years after a wild religious reformation took place in our town. It commenced in the east part of the same among the Methodists, then a new sect in those parts, and it soon spread through the whole community. They held frequent day and night and all-night meetings, where all took part in exhorting, singing, weeping and groaning, and even the falling power, as it was called, when persons would fall down apparently in a trance. To all this I was a spectator, still being but little moved, though I supposed others experienced all they showed, even most of my own family, though all my elders, seemed deeply moved. I felt an uneasiness that I was not also affected and secretly prayed that I might share and also be converted. For it was claimed that all in the whole place had been, but four, and I was one of that number. . . .

And from that time commenced serious doubts, whether the whole of it was not a matter of emotion, sympathy, and delusion. . . .

My next brother, Ebenezer, was in his boyhood a greater reader and more of a thinker [than Nathaniel]. I well recollect that sometimes he expressed doubts as to the opinion and ways of those around us, and considering his limited opportunity, showed talent by his acquisitions. He waited, not quite patiently, for his twenty-first birthday, that he might be his own man and leave home, which he did on the very day, and went first to Sterling, Massachusetts and there learned the business of chair-making. He afterwards worked in Boston, and was there at the coming of the war of 1812 and when the Militia was called out for service, he was stationed on one of the islands in the Harbor, where he took cold, sickened, and in the attempt to get him home, he died before reaching there, but his body was brought there for burial. Severely did I feel his loss. We had always corresponded and he had encouraged me in my efforts for an education by words and proposed aid.

My sister, Deborah, possessed a vigorous body and mind, quite self-reliant and early sought to carry it out, so went away from home and learned the tailor's trade, and worked at the same. She married William Powers. I knew his grandfather Willie and father William, of the neighboring town of Groton, and they, William the third and my sister, went to Lansingburgh, where he had been before, to reside. But of them I shall have occasion to speak more.

My brother William, who was but two years my senior, and with whom I always worked on the farm when boys, was strong, but rather slow in his movements. Still he would work on till the whole day's work was done, if it took to a late hour. Being the older he claimed the right to direct the work in a way that to me was not always entirely satisfactory. It seemed hard to work all day and part of the night in the long autumn days. At school he rather excelled in arithmetic, but had little taste for other studies, and never became much of a reader. He once made quite a sensible remark, which he applied to his son E. Morris, that he thought more conversation and less reading would be more profitable.

As I had determined to leave home if I could, I gave him to understand if he would stay and provide well for our parents I would set up no claim from that source, and he did stay and worked the old mountain farm while our parents lived. . . .

As for myself I early became quite dissatisfied at having so limited an opportunity for an education, so as soon as I deemed it safe to do so I broached the subject to my father. I knew he adhered strictly to the opinion that work and implicit obedience were the things most useful and needful in the education of boys, but after much importunity, he consented that I might go into the next town of Groton to a clergyman by the name of Rolph, who kept a kind of private school. It was eight miles distant by carriage road, but only half that by a foot-path across a mountain pass which was usually my route.

At first I took up arithmetic and English grammar in good earnest during the first fall and winter. And as poorly as I was qualified I taught a small school for a short time during the winter on Power's Hill. In the spring my said reverend teacher proposed, to my surprise, that I should take up the Latin grammar, which I did, though of English I knew so little; not the first rudiments of reading or spelling at all well, and nothing I might say of history or geography. I thought it strange that he should thus propose it, for I had not yet hardly dared to think it possible that I could think of anything more than a limited English education but his evident design was to lead me further.

Come summer, as always after, until I graduated from college, I went home and worked on the old farm at haying and harvesting. The next fall I returned to my school pursuing my Latin and some other studies, also writing under a special teacher of that art. And come winter, knowing that I must do something for my own support, I started out to get a writing school. I took my bundle and went, of course on foot, through Plymouth and Rumney to Oxford. At the latter place I recollect I offered my services in that capacity, but my showing was not satisfactory or they did not need the instruction. So I went on to Thetford, Vermont, where I had a lady cousin, with whom I was acquainted. I do not now recollect her husband's name. With their aid I got, for a time, my writing school.

But the time not being long that I was patronized in that line, I went to Vershire in the same state to visit my uncle John Ball, for whom I was named. We were all named for father and uncles. There I engaged in teaching a small district school at some very moderate compensation, how much I do not recollect. There to extend my knowledge of men and manners it was my lot to board around, as was usual in those times, from house to house, according to the number of scholars or some other rule of ratio. It proved a new and interesting experience for everywhere I was a favored guest, for they lived on their best while the master boarded with them and I had the society of the young ladies and all the members of each family in their most approved form, but to me it was sometimes embarrassing, for up to this time my acquaintances had been very few.

This winter was a notable one in the history of our country. The war had been conducted with few successes and some humiliating defeats, such as the taking of Washington, and now came the glorious news of the battle of New Orleans, and soon after the very welcome, and if I am right, unexpected news of peace. The overthrow of Napoleon and peace in Europe brought peace to us also. Oh! these wars and rumors of wars among people that in a boastful way call themselves Christians, claimed followers of the peaceful and loving Jesus Christ. Well might the Turk, of course a Mohammedan, say in satire when, a short time before this, he was witnessing from a neighboring eminence, the tremendous battle of Borodino near Moscow between the French and Russians, "See how these Christians love each other." Though I had then seen but little, very little for my age, even I had thought enough to give me then about my present views on that subject. . . .

The following winter I think I taught school in my native district on Tenney's Hill and in the following spring I returned to the academy, and went on with my studies, having made up my mind that I would try and fit for college. I studied hard, but from my prior limited opportunity and natural slowness my progress was not very rapid and I did not hope to be fit for admission to college before the next year; but to my surprise the tutor of the academy told me he thought if I studied well he could recommend me for an examination for admission at the close of the term about July. At that time, he said, President Brown of Dartmouth was coming there to examine some others for admission and he would propose me with the rest. Being so advanced in age it was very welcome news, and I, of course, exerted myself to be prepared for the trial. President Brown came and I was examined with the others and decided to be qualified. The college was the more desirous, at that time, to get students on account of the state's interference with its charter rights. My father had sent me word that he would be returning from a journey at the time of the closing of the term of the academy, and he would come that way and take me home. He did arrive the last of the week when the term had just closed, but the examination for the admission to college was not to take place till the next week, so I had to tell him what I was proposing to do and that I would wait and have the examination, and he might take my trunk, and, after President Brown had been there and examined us, I would walk home. And to show what my prospects were as to aid in my college course, I will state what he said. "What is that you say, John, if you are going to take that course you must not look to me for help." So he left me, taking my baggage, and I stayed, passed the examination successfully and walked home, and when there went as usual into the mow field.

As the time approached for the fall term at the college I well recollect the anxiety and trouble I experienced in procuring the means to meet my expenses. But how I did get them I do not now recollect. During my whole course my father did loan me to the amount in all, at different times, two hundred dollars, but whether any at this time I do not remember. Still, by some means, I managed to join my class in due time and keep along, but with the most rigid economy in everything. When I hired my board it was at the cheapest place and I often boarded myself, preparing my frugal meals in my room, a room I took in the old college building at some low rent, and for the first year George Richardson of our class was my room-mate.

On first meeting my fellow students for recitation, I well recollect my feeling of embarrassment for I fully realized my lack of language, hesitating ways, and the better preparation of all of them than myself. In all I had been in school hardly four years while they, with probably a more ready capacity, had been preparing all their school years. Of the languages, Greek and Latin, they had read and re-read the required authors while I had not in either read what the college rules required, of Greek, but part of the Testament and in Latin, Virgil and part of Cicero. By great industry I managed to get a pretty good understanding of the lessons, still recited but poorly. . . .

Dartmouth College is beautifully situated on a plain, high above the Connecticut River, which flows swiftly a half mile to the west, in which we bathed and such as could, swam, and I remember that I was usually the first in the spring to try its cold waters. The college building, for then there was but one, and a small chapel, was on one side of a broad green or common where the boys played football with great glee, and the best in the lot were the two or three Indian students, for by a condition of the charter and funds they still are required to have some of the people for whom the institution was founded in order to draw on certain funds in England and Scotland.

Come winter vacation I went to my winter occupation, teaching school, and this time to be the one on what is called the Groton intervale, some four miles up the valley from our own village. I boarded at a Mr. Heath's. At one time I came near getting into serious trouble for having punished a refractory scholar, but by the kindly interposition of my old friend Mr. Rolph, the matter was adjusted. . . .

When I entered, and most of the time while in college, there were two institutions on the ground, the college and the university. The state had passed a law changing the name to university, and making many changes from the old English charter to the college, but most of the twelve trustees and the faculty deeming this act of the State unconstitutional resisted its provisions and continued the college in operation as though no such law had been passed. A Mr. Allen was appointed president of the new state institution, and also able professors. They took possession of the building, library and all the property, but having at most but a dozen students they rented rooms in the main building to students that preferred, as ten-to-one did, the old faculty, and the old college people procured a hall for a chapel, and some private rooms so they continued their instruction at Hanover as in past times. The matter went before the Supreme Court of the United States and Webster, who was a trustee of the college, conducted the cause in its behalf, and the court decided that the old charter was a vested right and no more to be infringed upon than the title to a farm acquired before our independence. . . .

President Brown was then at the head of the college, and an able and worthy man. But very unfortunately for us he was all the while so out of health that he could not at any time fill his appointed place in our instruction. He finally, about the time of our graduation, died. I well recollect that after he had become very feeble he sent for our class to come to his room. And there he gave us some excellent advice as to our future lives. Part of it I well recollect, and if I have any claims to be in some degree learned, it has been by observing and following his suggestions. He said, "Young men, do not think you shall have completed your education, for it is but a beginning. You must still be pupils all your lives," or words to that effect. We lost much by not having his instruction.

There were two societies kept up by the students of the college. The Social Friends and Fraternity were the names, I think. They had libraries, and there arose a trouble at one time about them between the members of the societies, who belonged to the college and the university. They were in the old college building when the university had possession of it, and I think the university members of the societies claimed the libraries, and there was quite a battle on the subject; for the members of the societies belonging to the college were twenty to one, and claimed the ownership and moved the books away to another building. But before my course ended the United States Supreme Court decision was rendered, and buildings, libraries and all things were restored to their original status.

By the little I had earned and received from my father and friend Powers, I met my board and outside expenses, purchased second-hand books for my studies, and as for clothing I had little except what was supplied by mother, as I recollect. But my tuition had run on till there was something like a hundred dollars due. I called on the treasurer, Honorable Mills Olcott, to see what I must do about it, and he told me that if I could not pay I must get security. I told him there was no one whom I could get or at any rate was willing to ask and assured him that it should be paid if I lived long enough to earn the money, as I intended that that should be my first business. I explained that no one was in any way obligated to become my security, and I could not give it. I was answered, I could not then receive my diploma, parchment, as then called. As to that I thought it only a matter of form, and I could do without it.

But I went to the pews appropriated for the class in the church, at the commencement ceremonies and listened to the parts acted by some of my fellows; for I, of course, was not an orator, or scholar enough to at all expect any appointment in any of the performances. The last performance of all was to be our march over the stage, in front of the pulpit, where all the trustees and the faculty were seated, and each receive his parchment. But when my fellow students, almost at the last moment, found that I was not to get mine they drew up a note for the amount due for my tuition, had me sign it, then nearly all of them did the same. Nothing in my life more touched me than this expression of their confidence and regard. As I now relate it the tears came to my eyes. But they did not pay the note, or any part of it. So then by that means I, with the rest of them, marched up and received my diploma, which is in the Atlantic Ocean; but of that hereafter.

That same day I left for Lansingburgh, where my brother-in-law, Powers, resided, to visit them on my way, as I intended going further south to seek employment. I started out on foot by the most direct route, without regard to a good or public road. . . .

And I think it was at that time I first went to Saratoga, where then there were but few buildings, only one hotel of any account. There were the High Rock, Flat Rock, and Congress Springs; the last but lately found. Then, or later, I was at Ballston Spa, where I recollect of seeing Joseph Bonaparte.[1] I think he was often in summer stopping there at the Sansouci.

On my informing Mr. Powers of my intention first of all to seek employment to earn money to pay up my indebtedness to the college, to himself and to my father, he urged me instead to select my profession and to begin the study of the same. I had not yet decided what should be my future pursuit, but had left that to be determined when my debts should have been paid. As I had but little gift as a speaker my classmates had set me down for the profession of medicine. For all college students were supposed to be destined for one of the three learned professions, as they were then called. The study of medicine I thought I should like well, but the practice seemed intolerable. Being heterodox I could not take divinity, so the law only was left.

So I yielded to my friends' importunities to stop with them and take up the study, and make the earning of money to pay my debts a secondary matter. . . .

For my legal reading I of course was assigned Blackstone, which I pursued with due diligence, and also did some work in copying papers for the office. A Mr. Simmons, was also a student in the office. He taught in the Academy, and after a time I got a department in the same to teach. My pupils were some twenty girls and young ladies, to govern whom to my mind I found it troublesome. The next year I taught a school of primaries, and gained some credit for my success. I soon made the little folks, some eighty in all, understand that I intended to make it pleasant for them—had lessons on large cards that could be hung up about the walls of the room. They were the same Mr. Powers had used before in teaching school on the Lancastrian plan. Six would stand around looking on the same lesson with directions to correct each other as they read in turn. And the whole school would read at once, except the alphabets

---

1. Saratoga Springs later became one of the most famous resorts of the nineteenth century. Joseph Bonaparte, who had been both king of Naples and king of Spain, was Napoleon Bonaparte's older brother. He sought refuge in America after his brother's fall from power and lived in the United States from 1815 to 1832, taking the title of the Comte de Survilliers.

(little folks), who had sand smoothed down in which to make the letters with their fingers, with an older scholar to show them how. And I gave them liberal time outdoors, so it went merrily on. At the same time I kept up my reading in the office.

Though little in society for a time, I gradually got acquainted with the young people. There were a large number of young ladies accustomed to dance, but many of the young men were from the New England mountains, like myself, who knew nothing of the art, for there it was deemed very sinful. But having revolted from our education we employed a man, who was teaching some children, to give us a few lessons, intending to ask the young ladies to join us in the dance as soon as we were able to perform. But they mistaking our intentions, out of opposition some of them got up a sleigh ride with no men but the driver. At the first dance we had, we omitted to invite these, and the result was some unkind feelings, but before the winter closed it was all harmonious, and we got much reasonable enjoyment from our dancing.

The next spring after coming to Lansingburgh, the spring of 1821, I first went to the city of New York. I sailed down the Hudson in a sloop belonging to Mr. James Dougery of Lansingburgh. I had not before been below Albany, so it was all new and interesting to me—the varied shores, villages, the Catskill Mountains, West Point, highlands and palisades. Put up at a private boarding place on Pearl Street near the Battery, and the first evening I must see a theater, and went to some place up Broadway, for the Chatham had been burned. It seemed to satisfy my curiosity on that subject, for I never after felt much wish to go. The next morning, to see the city, I started up Pearl Street and some way crossed Broadway without observing it and came out into view of a broad water. And having started east I thought, of course, it was the East River, when in fact I had gone the circuit and come out on the Hudson. Then going up Broadway I came to vacant lots only two blocks above the Park. There was an open sewer in Canal Street and Greenwich was two miles out. Crossed over to Brooklyn and went onto quite a high hill, about I should think where the center of the city now stands, from which I got a very fair view of New York. There was little that you now see there except the City Hall and Trinity Church. Returned by steamboat to Albany, taking about twenty-four hours. . . .

When some two years or more had passed at hard work at Lansingburgh, I tired and longed for a change. So against all persuasion of friends I determined to put out somewhere, and perhaps the greater influence on my mind was to see something more of the world. So I went to New York with the view to ship to some place south, and on arriving there noticed on the North River a schooner advertised for Darien, Georgia. As that was about as far south as I could sail on the Atlantic side in the United States I engaged a passage aboard of her. She was to sail in a few days but was longer delayed than intended by a tremendous easterly November rain storm. It drove the water over the docks and into cellars. But at that time the lower part of the city about up to the Park had been deserted on account of the yellow fever. The disease had subsided, and the residents were then about to return into this deserted section. It was indeed a strange sight to thus see a city without people—no shipping at the docks for a long distance each way from the Battery. A great share of the city business had for a long time been in temporary shanty buildings erected on the then vacant grounds up the Hudson, the shipping lying opposite in the river.

I was now to take my first sea voyage. We sailed as soon as the storm was over, in a high sea, for the wind had shifted to the southwest and blew hard. Before we had reached the Narrows I had the new experience of sea sickness. . . .

Then came on a northeaster, which against the Gulf Stream current raised a tremendous sea, making our little vessel roll and pitch awfully. At night I could hear the water splashing and whizzing by my ears, as I lay trembling in my berth, and by day the look out was in the thick rain storm and the foaming sea. . . .

The vessel that saved us was bound for Darien, so the next day after the taking us up, they continued their voyage on to that place, where they arrived before night. On the way up we made from our scant means a purse, for the brave men who had risked their lives to save ours, and we soon by donation or otherwise, got what would make out one full suit. I escaped with shirt, coat, vest and pants and my small means which were in bank bills in my pocket. My hat, boots and baggage, in which was my college diploma, went to the waves.

I found Darien a small village with a few stores built in the Spanish fashion, they being the first people here. . . .

Well, at Darien I boarded at a Mr. Hunter's, and succeeded in raising a small private school, and there passed the winter of 1822 and 1823, and the spring till May. . . .

I was here in the midst of Negrodom, only a fifth of the people of the country being of the white race, and very few free negroes. But Butler plantation, on an island, in the river against the town, had its 400 slaves with only one overseer—the owner, Mr. Butler, living in Philadelphia. On Sunday they would come into town by thousands, usually bringing a chicken, tarapin, fish or some little thing of their procuring, for trade, the stores being kept open till ten o'clock. All the negro families have their little patch of ground by their cabins to cultivate and raise their chickens, etc. They would meet acquaintances in town on these Sundays and talk and laugh—a more happy, jolly set of creatures I never saw. There was one church in the place, and such of them as chose, but there were very few, could go into a small gallery.

At all times, at the ringing of the eight o'clock town bell, on all days, they had to go home, and any found in the streets after were taken to the guard house. And every white resident was enrolled to take his turn about once a week or two, to patrol the streets and guard the place on account of the slaves, fearing an insurrection or some mischief from them, and I had to take my part. I saw no severe punishment, the usual punishment for bad behavior being imprisonment in the public gaol or short feed till they promised, as they soon did, good behavior.

I witnessed a sheriff's sale of the whole people of a plantation, some 60 or 80 men and women and of all sizes. And there was great grief among them, that they would be bid off separately and thus parted. But the matter was compromised, and when they were told that they were all going home again together, you never saw a happier set. I noticed that when anything happened to them, like the loss of a child, their grief seemed deep and the manifestations boisterous. But in a few days, all was apparently forgotten and the afflicted mother as gay as ever.

Saw much that satisfied me that the African and Caucasian are constitutionally unlike, and cannot by any education be made, even to fully understand each other, any more than the ox and the horse. Each may have good qualities, but each in his own way. The negro docile or he could not be enslaved, cheerful under all circumstances, never committing suicide.

My landlord however, had a very capable slave, Sam. He was chief butler to the whole establishment, did the marketing and oversaw the cooking and dealt the rum to visitors—no, not rum, but good brandy or gin, and these we always had on the table to temper the poor water. In following this prescription I feared I might make it a needful habit, but it did not prove so, I left the habit when I left the country and without remorse. . . .

After thus spending nearly a year away from my legal studies in the state of New York, I returned to Lansingburgh and resumed them for another year. For by their rules no legal student could apply to be examined for admission to the bar as an attorney till he could produce a certificate from a practicing one, that he had studied in his office for three years. This certificate I obtained the next summer of 1824 and went to Utica, where the Supreme Court was in session, and was examined and admitted as an attorney of that court, but still no counsellor. I went from Schenectady by boat on the then new canal. It was not yet completed through to Buffalo. We arrived at Little Falls in the night, and there came on a thunder storm with most vivid lightning, so that during the flashes, the rocks and scenery thereabouts, could be seen as plainly as in full daylight, giving a more striking and lasting impression than seeing the same by day. The scenery all along the Mohawk is interesting and the spreading out of its valley about Utica with its fertility in that part truly so.

Spencer was then Chief Justice, and Platt and Woodworth Judges. But there was one attending the court at the time who attracted more notice than the court itself. This was Aaron Burr, who was attending to argue some important causes before the court as counsel. He was said then to be nearly eighty years old, small in statue, his head white, but erect and mentally in full vigor. When he came into the courtroom, there was shown a sensation by all, even the Judges on the bench. . . .

About a year later it was proposed that I should go in with another of the practicing lawyers, Jacob C. Lansing, one of the men with whom I had read, he and Walbridge having dissolved. He was much out and rather negligent of business, and his friends seemed to want someone they could find in the office. . . .

In that same year came on the political campaign when General Jackson was first elected president. And I was out and out a Jackson man, as I also was at the previous contest in 1823, when he, Clay, Adams and Crawford were candidates, resulting in no choice, and Clay and Adams joining, the states chose Adams.[2] At the election Jackson

---

2. This was the famous election when the surprise candidate, Andrew Jackson, won the most popular votes, but lost the election in the House after Clay and Adams

was my choice out of the four, but he received but two other votes in the village.

My friend Powers was then an Adams man. And he had now shifted his business from school teaching to the manufacture of floor oilcloth. There was then little if any made in this country, that used here being imported from England. He knew nothing of the business, but being of a mechanical and inventive turn, could make it. So after experimenting for a time in a small way he succeeded in making an article that was well received in the New York market. He then proceeded to make preparation to extend the business, by erecting a brick factory of five stories and 150 feet in length. And commenced his business in the same in the spring of 1829. . . .

For in a week from that time, news was brought me, that he was badly burned. I hastened to the factory, for the family residence was in a part of the same building, to witness a scene indeed of horror. He was burned to a crisp, almost from head to foot and my sister and one or two of the men badly burned in their effort to save him.

It was this way. He was making a copal varnish, a composition much used in his work, in a high sheet-iron kettle over coal on a movable, or hand furnace, standing at a fireplace in the opposite end of the factory from the dwelling part. The varnish caught on fire, and in his effort to extinguish it, his clothes caught, which being a cotton shirt and linen pants, he was soon enveloped in flames. His wife happened to be near on the sidewalk and some of the men, when they reached him, made the effort to get his clothes off of him, so they too were burned. . . .

Thus died William Powers the third, for I had known his father and his grandfather, who bore the same name. Not only his family but the whole community seemed paralyzed at the shocking manner of his death. All the business men of the place had full confidence in his punctuality and ability to accomplish what he had undertaken, and as far as asked by him, aided him in his enterprise. When we had laid him in his grave and looked about to see what was to be done to fill the large place he had filled, it looked hopeless. His very art seemed to have been lost with him. Some of the compositions for his cloth, he prepared with his own hands and the workmen did not understand them. My sister was

---

supporters joined forces to elect Adams. When Clay became Secretary of State in John Quincy Adams's cabinet, Jackson denounced it as a corrupt bargain.

suffering for some time from her burned hands, and the men had no heart to go to work. So for a time everything lay as he left it.

His two boys were young, Albert E. twelve, and Nathaniel B. but six. And it seemed so hopeless to even carry on the business so as to pay the debts, being some $8,000 and all the property besides the factory not amounting to near that sum, my sister offered the creditors the factory and all, if they would take it and say they were paid. This, most of them being neighbors, they promptly declined, saying they would give time for their pay and the business must go on, for the benefit of the estate, and said and did all they could to that end. So hopeless as it seemed, the men were induced to go to work and make the effort to carry on the business though it was even feared a merchantable article could not be made. . . .

As for myself, I at once proposed to assist in settling the affairs of the estate and do some of the outdoor's affairs in carrying on the business, little expecting at first that the death of my friend would result in the entire change of the business of my life and residence. I went to New York to purchase paints and all the credit I could get was to the amount of $300. The business was carried on in the name of my sister as administratrix and she soon put some cloth on the market, which was well received. And when we could give the creditors orders on good carpet merchant houses in the city, to pay for the stock of paints and other materials wanted, our credit became good and the business went along.

But I soon found that I was devoting so much time to the factory business, my own office business would leave me. So after consideration, feeling that I must abandon one or the other, I concluded to shut up my law office and give my whole time to the business left by my friend. So I went and boarded with my sister and gave my whole soul to the work of extricating her affairs. Acted as foreman in the factory, directing the whole business of the same. And from the aid of the kind neighbor painter, soon learned to compound paints and in fact to do any and all parts of the work. But I was engaged mainly in planning the work for the men so as to make the most of their labor. The greatest economy was practiced by my sister in all things to increase the means, being so limited, to carry on the business. She hired a woman to keep her house and went into the factory and in the ornamenting took the place of a man saving so much in wages. Even Albert was turned to account in running errands and doing chores, which he attended to faithfully, if he did not meet with a book, which if he got hold of, everything else was apt to be forgotten. . . .

And as for myself I never worked harder, for I saw daily more to do than could be accomplished. For I shirked no part of the work that I could lay my hands to. And when I went to New York on business I left by stage for Albany just in time to reach the night boat, so to be in the city in the morning for the day's business and probably returned by the next night's boat, neither using the means nor the time for theater going or other outside matters. In the spring after the death of Mr. Powers, I took some samples of the cloth and patterns stamped on paper, so as to make but a light roll to carry, and went to New York, Philadelphia and Baltimore to get orders. I was gone but a week or so, though I had to travel across New Jersey by stage and to Baltimore by the Delaware and Chesapeake canal, and in that one trip procured advantageous orders for a whole year's work. So that we now felt assurance that we should work out successfully, pay up the debts and go along if no disaster overtook us.

For the first year I claimed no compensation for my services but the next year proposed to my sister as her business was proving successful, that I should have one-third of the net profits, which gave me some $1,600. At first she seemed much to rely on me in all matters of business, but after a time she showed a readiness in taking a part in all the concerns of the establishment. We well agreed in all things except the working hours of the men, she thought ten hours not enough.

In the spring following, 1831, a Mr. J. E. Whipple came to the factory and engaged to work on the same terms as the other men, at one dollar per day. He was a brother of a Rev. Mr. Whipple, the Episcopal clergyman of the place, and who had been very friendly to my sister in her troubles, though she was not of his church, or indeed of any other. And it was through him his brother was introduced to us. I thought it a little strange that he should take the place, as he had been for some time a clerk in Boston and had some means. But it was not my business to inquire why, as he took hold of the work assigned him faithfully and in earnest. And the business continued to prosper. I made a proposition to my sister to rent the establishment, but she did not wish to, saying she wanted the boys to learn the business. I told her I did too and that need not be in the way.

When Mr. Whipple had been in the factory say six months he said to me one day, "Your sister has proposed to me to go into partnership with her, in this oilcloth business." And said, he thought considering my relation to it he ought first to speak to me on the subject. I told him at once, I hoped he would do so, if she wished it. And if he would, I would give him all the information I could about the business and introduce him to our customers. So the partnership was agreed on and the terms arranged, and to commence on the first of the coming January. Up to that time I was to continue to conduct the business.

My sister expected me to remain in the place and return to my law business, and proposed to give me a salary of $500 to aid them in sales and business outside. But I made up my mind that I would have no connection with the business unless a controlling one, and that I would not go back to hunt up my old law business, that had all gone into other hands. But having worked hard all my life so far, I would take a little recreation, and for that purpose having learned that a Mr. Wyeth of Boston, North Cambridge, was making arrangements to cross the plains and mountains to Oregon the next season, I wrote to him to inquire if I could join his party. . . .

While in New York I sought out and found some of John Jacob Astor's Oregon men for the purpose of gaining information from them about that country. There were the Messrs. Seaton's who sailed around Cape Horn and to the Columbia River and assisted in establishing the trading post Astoria, and Ramsey Crooks, who conducted the land party for him across the continent, reaching Astoria the second year. They told me much of their experiences there. I then went to Philadelphia and Baltimore and made collections in each place for the oilcloth contracts, for my sister, and sent her back after my leaving, in all, some three thousand dollars.

Having the time, before the arrival from Boston of my Oregon traveling companions, I went for the first time to Washington. Put up at Brown's Hotel, standing there almost alone, on the Avenue, Washington then being comparatively but a village. General Ashley, who had long been in the fur trade from Missouri to the Mountains, was stopping at Brown's. So I took the liberty to call at his room and inform him of my intended journey and asking from him advice and information. He kindly answered many inquiries. But finally said, "Young man, it would be as difficult to tell all about it, all that may occur or be needed on such a journey, as for a carpenter to tell every blow he had got to strike on commencing to erect a house." He had sold out his fur business to William Sublette of St. Louis and others, and had been elected a member of Congress.

While thus spending a few days at Washington I took the opportunity with other things to attend the sitting of the United States Supreme Court. And then I listened to Chief Justice Marshall's celebrated decision of the Georgia and Cherokee case, with regard to the Cherokee lands. And, of course, attended the sitting of the houses of Congress, Calhoun, then Vice-President, presiding over the Senate, in which Benton, Clay, Webster and other celebrities were then members. As a presiding officer I have never seen Mr. Calhoun's equal, or a finer man to look on. And, as then constituted, it was indeed an august body and in the House were then Adams and Choate. The latter I knew well at College and there were others in both houses with whom I might without impropriety have claimed acquaintance. But no, I poked about as a stranger. And as such presumed to call on General Jackson at the White House without any introduction. He however received me kindly.

Then, as always through life, I neglected to make use of men in place and of notoriety, as I perhaps might have done to my great advantage. Had I then told the President and others of my proposed journey they might have taken such interest, as to have given some aid, or more notoriety to my journey and personal advantage after its performance. But so it has always been, I have never felt much deference for men barely on account of holding office or claiming consequence. . . .

Having arranged matters for our journey, about the middle of March we left Baltimore on the Baltimore and Ohio Railroad for Frederick, sixty miles, by horse power. That sixty miles was then more than all the other railroads in the Union. It had been built at enormous labor, graded down, and part of the way through the mountains to a dead level and the stringers, on which was riveted strap iron, were of cut granite rock. . . .

From Pittsburgh we took passage in a steamboat bound for St. Louis. And as we descended the river I noticed its high bluffs, where at first the openings to the coal mines were high up the same, but as we sailed on, they gradually opened lower and lower, till the coal veins passed below the river. We stopped for a time at Cincinnati; which was then but a village, with few buildings but of wood and these of no great pretentions. That spring the river had been so high as to flood much of the town, doing a good deal of damage. Among the passengers on the boat, bound to Cincinnati was the Reverend Lyman Beecher, and one pleasant day, as we were smoothly gliding down the stream, he and also Wyeth and myself were promenading the deck which had no bulwarks.[3] We noticed that he turned many steps before he reached the stern of the boat, while we went so near that our next step would have been overboard. My companion remarked, "How is it that Mr. Beecher is so much more cautious than we sinners?" Implying that Mr. Beecher doubtless claimed that all would be right with him should he be drowned, while with us we made no pretentions in that direction. . . .

Arriving at St. Louis, I found it then but a village, mostly consisting of old French buildings along the levee and a street near the river, but few good buildings in the place. Draw a line then from there to, say Detroit, and the entire white population beyond I do not think was ten, if five thousand. I saw a steamboat sail, while there to go up the Illinois River, with the United States soldiers to fight Black Hawk, who was overrunning the country about where Chicago now is.

When all had arrived at Lexington, we went on to Independence, near which Mr. Sublette and his party were in camp. And on meeting him he readily consented that we might join them on this condition: that we should travel fully under his command and directions, and under the most strict military discipline; take our due part with his people in guarding camp and defense in case of attack by the Indians, which he rather expected, from a personal dislike they had to him. They charged him with leaving the year before a horse in the country packed with infected clothing, to give them the smallpox. I hardly think he could have been guilty of it. We then traversed the country and purchased horses and mules for our journey over the plains and mountains. Rigged them with saddles for riding and packing, made up those packs by sorting out the goods. . . .

And thus rigged and ready we started on our march from Independence, on what was then in much use, the Santa Fe road or trail, leading off in a southwest direction, crossing the west line of the state some twelve miles south of the Missouri. Our order of march was always double file, the horses led, the first attached to the rider's and the third to

---

3. Lyman Beecher was America's best-known minister and father of five famous children, among them Harriet Beecher Stowe.

him. So when under way our band was more than a hundred horses long—Mr. Sublette always giving all orders and leading the band, and Mr. Campbell as lieutenant bringing up the rear and seeing that all kept their places and the loose animals did not stray away.

Our last encampment, before crossing the west line of the state, was at a Mormon settlement. They had come and settled here the previous fall, on this extreme border of the settled world. We procured from them some milk and they otherwise treated us very kindly. They thought then that they had found a permanent home. But no, like all new religionists, they were doomed to much persecution. I remember when the Methodists were slighted. It was the 12th of May that we left this last settlement and continued our march on said Santa Fe road over a beautiful prairie country, some two or three days, then left it and turned to the northwest and in a few days more came to the Kansas river, at a point I think near where is now Topeka. Here we found means to cross the river and swam our horses. For here was one white man, acting I think as a gunsmith for the Indians. He was the last white man we saw except of our own party.

We continued our march up the Kansas river along the edge of the prairie back of the timber bordering the river. For on most the larger western rivers and often on the smaller, as far as the land is moist, there is timber, but beyond grass. And in the spring or fall, the fire sweeping through this grass kills the timber on its border. But then it will, if the seasons are wet spring up again. So there was a constant warfare between the fires and the trees till these prairie fires were stopped by the settlers. . . .

On this first part of our journey we did not depend at all on game for subsistence, but on supplies packed along on our horses. Mr. Sublette's party had also driven along cattle to slaughter on the way; as the horses never went faster than a walk, they could keep up. Then were some deer seen, but as yet no buffalo, so there was no reliance on game, or intended to be, till we should reach the buffalo. And now we continued our march over the smooth bottom of the turbid Platte river on the south side, the river Riley, broad and rapid, no falls, but a sufficient descent in the country to give a rapid current—from a half to a whole mile wide and very shallow. It gives its full share of the mud of the Missouri—some timber on its islands and on its shores, bottoms broad and rich, bounded by broken bluffs and all the country beyond rolling.

Our provisions were becoming nearly exhausted and we were daily expecting to see our future resource, the buffalo, but none were met with, till the day we reached the forks of the Platte, when nearly our last meal on hand had been consumed. And the same day too, we had the last shower of rain of any account. Up to this time, about the first of June, we had occasional rains, and the prairies had become green affording good feed for our animals and the wild ones too on their native range. . . .

We had now reached the region where there was no growing timber even along the river. And our fuel for cooking was the dry buffalo droppings. We usually in this part of our journey cooked our meat by boiling it in our camp kettles. And it was rather hard fare, for the buffalo were still lean in flesh, they getting quite reduced in flesh during the winter from their poor chance. The men felt the change from common food to this lean meat only and without even salt very severely, and rapidly grew weak and lean. The men would almost quarrel for any part of the animal that had any tallow, even the caul. But as soon as the buffalo improved in flesh and we got where there was wood to roast whole sides by, the men rapidly improved. I was a little surprised that I stood this change of life and living about as well as the mountaineers, and better than most of the new ones at it, and as to a camp life I rather enjoyed its ways. . . .

At times we would not see a buffalo for a day or two, and then in countless numbers. One day we noticed them grazing on the opposite side of the river on the wide bottoms and the side bluffs beyond like a herd of cattle in a pasture, up and down the country on that side as far as we could see, and continued the same during our twenty-five miles' march and no end to them ahead, probably, 10,000 seen in that one day. . . .

Now we came into a rough and mountainous country, more difficult than any we had experienced. And to add to our troubles our animals had become, from their long journey, much worn out, and the men though in like feeble condition had to walk. And food too became short, for we met but few buffalo, but some game of other kinds. And nothing came amiss. And we ate of everything that fell in our way, but the snakes, I think. Sublette had before this met with some of his mountain trappers who guided us on our way to their rendezvous. And in four days of hard working our way through ragged ravines and over steep ridges brought us out on to a fine grassy plain among the mountains, called Pierre's Hole and to the grand encampment, where they had for some time been awaiting our arrival. . . .

We were with these trappers more than a month, parting from them the 28th of August. I had during the time made many interesting observations of things around, the weather clear, and days hot and usually frost at night, ranging from say 30 to 80 degrees often. Soon after crossing the Lewis river I observed for the first strata of igneous or volcanic rock in conglomerate. And ever after met with it and saw beautiful white and variegated marble boulders, and lime and granite rock partially melted down, but still showing the original rock. The vegetation was much diversified, timber of various kinds and extended prairies. Though but little or no rain, grass was often good and occasionally we met with fruit, which, you may well think, was very acceptable to us—a berry growing on a shrub they called a service berry, resembling what is called in New England the robin pear, and red and orange colored currants, all of an excellent quality. I brought the seeds home, but they did not grow.

The said fort [Fort Walla Walla] was a small stockade of upright timbers set in the ground some fifteen or eighteen feet high with stations or bastions at the corners for look-outs. And the company kept here for the purpose of trade a clerk and some half-dozen men. We were kindly received and here for the first time since leaving the forks of the Platte the first of June ate bread, being now the 18th of October. The fort is at the mouth of the creek on the Columbia nine miles below the mouth of the Lewis river. It was an interesting sight to look on the Columbia, after the long, long journey to see the same and to get to it.

The country about looked barren, for the fall rains, if they have them, had not commenced—little or no timber or shrubs, except the Artemisia, wild sage, which grows from one to five or six feet high, and is found everywhere on the mountain plains. It has an ash-colored leaf as bitter as the garden sage; still when nothing else can be found it is eaten by the buffalo and deer. I am informed that there is now cultivation in these parts and crops raised; but I presume it must be by means of irrigation. Here we decided to leave our faithful horses and descend the river by boat. Oh! the horse is appreciated, when one for months has passed with him, his days and nights. . . .

We got a yawl and one of their men to sail it and crossed over to

Chenook Point and returned across the broad boisterous bay to Clatsop Point on the inside and encamped. And I urged the men, or some of them at least, to accompany me around the point to the seashore, but they declined. So the tide being down, I alone footed some three miles, fairly around on the beach to where I could look out on the broad Pacific, with not an islet between me and Japan, look far down the coast and Cape Disappointment across the mouth to the northwest. Here I stood alone, as entranced, felt that now, I had gone as far as feet could carry me west, and really to the end of my proposed journey.

There to stand on the brink of the great Pacific, with the rolling waves washing its sands and seaweeds to my feet! And there I stood on the shore of the Pacific enjoying the happiest hour of all my journey, till the sun sank beneath its waters, and then by a beautiful moonlight returned on the beach to camp, feeling that I had crossed the continent. Cape Disappointment is in Lat. 46.19 N. and 123.59 W. Mount Saint Helens being due east, majestic and symmetrical in its form. This was the 9th of November and we had left Baltimore the 26th of March, seven and one-half months before. We returned slowly up the river, seeing something of the Indians, always peaceable in their ways, for these traders had the good sense and tact to keep a good understanding with them, though they had to deal with them quite in their own way, the Indian always knowing just how much he was to get for his furs in the articles he wanted. I should mention the fact that the Columbia in parts, as we passed, seemed alive and white with geese and ducks. . . .

No immigrants arrived from the States, as I expected, and the Hudson Bay Company having control of the country, so I could do nothing but subsist in the way I was pursuing. And tiring of the life I was leading, I saw no object of staying longer in the country, than for an opportunity to get away by sea. For once crossing the mountains and plains, I thought enough. I had passed nearly a year there, and experienced its climate and seen its lands and waters, and become acquainted with the natives and traders. And the company being about to send a vessel to the bay of San Francisco and the Sandwich Islands, I exchanged my crop, now mostly harvested, for a passage in the same.

So about the 20th of September, 1833, I quit my home on the Willamette with something of regret after all, but on the whole gladly went down the river by boat, and when I got to the falls an Indian boy of perhaps eighteen assisted us in carrying our boat by. . . .

On October 18, 1833, we sailed from Astoria, the wind having subsided, but we still found the swell in crossing the bar tremendous, and much of wind and storm as we sailed down the coast. So with the combined seasickness and ague I was not able to leave my berth for some days. But after a time both left me and I was able to look out on the sea, and occasionally the land. Still we kept at so respectful a distance that we saw little of it, and no harbor was then known between Columbia river and the bay of San Francisco.

After a half month's voyage we neared the coast and on the 4th of November entered at the Golden Gate, but some fifteen years or more before it received that name.

The only buildings then seen about the bay were just at the turn, on the right, as you enter the same, called "The Presidio," which we passed and came to anchor some mile or so south, near the shore of little valleys and sandhills, all in their natural forest of bushes and trees. And here, and hereabout, they say is now the city of San Francisco. Some mile or two beyond and back from the bay was a mission called Dolores, consisting of a few, small adobe buildings; and back on the opposite side of the bay were some farmers. . . .

Upper California was then, and till acquired by our war with our neighboring Republic, a Mexican territory. One day its governor came aboard the ship to dine. He had come, I suppose, all the way from Monterey, his capital, for that purpose. His name was Figueroa. There is much said of John Augustus Sutter, as an early settler in this country, but this was long before his time. The only trade to these parts seemed to be by vessels from the States with calico and the like to exchange for hides, their only product, the country being full of cattle, and vessels came in for that purpose while we were there. And not having heard from that country for nearly two years, I inquired with much interest for the news, but was much disappointed in not getting more. He knew that Jackson was still President, and that the nullification business was all settled, but there came the puzzle, what nullification was. I had never heard the term, and he could not define it any further than it was something about South Carolina. . . .

And now we repass the Gate and bear away for the Sandwich Islands, not direct, but bearing southerly, so the sooner to fall into the trade winds. We had a diversity of weather, but none very bad, and with the aid of the sea air I soon got clear, and for good, of my ague. And so we sailed on prosperously and in three weeks, the 22nd of December, 1833, entered the port of Honolulu, having as we approached a splendid view of those high volcanic mountains that constitute all of the higher parts of all these Pacific Islands. I was told before, as I found when there, that all the rock were either coral or volcanic. The island is 14 miles long, and some half that in its widest part, and the mountains 3,000 feet high, a portion of the valley and side mountain, susceptible of cultivation, well watered by streams from the mountains. An old crater called the "Punch Bowl" immediately in rear of the town, say some two or three hundred feet high, was used as a fort, being a basin some half mile across with a grass plot and rocky border.

Before I went on shore myself, the officers of the ship who had been, informed me that they met a man on shore who knew me, and that his name was Brinsmade. As I knew no person of the name except Dr. Brinsmade of Troy, who was my most intimate friend and correspondent, and his two brothers who were clergymen, I took it for granted that one of them was there as a missionary, but when they told me that he was a merchant it seemed a great puzzle. But on meeting him I found that one of the clergymen, from loss of voice or some cause, had changed his business and joined a brother-in-law, a Mr. Ladd, who had come there before, and my friend was indeed a merchant. I will mention here that they had two Chinamen, as clerks in their store, who dressed in their native costume and had the cue of hair. My friend told me that one of them was a great accountant, quick and accurate. Their trade was mostly cash, receiving in a day some hundreds of dollars in Spanish gold ounce pieces, and dollars and shillings in silver. To test his accuracy and honesty he had abstracted from his drawer a sixpence, and after fussing a long time over it would tell him he could not make his accounts balance.

There were strangely here too, four Japanese, and in this way. A strange looking craft was seen off the harbor, and it was found to be a Japanese junk or vessel with but four men alive on board. They were brought in and were kept by a Mr. French, an American merchant, and when they had so far learned English that they could talk with them, they said they got lost, had been out so many moons, that being their way of reckoning time; that the rest had perished for want of food. . . .

The American consul's name was Jones, a Boston man. Mr. Reynolds was from Charlestown, Massachusetts. When the first missionaries,

Mr. Bingham and others, first arrived there in 1818, he received them kindly and did much for their comfort. But when he found they had written home, and their letters were published to be read by his family and friends, representing the resident whites as being a dissolute and wicked set of men, he felt that they had acted an ungrateful part, and in fact, there soon grew up a great dislike between the merchants and missionaries, their business and views clashing severely. So when there I found there was no friendly intercourse between them, the residents having their own minister, a Mr. Deal. I am of the opinion, that as to the change in the ways and opinions of the natives, the missionaries claimed more than their share of being the instruments. Kamehameha First, a short time before their arrival, had abruptly at a feast gone over to the women's table and eaten. And then, in the surprise and commotion arising from a violation of all their fixed customs and usages, he came out in an able speech showing the folly of this and many of their customs and opinions, which so satisfied his people of the truth of his views that on the ground they assailed and broke down their images.

The Catholics of Mexico also sent missionaries to the Islands. But when it was found by the Protestants, that they were rapidly gaining ground, they induced the native government to send them away and punish their adherents by putting them to hard labor on the public roads. This looks a little like persecution.

An American merchant by the name of Hinkley occupied their mission building, one of the best there. To this, for a Christmas dinner, he invited all the resident white gentlemen and ladies, except the missionaries, and the King Kamehameha Third and a few men of his cabinet, but none of the native women. And I was informed that they found them so easy in their manner that the whites, even the missionaries, could not tolerate them in general society. . . .

The natives are indolent and apparently happy in their ways. You would hear them chatting late of the moonshine nights. Still they are strong and enduring. They are often employed aboard whale vessels, and a whaler told me that they were so docile and obedient that if you put a gang in a boat they would row all day long unless told to stop. Still these people, like our Indians, are fast passing away. Mr. Bingham told me they had been dwindling, but he thought at that time, under their influence, they were keeping their own. And that then he estimated the population of the island at 200,000 but he was greatly mistaken. They have constantly dwindled in number, swept off by, to them, new diseases. The measles proved to them as fatal as the plague, in times past, to whites. The same disease very differently affects it seems different races of men. And so it seems there must be an eternal round of races to inhabit this, our earth, island and continent. All races have and probably will have their turn.

I found, on arriving at Honolulu, a trunk so far on its way to the Columbia river from Boston, for me, it being my directions, when I left Lansingburgh that they should thus send to me, if opportunity offered. It contained some clothes and other things, but what just then proved most interesting to me was a file of newspapers. For though all of them a year old or more, I never read news with greater interest. And among the other documents I found General Jackson's nullification message, by the reading of which I learned fully what nullification meant. And that very able state paper added to my great faith in my always favorite statesman. Had we had a Jackson at the helm, when the Rebellion was brewing, I have always thought that things would have taken a different turn. . . .

I did not come here with the expectation of staying long, but to find the means of further return toward home, which I expected would probably be by an American whale ship. I was pleased with the country, and would perhaps have stayed had I found anything to do, and as it was, thought that I would probably return with goods for merchandising. In no place of my long journey was I so much interested, or enjoyed myself so well, but I must go, so I sought a vessel in which to take a passage. And I found the whale ship *Nautillus,* whose captain was named Weeks, and the first mate, Harding. It was nearly full of oil and bound home to New Bedford, would only stop to catch any whale they might meet with on their way. So with the scant money I had, I engaged a passage on her around Cape Horn.

After spending two weeks on this island of Oahu, including Christmas and the New Year of 1834, on the sixth I bade farewell to my Columbia and Honolulu friends, by all of whom I had been treated most kindly, and went aboard ship and sailed. It was a great change indeed, from the society of intelligent men and the agreeable family of my friend Brinsmade, to that of Captain Weeks only, a man who never in his life had been three miles from the sea—born on Martha's Vineyard and raised almost from childhood on shipboard. He knew well how to sail a ship and to catch a whale, but little more. . . .[4]

And now came up strongly the question, "What next is to be done?" I had up to this time rather expected and wished to return to the Sandwich Islands, and received a schedule of goods fitted for that market from the Mr. Brinsmade I met there, by the mail from Valparaiso over to Buenos Aires and so on. But my friends would not aid me in that project, and I gave it up. As to means I brought none back with me, but instead had to economize severely to get around, and all I had was about $400, due me from the avails of the sales of cloth at the factory made before I left, my one-third. . . .

It is but little that one can recollect, or say of himself, when living a life, the daily routine of which is the same. My friend, Dr. T. C. Brinsmade, was now living in Troy, and of course, I often saw him. And he, Dr. Leonard, of Lansingburgh, J. A. Whipple, my sister Powers' partner, and a Mr. Webster proposed to me, as my business was not lucrative, to furnish me with some means to go west and operate in lands, there being then much doing in that line. It was the great year of speculation and I have always thought strange that so sober men as those should have yielded to the mania that so pervaded the country.

When they proposed the project, I fell in with it, for I was glad of an excuse for a change of life. Anything lawful, that would give me occupation, and a possible chance for making something for myself, though my expectations were not as high as theirs. So the agreement was this: that I should take such amount of money as they should furnish from time to time, the amount not limited; go anywhere West, north of the slave states, and operate in real estate, wild Government lands, second hand, village or city. Anything and everything that should promise a safe investment, and probable quick and good and great return. Buy and sell in my own name, as though the money was all my own, and have one-fourth the profits. Though I had none, not even enough to meet expenses.

---

4. After rounding Cape Horn, Ball desperately wanted off the whaler and in Rio de Janeiro was able to secure passage on the American man-of-war *Boxer* by agreeing to serve as the clerk to its commander, Lieutenant David Farragut. Ball returned home to Troy in the summer of 1834.

And I first started out on the 27th of July, 1836; just about two years from my return from the Pacific. I went with a Mr. Mann, who had before been West. Went by railroad to Utica, which was as far as I had ever been in that direction. . . .

And now I procured at the office maps of unsold lands and prepared to go forth to look up the same. And now I left my funds behind, for I had made thus far my journeying with some $1,000 in gold and drafts, I do not remember to what amount, in my saddle bags, but had not been robbed nor did I hear of anything of the kind during all those times of wild speculation. Everyone knowing that each one he met whether on the byroads or in the lone cabins, had money. But in this speculative deal in corner lots and broad wild acres, there was not the same circumspection. No scruples as to exaggerated representation. If one bought today and gave the full value, he had no scruple in taking for the same tomorrow five or ten times the amount from you, his dupe, and all seemed deluded. . . .

Half the population of Grand Rapids was then French, people who had followed Mr. Louis Campau, who had been here as an Indian trader ten years, many of them mechanics, but most of the rest of the white population were here to make their living, like myself, by their wits. And all were full of life and hope as though it were a sure thing. Seeing it was no place for me I stopped but a day and then out again for the woods and looked some lands out in the northeast part of Allegan and western part of Barry and purchased the same.

The rush for Government lands was so great and the soundness of the state banks, the bills of which was the main currency, so doubtful that the Government issued an order that specie only should be received in payment for United States lands. For which President Jackson was much abused; but time showed that that was a much needed measure. Still the purchases went rapidly on and the specie paid in for the same, much or mostly in silver. . . .

And here perhaps I ought to describe the manner of Government surveys. In Michigan all the lands reckon from one point, the intersection of a due east and west and north and south line. These lines intersect on the north line of Jackson County. A township is six miles square making thirty-six square miles. Reckoning north and south from this first east and west line is called 1, 2 and so on, town N. or S. and from the meridional, or N. and S. line they say range 1, 2 and etc., W. or E.

So all this Grand River country reckons north and west. And each township is subdivided into square miles. So each way are lines marked by the surveyor cutting off a chip from each side of trees along the course. And at the mile intersections of these lines, marks on trees with just the initials of the township, range and section. So the land looker, if he knows he is in the state of Michigan thus knows in just what part. . . .

And returning to the land office at Ionia, the question arose as to the division of these lands we had together found. And after some negotiation on the subject the Messrs. Anderson sold me their right in the same, for a few lots I had before bought in Allegan County. I think they were induced to do so from their want of funds. So I made the purchase of the whole tract in my own name. In exploring the Ottawa land the last time we were in the woods about a week, and coming out we stopped at Ezra Chubb's, on his farm in a log cabin between Grandville and Grand Rapids, on whose place near the Grand River are some Indian mounds as well defined as I have ever seen.

I continued my explorations about the country, stopping when not so engaged mostly at Ionia, and there was, all the fall, a great crowd of land lookers coming there to make purchases and often a greater number than could be well accommodated. . . .

When in Detroit that winter I stopped at the American, the same house that was Gov. Hull's before he surrendered the place to the British. Among the boarders were Gov. Mason, unmarried, and Mr. Schoolcraft, whose wife was a half-breed of the Johnson family.[5] She did not often appear at the table, though well educated in England and a real lady in her manners. When she found herself cut by some of the white ladies when at Washington, she could never get over it, but rather retired from company. I now became well acquainted with some of the members of the Legislature from different parts of the state, territory I should say, and the Detroit people and travelers whom I again met. But, just about this time, it was declared a state by an act of Congress, for the Toledo war, for Toledo and the six mile trip, had passed and Michigan

---

5. General William Hull, a Revolutionary veteran placed in command of the defense of Michigan in the War of 1812, surrendered Fort Detroit and his army without a fight. This humiliating event figures also in the autobiographies of Alfred Lorrain and Allen Trimble. Henry Rowe Schoolcraft was Superintendent of Indian Affairs for Michigan when Ball met him, but made his reputation as a distinguished mineralogist.

had consented to take the Upper Peninsula. And when the news reached Detroit it was celebrated by discharge of canon, etc.

Going along Jefferson Avenue I noticed two boys ahead of me talking earnestly, but all that I understood, one said to the other, immediately after the discharge of a cannon, "Now Michigan is a state."

DANIEL DRAKE

1785–1852

DANIEL Drake grew up on the Kentucky frontier surrounded by a farming community of relatives and friends who had migrated west from New Jersey with his parents. Drake provides a wonderfully detailed picture of the round of chores that absorbed his every hour as a boy. As the eldest child, his laboring capacity was quickly incorporated into the yearly round of tasks both in the house and on the farm. By the time he was twelve, Drake knew how to make brooms, soap, cheese, and sausage; slaughter hogs; wash sheep; shear, card, dye, and spin wool; and churn cream into butter—all activities lovingly described in his autobiography.

Drake's father, perhaps sensing his son's ability, pledged to educate him so that he could become a benefactor to society; by his fifth birthday, it had been decided that Drake would become a physician. Despite the remoteness of their Kentucky home from any center of learning, Drake scraped together an education based on his reading of Aesop's fables, Benjamin Franklin's *Autobiography*, John Dickinson's *Letters from a Farmer in Pennsylvania*, and Lord Chesterfield's *Letters to His Son*. Drake's eager embrace of a larger world is reflected in his comment that Chesterfield's ideas "fell in mightly close with my tastes, and not less with those of father and mother, who cherished as high and pure an idea of the duty of good breeding as any people on earth."[1]

---

1. Daniel Drake, *Pioneer Life in Kentucky: A Series of Reminiscential Letters,* ed.

Like Ball, Drake greatly admired his mother, giving her credit for religious education. Although she could not write, she could read the Bible and John Bunyan's *Pilgrim's Progress.* "Her theory of morals was abundantly simple," Drake explains, *"—God has said it!"* It was she who taught him the household tasks that he had to perform until his young sisters were old enough to take over.

In 1800 Drake went to study medicine with a doctor in Cincinnati, when the town, scarcely a dozen years old, had fewer than 400 inhabitants. After three and a half years he became a partner of his mentor. They charged from three to four dollars a day for their services at a time when manual laborers earned from seventy-five cents to a dollar, but Drake figured that they would collect only a quarter of their billing.

A zealous student, Drake went to Philadelphia to attend medical lectures in 1805, then returned to practice in Cincinnati, where he married Harriet Sisson of New Haven, Connecticut. After his wife's death in 1825, Drake poured out his heart in an essay, "Emotions, Reflections, and Anticipations." In it he explains that they had been "cojoined on principles of equality." "We began the world in love and hope and poverty," he writes. "It was all before us, and we were under the influence of the same ambition to possess it; to acquire not wealth merely, but friends, knowledge, influence, distinction." Describing his wife's growing intellectual development, he stresses their parity: "We had equal industry and equal aspiration."

During the early years of his marriage, Drake became interested in writing, and his wife became his first reader, bringing "taste, judgment, severity, and love" to her role as critic. She accompanied him on house calls, waiting for him in their "gig" while reading. Eloquently expressing his grief at her loss, Drake concludes the essay with a poignant declaration that he "had no separate social or sensual gratifictions, no tavern

---

Charles D. Drake (Cincinnati, 1907), p. 165. Lord Chesterfield was a distinguished political figure in eighteenth-century England and a man of letters whose name became synonymous with elegant manners and good taste because of the witty and elegant advice he wrote to his son.

orgies, no political club recreations, no dissipated pleasures nor companions. Society was no society to me without her presence and cooperation."[2]

Drake became the most important intellectual and scientific figure in Cincinnati. His *Notices Concerning Cincinnati* of 1810 represented the fruits of his direct observations of his surroundings, a talent he amply displays in the autobiographical reminiscences of his childhood. He followed his first publication up in 1815 with his *Natural and Statistical View, or Picture of Cincinnati and the Miami Country.* During this time Drake worked hard to establish a western museum to display the artifacts of the Ohio River Valley. He was also instrumental in establishing the School of Literature and Arts in 1813, when Cincinnati had a population of 4,000.

A man of extraordinary energy, Drake also became the first professor of materia medica at Transylvania University in Lexington, Kentucky, in 1817. Preferring to practice in Cincinnati, he started the Medical College of Ohio as president in 1820 and next turned his attention to the building of a hospital with $10,000 from the state in depreciated bank currency. The center of a stormy controversy over this effort, Drake was thrown out of his medical college by the four other professors, a turn of events he describes in *Narrative of the Rise and Fall of the Medical College of Ohio.* For the rest of his academic career, Drake went back and forth between the medical schools of Lexington and Cincinnati (where he was reinstated as a professor).

In 1827 Drake became the editor of the *Western Medical and Physical Journal.* Not content with the four careers of physician, professor, writer, and naturalist, Drake became an active promoter of railroads in 1835. As his autobiography so graphically demonstrates, he was indeed what his son described him to be: "by nature a pioneer and projector." He began his memoirs when he was sixty-two, casting them as affection-

---

2. Drake, *Pioneer Life*, p. xv–xvi. Charles Drake published the essay in the preface.

ate letters to his son, two daughters, two sons-in-law, and adopted daughter. The first letter was dated December 15, 1847.

⤳ ℰ ⤳

*T*W O hours more, my dear Harriet, will complete forty-seven years since I left the log cabin of my father and the arms of my mother, to engage in the study of medicine in the village of Cincinnati, often, at that time, called Fort Washington. Two years ago, on the anniversary of my departure, I took it into my head to give your sister an off-hand sketch of that, to the family and myself, memorable event, and of my journey, and introduction into the family of Dr. Goforth. . . .

After the marriage of my parents, about the year 1738, they went to housekeeping near my grandfather Drake's, on his land, where the town of Plainfield now is. He owned a small grist mill on a branch of the Raritan river called Boundbrook, and my father's occupation was to "tend" it. The first born of the family was a daughter, who was named Phebe, and died in infancy. The next in order was myself, which in some countries, would have made me a miller. . . .

His [my father's] father and the neighbors were generally Baptists. Mr. Wood visited among them, and gave such glowing accounts of Kentucky, that old Virginia was soon forgotten. The Rev. Mr. Gano, of New York, another Baptist minister, or some of his sons, had visited Kentucky, and his breath of praise still further fanned the flame; till at length the iron ties of affection for home and friends were melted, and a departure was determined upon. The decision extended to five families. . . . The time fixed on for their departure was the latter part of the spring of 1788. Their first point was Red Stone Old Fort, where Brownsville, Pennsylvania, now stands. Their mode of traveling was in two-horse wagons. The family of my father consisted, after himself and my mother, of myself, about two years and seven months old, my sister, Elizabeth, afterward Mrs. Glenn, then an infant at the breast, and my mother's unmarried sister, Lydia, who chose to accompany her into the wilderness, rather than submit to the caprices of a stepmother for a longer time.

Behold, then the departure! These five persons, three of whom were adults, with all their earthly goods crowded into one Jersey wagon, to

be hauled by two horses over the yet steep and rugged Alleghany mountains, and throughout an overland journey of nearly four hundred miles.
Their travel was by Corryell's ferry, on the Delaware, and Harris' ferry,
now Harrisburg, which you have visited, on the Susquehanna. There
were but few taverns on the way, and if there had been many, we should
not have been much the better for them, as father's means were too
limited to admit of a participation in their comforts. He could only purchase necessary food, which was cooked when we stopped at night and
before we started in the morning. As the weather was mild, our lodgings
were often in the wagon. In this important and difficult enterprise I no
doubt played, to others, a troublesome part; but I can say nothing from
memory. . . .

The first residence of our family was in a covered pen or shed, built
for sheep, adjoining the cabin of its owner. How long we continued in it
I am unable to say. While occupying it, my mother one day made a call
at a neighboring cabin, where a woman was churning. Tired out with a
diet of bread and meat, mother fixed her heart on a drink of buttermilk,
but said nothing. When the butter was ladled out and the churn set
aside, with the delicious beverage, for which she was too proud to ask
(and which the other perhaps did not *think* of giving), she hastily left
the house, and took a good crying spell. Thus you see whence came my
propensity, and Dove's and Charlie's, for crying. We all, in fact, resem-
ble my mother in temperament, of which this is one of the proofs; while
another is our hereditary propensity to go to sleep in church! Your
brother Charles and yourself have the temperament of your mother and
my father. . . .

From the day of the landing of the little colony, composed of the
three Drakes and Shotwell and Morris, the older and more intelligent
men had been casting about for a tract of land, which they might purchase, and divide among themselves. At length they fixed upon a "settlement and preemption," eight miles from Washington, on the Lexington
road. Hard-by the latter there was a salt spring, and the deer and buffalo
were in the habit, as at other salt springs, of "licking" the surrounding
earth. This tract of fourteen hundred acres they purchased from a man
by the name of May, and decided on calling their new home Mayslick—a
decision sufficiently indicative of uncultivated taste. . . . The purchase
being made, the next thing was to divide the tract, and give to each of
the five a portion equal to his means of payment. That of my father was

thirty-eight acres, which I believe he afterward contrived to augment to fifty. How he paid even for this small participation, I am unable to state; most likely, by selling his wagon and one of his horses. . . .

There are events in our lives of such moment, that when the anniversary of their occurrence returns, the memory of them seems to bring with it the memory of many others, no way connected with them but in the continued consciousness of the individual. The same is true of nations, or the national mind. When the anniversary of the battle of Saratoga or Trenton comes round, if we notice it at all, our range of thought on the war of the Revolution is quite limited; but on the 4th of July we are incited to a review of the causes, events, and consequences of that war. . . .

In my own life, my departure from the house of my father for the study of medicine was the governing event; and when the anniversary of that act comes round, it calls up a multitude of reminiscences, by no means limited to the act itself, but ranging far up and down the chronography of my life. It was the 16th day of December when I started; this day, the 17th, I entered the State of Ohio; to-morrow will be the anniversary of my arrival in Cincinnati; and two days after (the 20th) that on which I began my studies, forty-seven years ago, and also the day of my marriage, seven years afterward. Thus, you see, I am in the midst of my greatest anniversary epoch, and, of course, in the state of thought and feeling into which I find it precipitates me deeper and deeper with each rolling year. . . .

The first event I can remember I have described in my letter to Harriet Echo. It occurred in the autumn or beginning of the winter of 1788, when I had entered on my fourth year. For the next six years my father continued to reside at the same place, in the same original log cabin, which in due course of time acquired a roof, a puncheon floor below and a clap-board roof above, a small square window without glass, and a chimney, carried up with "cats and clay" to the height of the ridgepole. These "cats and clay" were pieces of small poles, well imbedded in mortar. The rifle, indispensable both for hunting and defense, lay on two pegs driven into one of the logs; the axe and scythe—no Jerseyman emigrated without those implements—were kept at night under the bed as weapons of defense, in case the Indians should make an attack. In the morning the first duty was to ascend, by a ladder which always stood leaning behind the door, to the loft, and look out through the cracks for *from attacks* Indians, lest they might have planted themselves near the door, to rush in when the strong cross-bar should be removed, and the heavy latch raised from its resting place. But no attack was ever made on his or any other of the five cabins which composed the station. . . .

From the time of their arrival in Kentucky, fourteen months before, they had suffered from want of bread, and now they found themselves doomed to the same deficiency for another year. There was no fear of famine, but they cloyed on animal food, and sometimes almost loathed it, though of an excellent quality. Deer were numerous, and wild turkeys numberless. . . .

About the same period, the Indians one night attacked a body of travelers, encamped a mile from our village on the road to Washington. They were sitting quietly round their camp-fire, when the Indians shot among them and killed a man, whose remains I remember to have seen brought, the next day, into the village on a rude litter. The heroic presence of mind of a woman saved the party. She broke open a chest in one of the wagons with an axe, got at the ammunition, gave it to the men, and called upon them to fight. This, with the extinction of their camp-fires, led the Indians to retreat. That night made an unfading impression on my mind. We went, with uncle Abraham Drake's family, I think, to uncle Cornelius' for concentration and greater safety. Several of the men of the village went to the relief of the travelers, and one of them, a young married man, ran into the village and left his wife behind him! The alarm of my mother and aunts, communicated, of course, to all the children, was deep, and the remembrance of the scene was long kept vividly alive by talking it over and over.

Up to the victory of Wayne in 1794, the danger from Indians still continued; that is, through a period of six years from the time of our arrival. I well remember that Indian wars, midnight butcheries, captivities, and horse-stealings, were the daily topics of conversation. Volunteering to pursue marauding parties occasionally took place, and sometimes men were drafted. This happened once to father. Whether it was for Harmar's campaign in 1790, or St. Clair's in 1791, I can not say; but he hired an unmarried man as a substitute, and did not go. At that time, as at present, there were many young men who delighted in war much more than work, and therefore preferred the tomahawk to the axe. I remember that when the substitute returned he had many wonderful tales to tell, but am unable to rehearse a single one. . . .

At that period, the Shawnees residing on the Scioto, and the Wyandots on the Sandusky, were our great enemies. The children were told at night, "lie still and go to sleep, or the Shawnees will catch you.". . .

My first school-master had the Scotch name of McQuitty, but whether he was from the "land o' cakes," I can not say. He taught in a very small log cabin in sight of father's, up the creek which flows through Mayslick; and a beautiful stream it was when it had any water running in it. My dim recollections suggest that I was about five years old when I was his pupil for a short time. Of my progress I can say nothing. . . . Under his tuition I presume I made some progress, for in 1792 and 1793 I was a pretty good reader, and maintained my place respectably when we stood up to spell, before school was "let out" in the evening. My teacher then was Hiram Miram Curry, who, I think, had been a Baptist preacher, and made us, I remember, "get by heart" the catechism. He taught at first in the village, south of the brook, and then up the road beyond the meeting-house, where hickory switches were abundant. I think I went to him as late as 1794, and had begun to write before I left him. . . .

It was father's business, of course, to do the heavy chopping; mine, to hack down saplings, and cut off the limbs of trees, and pile them into brush heaps. The forests consisted chiefly of blue-ash, tall, straight, soft while green, easily hewed, and easily split into rails and puncheons; of sugar trees—generally preserved; of several kinds of hickory and walnut, and of buckeye. The last was so soft that it soon became my favorite, and to the readiness with which it yielded to my axe. . . .

The brush was of course burnt up as fast as it was cut, and of all the labor in the forest, I consider that of dragging and burning the limbs of trees the most delightful. To me it made toil a pleasure. The rapid disappearance of what was thrown upon the fire gave the feeling of progress; the flame was cheering; the crackling sound imparted animation; the columns of smoke wound their way upward, in graceful curves, among the tall green trees left standing; and the limbs and twigs of the hickory sent forth a balmy and aromatic odor, which did not smell of the schoolhouse.

In due time a "log-rolling" frolic was gotten up, when the buckeye showed that, if pressed too far, it could resist; for its consumption by

---

fire was effected with more difficulty than that of any other tree. The ground being prepared, and the logs collected and hewed on one side, the new cabin, a considerable improvement on the old, was "raised," and brought to some degree of finish; though glass could not be afforded, and a kitchen could not be put up till a stable had been first built. At length the day for removal arrived, and we left the village and public roadside, with its cavalcade of travelers, for the loneliness of the woods; a solitude which very soon was deeply felt by us all, but most of all, I think, by mother. . . .

Twelve hours ago, I finished a letter of eighteen pages to your brother Charles, which I shall send off to-morrow. It was preceded by one to your sister Echo, of fifteen pages, which must have reached her this morning. At the end of each I determined to write no more this winter on the same subject, but here I am already violating my good resolution. . . .

To prepare the new field for cultivation required only the axe and mattock, but the cultivation itself called for the plow and hoe; both of which I recollect were abundantly rude and simple in their construction. Deep plowing was not as necessary as in soils long cultivated, and if demanded would have been impracticable, for the ground was full of roots. After a first "breaking up" with the coultered plow, the shovel plow was in general use. In such rooty soils it was often difficult to hold the plow and drive the horse; it was the employment of small boys, therefore, to ride and guide the animal—a function which I performed in plowing time for many years; and it was, I can assure you, no sinecure. To sit bareback on a lean and lazy horse for several successive hours, under a broiling sun, and every now and then, when you were gazing at a pretty bird, or listening to its notes, or watching the frolic of a couple of squirrels on the neighboring trees, to have the plow suddenly brought to a dead halt by running under a root, and the top of the long hames to give you a hard and unlooked-for punch in the pit of the stomach, is no laughing matter, try it who may. . . .

But I must reconduct you to the cornfield, the scene of my earliest labors and most cherished recollections. Nothing is equal to the Indian corn for the settlers of a new and isolated spot. At the present time, when steamboats not only transport the movers to every point, but afterward supply them with flour and every needful article of food, the value of corn to the first settlers of Kentucky can only be estimated by those who witnessed the pressure of the arm of civilization against the resisting forest, and saw that men had to support themselves while they were performing the very labor from which support must come. In the new soil, corn, with moderate cultivation, yielded from sixty to eighty bushels to the acre. Every domestic animal fed and flourished on it—the horse, the cow, the sheep, the hog, and the dog, who, as wheat-bread came into use, would not eat it. The blades of corn up to the ears were "pulled," as the latter began to harden and when partly dried were tied, with blades, into bundles; the tops above the ears were cut off and "shocked." After the corn was pulled, the tops were hauled in, and covered the long fodder house, in which the blades and husks were stowed away, while the corn was measured and thrown into a crib of long round poles. Here, then, were provender and provision for the coming winter. Neither wheat, nor rye, nor barley, nor the far-famed potato, could have been substituted for the admirable maize. Several things in its cultivation can be done by small boys, and from my eighth year I participated in them. When the field was "cross-furrowed," the furrows being about four feet apart, dropping the corn was a simple task, and father, following with the hoe, would cover it. When I was a little older and the furrows ran in one direction only, much greater skill was requisite; for the rows must be kept straight and parallel, that cross-plowing might be practiced. The method then was, as it still is, to cross the furrows at right angles, in lines four feet apart, by the aid of stakes or sharpened poles, generally of hickory or pawpaw, with the bark peeled off, so as to be white and easily seen. To drop by the range of these stakes, had something in it that was intellectual or scientific, though I knew not then that there were such terms. . . .

But I must pass on to the antagonisms of the corn-husking. When the crop was drawn in, the ears were heaped into a long pile or rick, a night fixed on, and the neighbors notified, rather than invited, for it was an affair of mutual assistance. As they assembled at night-fall the green glass quart whisky bottle, stopped with a cob, was handed to every one, man and boy, as they arrived, to take a drink. A sufficient number to constitute a sort of quorum having arrived, two men, or more commonly two boys, constituted themselves, or were by acclamation declared captains. They paced the rick and estimated its contractions and expansions with the eye, till they were able to fix on the spot on which the end of the dividing rail should be. The choice depended on the tossing of a chip, one side of which had been spit upon; the first choice of men was decided in the same manner, and in a few minutes the rick was charged upon by the rival forces. As others arrived, as soon as the owner had given each the bottle, he fell in, according to the end that he belonged to. The captains planted themselves on each side of the rail, sustained by their most active operatives. There at the beginning was the great contest, for it was lawful to cause the rail to slide or fall toward your own end, shortening it and lengthening the other. Before I was twelve years old I had stood many times near the rail, either as captain or private, and although fifty years have rolled away, I have never seen a more anxious rivalry, nor a fiercer struggle. It was there that I first learned that competition is the mother of cheating, falsehood, and broils. Corn might be thrown over unhusked, the rail might be pulled toward you by the hand dexterously applied underneath, your feet might push corn to the other side of the rail, your husked corn might be thrown so short a distance as to bury up the projecting base of the pile on the other side:—if charged with any of these tricks, you of course denied it, and there the matter sometimes rested; at other times the charge was re-affirmed, then rebutted with "you're a liar," and then a fight, at the moment or at the end, settled the question of veracity. The heap cut in two, the parties turned their backs upon each other, and making their hands keep time with a peculiar sort of time, the chorus of voices on a still night might be heard a mile. The oft-replenished whisky bottle meanwhile circulated freely, and at the close the victorious captain, mounted on the shoulders of some of the stoutest men, with the bottle in one hand and his hat in the other, was carried in triumph around the vanquished party amidst shouts of victory which rent the air. Then came the supper, on which the women had been busily employed, and which always included a "pot-pie." Either before or after eating the fighting took place, and by midnight the sober were found assisting the drunken home. Such was one of my autumnal schools, from the age of nine to fifteen years.

And now, I suppose, you hope I am done with Indian corn, but not so; I am only done with the field and frolic. Its preparation for the table must not be overlooked; I mean preparing it for the hands of the cook. . . .

Our first and cheapest implement was the tin grater eight or nine inches long. It was used to reduce to a sort of pulp the unripe corn, when it had got too old for roasting ears, and was too soft to pound or grind. The ear was rubbed up and down on this instrument, over which, at the age of seven or eight years, and still later, I often tired my right arm and sometimes lacerated my fingers. When the corn had got ripe and dry, it was sometimes thrown into the hominy block, and sometimes taken to the hand-mill. The concavity or mortar of the block was made by burning; the pestle was an iron wedge (used for splitting rails) let into a wooden handle. Many a long hour did I toil over this mortar, which, for aught I know, was one cause why I was adverse to the study of medicine. As this was not the mortar Shakespeare had in his eye, I can not (classically) lay the blame of my cramped genius upon it, and still I must be indulged in the opinion, that its power in developing the mind is not equal to its efficacy in developing the muscles of the arms.

Mary Wolstoncraft remarks of girls that in her day were compelled to sew a great deal as a part of their education, that their ideas at length came to follow their needles.[1] In like manner mine went up and down with the pestle. The needle made progress, but the pestle, like a paper dancer between two electrified plates, still continued to move up and down, forever up and down! Time, however, which cures everything except egotism and garrulity, so applied his skill to my feelings against the hominy block, that forty-five years afterward, when I saw, at Mackinaw, two Chippewa squaws pounding their corn in the same mortar (in the manner of the two Jewish women), I felt no repugnance at the sight. To the wedge and mortar succeeded the hand-mill. A rod with its upper end run through a hole in the board, and its lower resting in a cavity or hollow, pecked out near to the circumference of the upper millstone, was seized with the right hand, while the left threw the corn into the large opening at the center. Here again was motion without progression; but the meal flowed out, and its stream was augmented as the velocity of the stone was increased, giving to effort *immediate* reward, which, down to the present hour, I have observed to be its greatest stimulus. My father never owned a hand-mill, but on those of his neighbors, when ten or twelve years of age, I have ground many a small grist, often taking

---

1. Mary Wollstonecraft was the famous English author of *The Vindication of the Rights of Woman* (1792). Drake's reference to her is rather surprising, for Wollstonecraft, who had a well-publicized affair before she married the English philosopher William Godwin, was considered too audacious a figure for Americans, like Drake, who emulated Victorian cultural models.

my sister Elizabeth to lend a hand to the work. We, of course, went on foot, and I "toted" the peck of corn on my back. Water and horse-mills had been built before I was old enough to perform the labors I have just noted; but they were for many years few and feeble. . . .

Father and mother, however, like the other immigrants, longed for wheat bread, and as soon as practicable wheat was sown. The fallow was but little attended to, and the sowing was generally in the cornfield, sometime after the corn had been "laid by." The ground had to be plowed with the shovel-plow, and until I was twelve years old it was my function to ride the horse, and have both legs stuck with Spanish needles up to my knees. Having no shoes and stockings (superfluous things in early autumn), and tow trousers, which would slip half way to the knee, the service was not the most enviable. After about my twelfth year I was able to hold the plow and guide the horse. A narrow wooden harrow or a brushy limb of a tree, and subsequently the hoe, covered up the grain and finished the rude "seeding."

Harvest was a social labor, a frolic, a scene of excitement, and therefore a much more desirable era than that of seeding. My first labor in that field was to carry the sheaves to the places on which they were to be shocked. The next was to bind up the handsful of cut wheat, a more difficult task for a small boy. My ambition was to wield the sickle. . . . In the harvest field my greatest ambition was to sweat so as to wet my shirt. I then first noticed, that, under the same circumstances, men sweat more than boys; but the circumstances were not precisely the same; for the former drank more whisky than the latter, and it contributed to the sudorific effect. . . .

In winter rural economy, at nightfall, is, in a new country, before barns and stables and sheds have been built, an interesting period of the day. The stock must be collected, fed, and disposed of in the best manner possible for the night. Did you ever pass an evening under such circumstances? The memory of such evening scenes can never fall out of my mind. The voice of the hungry and impatient calf still rings in my ears. As the evening approached its cry was sent forth, and the tones, slightly tinged with the mournful, when I chance to hear them repeated, awaken to this hour in my heart a kind of romantic melancholy. Father and mother were early risers, and I was drilled into the same habit before I was ten years old. In winter we were generally up before the dawn of day. After making a fire, the first thing was feeding and foddering the horses, hogs, sheep and cattle. Corn, husks, blades, and tops had to be distributed, and times without number I have done this by the light of the moon reflected on the snow. This done at an earlier hour than common, old Lion and I sometimes took a little hunt in the woods; but were never very successful. I had a taste for hunting, but neither time nor genius for any great achievement in that way. Among the pleasant recollections of those mornings are the red-birds, robins, and snow-birds, which made their appearance to pick up the scattering grains of corn where the cattle had been fed. I well remember my anxiety to get some fresh salt to throw on their tails. I often made conical lattice-work traps, and set them; but not, I believe, with any great tact, for my captures were not numerous.

Our stock required attention in other seasons of the year than the winter. For several years our fences were low and open, and the corn-field was a place of irresistible attractions. The horses and sheep would jump the fence, the cows would throw it down with their horns, and the hogs would creep between the rails; when the cry would be "Run, Dannel, run!" and away went "Dannel" with his fellow laborer, old Lion. . . .

Up to the time of my leaving home, at the age of fifteen, my mother never had a "hired girl," except in sickness; and father never purchased a slave, for two substantial reasons: *first,* he had not the means; and, *second,* he was so opposed to slavery that he would not have accepted the best negro in Kentucky, as a gift, provided he would have been compelled to keep him as a slave. Now and then he hired one, male or female, by the day, from some neighboring master (white hirelings being scarce), but he or mother never failed to give something to the slave in return for the service. In this destitution of domestic help, and with from three to six children, of which I was the oldest, you will readily perceive that she had urgent need, daily and nightly, of all the assistance I could give her. To this service, I suppose, I was naturally well adapted, for I do not now recollect that it was ever repugnant to my feelings. At all events I acquiesced in it as a matter of duty—a thing of course; for what could she do, how get on, without my aid? I do not think, however, that I reasoned upon it like a moralist, but merely followed the promotings of those filial instincts of obedience, duty, and co-operation, which are among the elements of a system of moral philosophy. . . .

I have already spoken of grating and pounding corn, toting water from a distant spring, holding the calf by the ears at milking time, going to the pond on wash-days, and divers other labors with which mother was intimately connected. But my domestic occupations were far more extensive than these. To chop, split, and bring in wood, keep up the fire, pick up chips in the corn basket for kindlings in the morning, and for light through the long winter evenings when "taller" was too scarce to afford sufficient candles, and "fat" so necessary for cooking, that the boat-lamp, stuck into one of the logs of the cabin over the hearth, could not always be supplied, were regular labors. To bring water from the spring, which was but a short distance from the house, was another. To slop the cows, and, when wild, drive them into a corner of the fence, and stand over them with a stick while mother milked them, was another. Occasionally I assisted her in milking, but sister Lizzy was taught that accomplishment as early as possible, seeing that it was held by the whole neighborhood to be quite too "gaalish" for a boy to milk; and mother, quite as much as myself, would have been mortified, if any neighboring boy or man had caught me at it. In 1842, when I was sailing on the northern lakes in quest of information on the condition, customs, and diseases of the Indians, a gentleman who had been much among them told me, that as he was once traveling a bridle path, he saw, some distance ahead, an Indian family about to meet him. The man had on his shoulders a heavy pack, and his wife was following him. They instantly stepped aside into the woods, and when they resumed the path, the burden was on her shoulders. It is evident that he had some tenderness of heart, and while they were alone he was willing to relieve her, and she willing that he should do it; but neither could consent to his performing so feminine a labor in the sight of others. The rifle was his appropriate burden. Thus it is that from the bark wigwam to the log cabin, and thence to the palace, public opinion displays its fantastic tyrannies. By a strange inconsistency, while it proscribed milking by boys, it permitted churning; and if I had as many dollars as times I have lifted the "dasher," I might give up teaching, and devote the remainder of my days to writing nonsense for the amusement of my grandchildren. If I could have as many rational wishes gratified as I uttered wishes that the butter would come, I should have nothing more to wish for in this life. But, in truth, like pounding corn into meal in a hominy block, it was a hard and monotonous employment, especially in the latter stages of the process, when the butter rises on the dasher.

Friday was mother's wash-day, and then, when the duties of the field were not urgent, I left it for the house. A long trough dug out of the trunk of a tree stood under the back eaves to catch rain-water for washing, and during times of drought, when a shower came up, all the wash-tubs, and buckets of the house were set out. Still it often happened that much had to be brought from the spring. . . .

When speaking of milk and butter I forgot to tell you that I knew the art and mystery of cheese making, often prepared the rennet, and assisted in squeezing out the whey from the curds; and, although father made the press, I was mother's right-hand man in managing the long lever, while she placed the cheese beneath as its fulcrum.

December was our "killing time." I shall not take you to the hog pen, nor the scalding tub, but begin with cutting up the fat, a work to which boys are well adapted. The fat being "tried" out, the next labor was chopping sausage meat, which I began with a hatchet because too small to lift a heavier tool, and continued till I could use the axe with a vigorous arm. The stripping, twisting into links, hanging on poles, and moderate smoke-drying succeeded. Lastly, the frying and the *feast;* for in those days of simple fare, the annual return of the sausage season was hailed by the whole family. To this hour I prefer good, and especially *clean* sausage, to any other meat.

The same season and the same killing were followed by other labors of an interesting kind. A Jersey housekeeper could never neglect or forget the delicious mince pie, in the manufacture of which I have wielded the chopping axe full many a hour. For a long time, however, apples were too "dear" and scarce to justify a large application of them to that object. Our compositions, compared with those of modern times, were abundantly simple, but on that account more salubrious, and as our tastes were formed to no more savory mixture, they were eaten as delicious. . . .

When I look back upon the useful arts which mother and I were accustomed to practice, I am almost surprised at their number and variety, and although I did not then regard them as anything but incidents of poverty and ignorance, I now view them as knowledge, as elements of mental growth. Among them was coloring. A standing dye-stuff was the inner bark of the white walnut, from which we obtained that peculiar and permanent shade of dull yellow—the butternut—so common in these days. The hulls of the black walnut gave us a rusty black. Oak bark, with copperas as a mordant (when father had money to purchase it), afforded a better tint of the same kind, and supplied the ink with which I learned to write. Indigo, which cost eighteen pence an ounce, was used for blue; and madder, when we could obtain it at three shillings a pound, brought out a dirty red. In all these processes I was once almost an adept. As cotton was not then in use in this country (or in Europe) and flax can with difficulty be colored, our material was generally wool or linsey woolsey; and this brings me once more to the flock.

It was common, as a preparation for shearing, to drive the sheep to some pond or stream, where there was sufficient water—that which was running answered best—and wash the wool while on their backs. Too weak to hold and wash a sheep, it was my function to assist in driving, and to keep the flock together at the water's edge; no very easy task, from their instinctive aversion to that fluid. Yet such a labor was a frolic, and broke in upon the lonely routine of daily life at home. In the shearing I could do something more, for then the animal is thrown upon the ground and tied. At eleven or twelve I could handle the shears very well, and felt proud of the accomplishment. The shearing and weighing done, then came the very different task of picking. At that time our little fields were badly cultivated, and whether the sheep were kept up or suffered to run at large in the woods, their wool became matted with cockles and other burs, which could only be disentangled with the fingers. In this wearisome labor I have toiled through many a long rainy day, with my sisters and sometimes father and mother around the same fleece. There is no labor of boyhood that I look back upon with less satisfaction than this. To the carding I lent a cheerfuller helping hand, and could roll out as many good rolls in a given time as any "gaal" of the neighborhood. Mother generally did the spinning; but the "double and twisting" was a work in which I took real pleasure. The "buz" of the big wheel, rising (as I walked backwards and turned the rim with increased velocity) from the lowest to the highest note of the octave, still seems like music in my ear. To this process succeeded the reeling into skeins, and afterward the winding of a part of these into balls, for stockings. In the last operation, I got my first lesson of patience under perplexity. When a tangled skein fell into my hands, fretfulness and impatience, its first fruits, were utterly at war with progress. Alas! how long it takes us to become submissive to such simple teachings. In the long and chequered life through which I have passed since those days, how many tangled skeins have fallen into my hands, and how often have I forgotten the patience, which my dear mother then inculcated upon me. Human life itself is but one long and large tangled skein, and in untwisting one thread we too often involve some others more fatally. Death, at last, untangles all. To the eye of common observation the spacious firmament appears not less a tangled, than a shining frame, and yet, Newton, *by patience,* as he himself declared, reduced (for the human mind) the whole to order. . . .

I was preserved from many temptations, and practically taught self-denial, because indulgence beyond certain narrow limits was so much out of the question as not to be thought of. I was taught to practice economy, and to think of money as a thing not to be expended on luxuries, but to be used for useful ends. I was taught the value of learning, by being denied the opportunities for acquiring more than a pittance. I was taught the value of time, by having more to do day after day than could be well accomplished. I was molded to do many things, if not absolutely at the same time, in such quick succession as almost to render them identical; a habit which I have found of great advantage to me through life. But better than all these, I grew up with love and obedience to my mother, and received from her an early moral training, to which, in conjunction with that of my father, I owe, perhaps, more of my humble success in life, and of my humble preparation for the life to come, than to any other influence. She was still more illiterate than my father, but was pious, and could read the Bible, Rippon's hymns, and *Pilgrim's Progress.* Her natural understanding was tolerable only, but she comprehended the principles of domestic and Christian duty, and sought to inculcate them. This she never did by protracted lectures, but mixed them up with all our daily labors. Thus my monitor was always by my side, and ready with her reproof, or admonition, or rewarding smile, as occasion required or opportunity arose. Unlike many (so called wiser) teachers, she instructed me as to what was *sin.* Her theory of morals was abundantly simple—*God has said it!* The Bible forbids this, and commands that, and God will punish you if you act contrary to his word! What philosopher could have risen so high? How simple and yet how sublime! How often did I and my sisters and brothers hear that impressive word *"wicked"* fall from her lips in the midst of her toilsome and never ceasing household duties! How seldom does it fall on the ears of many children, born under what are called happier auspices! It was wicked to treat anything which had life with cruelty; it was wicked to neglect the cattle or forget the little lambs in winter; it was wicked to

waste or throw away bread or meat; it was wicked to strike or quarrel
with each other; . . . it was wicked to be lazy, to be disobedient, to work
on the Sabbath, to tell a falsehood, to curse and swear, to get drunk, or
to fight. To this last she had a constitutional as well as a moral repugnance, and to my participation in her temperament, not less than to her
precepts, I may ascribe that peaceful timidity of character, which often
painfully embarrassed me in boyhood, but at the same time preserved
me from many scenes of violence and profanity. . . .

When, two years ago, on the forty-fifth anniversary of my departure
from home to study medicine, I yielded to the old man's instinct to the
past, and gave you, in twelve or fourteen pages, some account of that
departure, the transition to a new kind of life, the beginning of a different
career, I did not intend (for I did not even debate the matter with myself)
to follow that letter up with any more of the same sort. Nevertheless, I
have done it this winter, till passing round the family circle I have come
to you, with whom I started, and now propose to write you a second
time. In my former letter I told you that I was put to the study of medicine without the requirements which are now made by the scholars of
our most ordinary public schools. . . .

With Master Smith I began my classical studies. True, he knew nothing of grammar, etymology, geography, or mathematics; but he had
picked up a dozen lines of Latin poetry, which I had an ambition (carried
out) to commit to memory. I was much taken with the sounds of the
words—the first I had ever heard beyond my mother tongue. From the
few I now recollect, I presume the quotation was from the eclogues of
Virgil. Master Smith changed his locality, and another long vacation ensued.

My next school-house was east of Mayslick, but in the edge of the
village, about a mile and a quarter from father's. It was kept in a cabin
built by Lawson, a tenant of his while living in the Lick, and my play-
ground now was, in part, the cucumber patch in which Tom and I stole
the cucumbers. I went to this school in winter, and had many a cold
tramp through deep snows, which filled my shoes in spite of old stocking
legs drawn over them. Of my progress here I can not recollect anything.
I only know that I did not enter on any new study, and that I extended
the old a little. Two incidents, however, remain in my memory, and I
will mention them as illustrating my character at that time. A boy by the

name of Walter, from mere mischief (for we had a quarrel), struck me a hard blow and cut one of my lips, which I did not resent, as most boys would have done; but quietly put up with it. When I went home at night, and was asked the cause of the assault, father blamed and shamed me for my cowardice. I felt mortified, but was not aroused to any kind or degree of revenge. The other incident was this. In the open field in which the school-house stood, the boys were accustomed to roll great balls of snow, and then dividing themselves into two parties, one was to have possession of the mass, and the other try to take it from them. On one of these occasions, when I belonged to the former battalion, the battle waxed hot enough to melt all the snow in the field. But it was, in fact, a little softened already, and hence our balls were hard and heavy. With these missiles we came to very close quarters, and the small boys, like myself, were sorely pelted on head and face by the larger. However, I never thought of flinching, and if it had come to fists, feet, and teeth, I am quite certain I should have fought until placed *hors de combat* by some overpowering contusion; yet I am equally certain that the admonition of father did not prompt me on this occasion, in which I was hurt much worse than I should have been in half a dozen ordinary school-boy fights.

Now, how are these two displays of character to be reconciled? They appear to stand in direct opposition. As they involve principles which have run through my whole life, I will offer you my speculations concerning them. Naturally, I took no pleasure in witnessing a combat of any kind, not even that of dogs or game cocks, the fights of which were in those days common amusements. The fights of men, which I often saw, also affected me unpleasantly. Thus I had not a pugnacious temper. Again, I was rather slow to anger, that is, to the point of resentment. Again, mother had taught me to regard fighting as wicked, and had not established in my mind any distinction between fighting in aggression and fighting in defense. She was, *in extenso*, a non-combatant. Finally, when not adequately aroused, I was timid, and the aggressions which are so often productive of fights among boys did not arouse me. The opposite emotion counteracted my anger. In the snowballing my ambition, not my anger, was up. I was under an adequate motive, one which excited me, and no fear or thought of personal danger came into my mind. . . .

During my boyhood there was in the country, except among wealthy emigrants from Old Virginia (of whom, however, there were none about Mayslick), a great deficiency of books. There was not a single book-store north of Licking river, and, perhaps, none in the State. All the books imported were kept in what were called the stores, which were magazines of the most primitive character, variety shops, if not curiosity shops—comprehending dry-goods, hardware, glass and earthenware, groceries, dyestuffs, and drugs, ammunition, hats, manufactures of leather, books, and stationery; the last consisting generally of coarse foolscap, wafers, slates, and pencils. The era of division of labor and distribution of commodities on sale, had not yet arrived; and, of course, no particular branch was pushed very far; and least of all, that which ministered to intellectual improvement, for its articles were least in demand. Bibles, hymn-books, primers, spelling-books, arithmetics, and almanacs, in fact, composed, in most instances, the importation, which was always from Philadelphia, the only city of the seaboard which maintained any commercial intercourse with the infant settlements of the interior. Our preachers and teachers were, in general, almost as destitute as the people at large, many of whom could neither read or write, did not send their children to school, and, of course, kept no books in the house. Of our own library I have already spoken incidentally. A family Bible, Rippon's *Hymns,* Watts' *Hymns for Children,* the *Pilgrim's Progress,* an old romance of the days of knight-errantry, primers, with a plate representing John Rogers at the stake, spelling-books, an arithmetic, and a new almanac for the new year, composed all that I can recollect, till within two or three years of my leaving home. . . .

A couple of years, or thereabouts, before leaving home, I got Entick's (a pocket) *Dictionary,* which was, of course, a great acquisition. I also obtained Scott's *Lessons,* which afforded me much new reading, and I used to speak pieces from it at Master Smith's school, when I went to him the second time. In addition (but not to my school library), father purchased I remember (when I was twelve or thirteen) the *Prompter,* Esop's *Fables,* and *Franklin's Life*—all sterling books for boys. The first was a collection of proverbs and maxims. A puzzle growing out of the last was his being called *doctor,* when he had not studied physic.

Occasionally, father borrowed books for me of Dr. Goforth. Once he bought me the *Farmer's Letters,* a work by Dickinson, secretary to congress during the Revolutionary war. Much of it was above my comprehension, but it made the mind strain forward; an effect produced about the same time by Guthrie's *Grammar.*

Another book from the same source, borrowed, I think, a year or so earlier, was Lord Chesterfield's *Letters* to his son, inculcating politeness. This fell in mighty close with my tastes, and not less with those of father and mother, who cherished as high and pure an idea of the duty of good breeding as any people on earth. The principle of politeness was deeply rooted in both; and their manifestation of it, in the form of deference, in their way, was sometimes, as I thought (even at that early period) carried too far. . . .

In the olden time newspapers, now the cumbersome pests of so many families, were almost as scarce among the country people around us as Sibylline leaves, and no tracts were spoken of in any house, but those of land. The first newspaper published in the State of Kentucky was begun at Lexington in 1787, the year before our immigration. It was called the *Kentucky Gazette,* and was edited, printed and published by John Bradford. Another was started in Washington, when I was eight or nine years old; but father did not take it. It was called the *Palladium.* Occasionally a number of it fell into my hands and was, from its novelty and variety, a great treat, although much of it was, of course, unintelligible to me. It spoke, I remember, a great deal about the French Revolution, Bonapart, and the war between France and England; in reference to which father and his neighbors were in close sympathy with the French. I recollect getting a number of it when I was about eleven years old. It was soon after corn planting, and I was sent into the cornfield to keep out the squirrels. I took the paper with me, and leaving the young corn to defend itself as it could, sat down at the root of a large tree near the center of the little field (where of course the squirrels would not disturb me), and beginning at the head of the first column on the first page, read it through, advertisements and all. This may seem to you rather laughable, but it was all right (the neglect of the corn excepted), for it gave me a peep into the world and excited my curiosity. . . .

Father, as well as myself, was aware that I was about to go to the study of medicine without due scholastic preparation, and if there had been a classical school in our neighborhood, I should, no doubt, have been sent to it, for some months at least. Under the conviction which I have assigned to him, he stipulated with Dr. Goforth that I should be sent to school for six months, to learn Latin; but by some great absurdity this was not done till I had studied for eighteen months that which, for want of Latin, I could not understand. But to dwell on this would be foreign to my present object. . . .

None but those who have lived where they saw many persons every hour in the day, can fully estimate the feeling of loneliness which comes into the heart when only trees and a few domestic animals can be seen. This feeling was ours, and especially mother's, for the first year or two after we left the young but somewhat stirring village . . . , for the seclusion of our new home. A day would often pass without our seeing any one, while before our removal we saw many every hour. Moreover we no longer saw the great wagons, laden with merchandise for the interior; the caravans of travelers, mounted on horseback; and the gangs of negroes on foot; all moving on to the south. This solitude, however painful (as it was at the time), had its advantages, for it drew us more closely together, and compelled us to rely more intimately on each other; while it enabled us to extract from the visits and company we did have a high degree of enjoyment. . . .

Mayslick, as I told you in my former letter, was a colony of East Jersey people, amounting in the aggregate to fifty-two souls. . . . The immigrants from other States were almost entirely Virginians and Marylanders. All were country people by birth and residence; all were illiterate, but in various degrees; and all were poor or in moderate circumstances; a majority or, at least, a moiety, however, were small freeholders. As to religious and moral refinement and a knowledge and use of the domestic arts of civilized life, the Jersey emigrants, as a body, were superior. Next came the Virginians, and last and lowest, the Marylanders; who in many respects were not equal to the Kentucky negroes of the present day. Of such was my old dominie, Master Beaden. The Jersey people were generally without slaves, partly from principle, and partly from the want of means. Most of the settlers from Virginia and Maryland brought slaves with them, though the number in each family was small, often one only. . . . It is a remarkable fact that in the early period of which I am writing, from 1794 to 1800, the white population was greater in that neighborhood than I found it in the visit referred to. . . .

The loss of white population, so impressively shown forth by what I have said, has occurred in various parts of Kentucky, and must be referred to the influence of Slavery. As bodies of different specific gravity rise to the surface in different times, so in every community some will rise in the world more rapidly than others. In a Slave state, new investments are constantly made in land and negroes, and hence the soil is constantly passing from the many to the few; slaves take the place of freemen, "negro quarters" replace the humble habitations of happy families; he who had a stirring and laborious father rides over the augmented plantations as a lord, and the hired man with his axe or sickle is replaced by the overseer with his thong.

But you must return to the primitive settlement, and meditate on the social circumstances under which I passed what, I suppose, in reference to the formation of character, to have been the most important period of my life—that in which it got its set. To aid you in the estimate of influences, I must give some details. Immigrants into the wilderness are, or rather become, social and hospitable; for their insulation makes them glad to see each other. They have private or family visiting, with abundance of small talk about the countries they had left, about their pursuits, their children, and their neighbors, in the last of which, according to my experience, they do not yield to people under any other circumstances. They also have many gatherings. Some are composed of men and boys only, for raising houses, stables, and barns, for rolling logs, for husking corn, for opening new roads, and other purposes; all of which I have repeatedly attended, and well recollect that profanity, vulgarity, and drinking were their most eminent characteristics. . . .

We had other gatherings composed of females only, or of the two sexes united. Dances were not common; I was never present at one. Weddings, commonly in the daytime, were scenes of carousal, and of mirth and merriment of no very chastened character. . . .

Another kind of gathering was the quilting party. Toward evening the young men would assemble, and amuse themselves by athletic exercises without, or talking to and "plaguing the gaals" within, the cabin. The quilt being removed, the supper-table took its place, and after the ladies had risen from the cream of the feast, the gentlemen, who had whetted their appetites by drinking whisky and looking on, proceeded to glut themselves on the *reliquioe.* Then came on plays of various kinds, interlarded with jokes and bursts of laughter, till bedtime, when the dispersion took place.

At other times small parties were made up by invitation, which were, of course, more select and conducted with greater decorum. If on the week day, they were generally in the evening, for the men had to work in the daytime; but on Sunday they began in the afternoon; for, among the most pious, Sunday, after worship, was regarded as a fit time for visiting, even in considerable parties. They were, however, conducted with greater propriety, and hymns and spiritual songs often made a part of the entertainment. Sunday was also the time for the visits of the young people, especially of young gentlemen from Washington, many of whom sought our community for amusement, and to be among those whose lower rank would allow them wide latitude of manners and conduct. . . .

Mayslick, although scarcely a village, was at once an emporium and capital for a tract of country 6 or 8 miles in diameter, and embracing several hundred families, of which those in father's neighborhood were tolerably fair specimens. . . . It was the place for holding regimental militia musters, when all the boys and old men of the surrounding country, not less than those who stood enrolled, would assemble; and before dispersing at night, the training was quite eclipsed by a heterogeneous drama of foot racing, pony racing, wrestling, fighting, drunkenness and general uproar. It was also a place for political meetings and stump conflict by opposing candidates, and after intellectual performances there generally followed an epilogue of oaths, yells, loud blows, and gnashing of teeth. Singing-schools were likewise held at the same place in a room of Deacon Morris' tavern. I was never a scholar, which I regret, for it has always been a grief with me that I did not learn music in early life. . . .

The infant capital was, still further, the local seat of justice; and Saturday was for many years, at all times I might say, the regular term time. Instead of trying cases at home, two or three justices of the peace would come to the Lick on that day, and hold their separate courts. This, of course, brought thither all the litigants of the neighborhood, with their friends and witnesses; all who wished to purchase at the store would postpone their visit to the same day; all who had to replenish their jugs of whisky did the same thing; all who had business with others expected to meet them there, as our city merchants, at noon, expect to meet each other on 'change; finally, all who thirsted after drink, fun, frolic, or fighting, of course were present. Thus Saturday was a day of largely suspended field labor, but devoted to public business, social pleasure, dissipation, and beastly drunkenness. You might suppose that the presence of civil magistrates would have repressed some of these vices, but it was not so. Each day provided a bill of fare for the next. A new trade in horses, another horse race, a cock-fight, or a dog-fight, a wrestling match, or a pitched battle between two bullies, who in fierce rencontre would lie on the ground scratching, pulling hair, choking, gouging out each other's eyes, and biting off each other's noses, in the manner of the bull-dogs, while a Roman circle of interested lookers-on would encourage the respective gladiators with shouts which a passing demon might have mistaken for those of hell. In the afternoon, the men and boys of business and sobriety would depart, and at nightfall the dissipated would follow them, often two on a horse, reeling and yelling as I saw drunken Indians do in the neighborhood of Fort Leavenworth, in the summer of 1844. But many would be too much intoxicated to mount their horses, and must therefore remain till Sunday morning.

I need scarcely tell you that these scenes did not contaminate me. They were quite too gross and wicked to be attractive. On the other hand, they excited disgust, and received from father the strongest condemnation. I turn from them with pleasure to others of a very different kind.

All the first settlers of Mayslick were, either by association or profession, Baptists, and had belonged to the church at Scotch Plains, of whom the Rev. Wm. Van Horne was the worthy pastor. At what time after their immigration a house of public worship was erected, I do not remember, but recollect to have attended public worship in Mr. Morris' barn. It happened that most of the Jersey and Virginia families around the village were likewise Baptists, and therefore it was the predominant sect. Hence all my early ideas of Christian doctrine, worship, and deportment, were derived from that denomination. The "meeting-house," as it was always called, was built on a ridge a quarter of a mile south of the village, hard-by the great road leading to Lexington. A couple of acres surrounding it constituted the burying ground for the station and its neighborhood. A number of walnut and flowering locust trees had been left standing within the inclosure, and between it and the "big road.". . .

The first Constitution of Kentucky was adopted in 1791, three years after we entered the State; the second, eight years afterward. Pending its adoption, a very strong effort was made over the State to elect members of the convention who would favor the gradual abolition of slavery. Mr. Clay, who had just then arrived at Lexington, united himself with that party, and labored in the good cause. I need scarcely tell you that your grandfather was of the same party. In fact, he was one of its most impassioned members; and all my own thoughts and feelings took the same direction. The discussions, public and private, were numerous, and the excitement ran so high that Phil. Thomas, a politician of some note, declared that he would wade to his knees in blood before it should take place. He lately died at Baton Rouge, La., in his eightieth year, under the title of General Philemon Thomas.

For several years before I left home, father with some of his neighbors talked a great deal of moving off to Ohio, then called the Territory, and actually made a visit of exploration into the valley of Paint Creek and to Chillicothe, then a new village, extending it thence to the Miami country. They returned loud in their praises of the Paint Creek bottoms (on which you and I have so often taken drives), and also of the Little Miami valley. Why they did not remove, I can not tell; but I remember the motives for removal, which led them to meditate it: 1st. The existence of slavery in Kentucky; 2d. The uncertainty of land titles; 3d. The want of good water. Had he removed at that time, when I was about thirteen years of age, the necessity and value of my services in opening a new farm would have no doubt prevented my studying medicine, and I might now have been a farmer, supplying families in Cincinnati with good clean butter, and acting at home as a justice of the peace, a school trustee, or an overseer of the poor! . . .

The outbreak of the French Revolution occurred when I was about four or five years old, and excited a deep emotion over the United States. [French Rev.] The aid which France had rendered us in our revolutionary struggle was still fresh in the memory of the people, and their hearts were of course in sympathy with the French, whom great masses of our citizens would have willingly assisted by going to war with England. General Washington opposed himself to this policy. John Adams succeeded him; and both were regarded by the zealous and grateful well-wishers of struggling France, as leaning to England, from which the sword had so lately severed us. To raise money for the support of our Government, as we had but little commerce to afford impost duties, certain direct taxes were levied by Mr. Adams' administration, among which was an excise duty on distilleries and their products; also, I believe, a "stamp act" or duty on paper to be used for deeds, notes, and other documents; all of which had been among those measures of the British Government which led us to rebel. These acts of Mr. Adams' administration were attacked with violence and virulence by the Republican press, as it was then called; and to defend itself from these assaults, that administration had the weakness to enact a sedition law. Such was the highly exciting state of national politics from my tenth to my fifteenth year inclusive. . . .[2]

Now, as from my earliest recollection of public affairs, I had a great deal of feeling and sympathy with them, I could not fail to be an attentive listener, and, of course, an apt scholar, throughout the period which has been designated; and in looking back upon it, I am persuaded that the school was a real source of intellectual improvement. Mr. Jefferson became the candidate of the party to which I, at the age of twelve, belonged, and on the 4th of March, 1801, when he was inaugurated President of the United States, three months after I commenced the study of medicine, I wrote, and sitting alone in my chamber in a small white farm house, where Mrs. Gen. Lytle now resides, drank, in cold water, thirteen toasts in celebration of the triumphant event. This little piece of veritable history shows that the workings of our popular institutions are in fact efficient causes of intellectual growth in our boys, and explains why we have so many able statesmen, lawyers, and divines, who have never submitted to the teachings of the university.

In a despotic country, such a country boy as I was could never have heard any of the discussions in religion and politics to which I had so many opportunities of listening, nor could he have had any of the lively sensibility to those or other great interests, which, like a healthy appetite to the body, favor the development of mind. I had not only variety of character, but variety of topics, presented to me; and while none of the former was intellectually high, many of the latter were of great magnitude, and the very apprehension of them served to enlarge the horizon of my childhood; while the diversities of character greatly augmented

---

2. The Alien and Sedition Acts were exceedingly unpopular because the preponderance of prosecutions under them were directed at newspaper editors supporting Thomas Jefferson, thus proving the Jeffersonian Republicans' contention that the Federalists were against popular political participation. Jefferson defeated Adams in the presidential election of 1800, although the tie vote that he and his running mate, Aaron Burr, received threw the election into the House of Representatives. Jefferson's victory, followed by the elections of his close friends, James Madison and James Monroe, brought to an end seven years of fierce debate over the Federalists' pro-British policies and the operative meaning of popular sovereignty.

the area of my social sympathies, especially in the humbler walks of life. . . .

I might multiply my recollections of characters and events connected with society, which exerted on me an influence, good or bad, but have resolved to forbear, as my letter has already reached an appalling length. I might also trace out the history and fate, or present condition, of several of my playmates and cornfield companions; but, for the same reason, shall not. Indeed a letter of sixty pages ought, I think, to be regarded, under the law, as carried to the maximum; and therefore I subscribe myself your loving

PA.

JULIA ANNE HIERONYMUS TEVIS

1799–1879

*S*CHOLARS have characterized women's memoirs as being distinguished by their depiction of life as a flow of experiences rather than as a dramatic narrative. Such is not the case with Julia Tevis, suggesting that it is perhaps the life led rather than the sex that determines the structure of the autobiography. Young Julia Anne Hieronymus developed such a confident, self-assertive personality that it is hard not to pore over her life story for clues as to how such a strong-willed woman could have emerged from the frontier of Kentucky in the first decades of the nineteenth century.

Her much-adored father was born in Germany, where he apparently acquired very advanced views of women's need for education. At least, his daughter ascribes such views to him when she looks back on his assiduous interest in her intellectual development. Her mother's family, the Bushes, were Virginia Baptists who had emigrated to Kentucky with their pastor in the 1780s, when Indians still protested the incursion of white families. As a child, Tevis listened with awe to old-timers' stories, the grimness of which can be assessed by her comment that the "whites scarcely ever took prisoners; they considered it safer to dispatch them [the Indians] at once to another world."[1]

After moving back to Virginia for their children's education, the

---

1. Julia A. Tevis, *Sixty Years in a Schoolroom: An Autobiography of Mrs. Julia A. Tevis* (Cincinnati, 1878), p. 50.

Hieronymuses finally settled in Washington, D.C. It is never quite clear what Tevis's father did to provide for the family. He apparently had enough money to build a handsome house and send his daughter to a private academy, yet the family also took in boarders from the congressional community.

In Washington Tevis led a rather glamorous life, attending the balls and receptions that enlivened the season when Congress was in session. She describes the great "illumination" in celebration of General William Henry Harrison's victory over the Indian confederation led by Tecumseh and reveals that she barely escaped the city before the British troops arrived to burn the Capitol. Tevis's brother got a lieutenancy in the army during the War of 1812, serving in a regiment with Sam Houston.

Torn between delight at witnessing the affairs of famous people and her dismay at perceived immorality, Tevis gives a mixed picture of life in the capital city. She recounts the derring-do of notorious duelers meeting at Bladensburgh, Maryland, "the Congressional duelling grounds." The display of wealth and splendor at the inauguration *fête* of President Monroe in her view was "little in accordance with the republican simplicity which should constitute the dignity of a nation so utterly rejecting high sounding titles and oriental magnificence." Yet it is with some awe that she describes how the girls at her school in Georgetown learned to do elaborate embroidery work sometimes "half a yard in depth" for the bottoms of their white muslin dresses.

Eventually her father lost all of his money when he cosigned a note for a friend who went bankrupt; the Hieronymus family's house and goods were sold at auction.[2] Tevis left home to take up a job teaching school, while her father went to St. Louis seeking work, soon thereafter dying in New Madrid, Missouri, where he was serving as an Indian agent. Thus Tevis became the virtual head of her family, her brother

---

2. Borrowing money was exceedingly common in the early nineteenth century, and creditors required cosigners on the loan papers (notes) of most people. If the borrower could not pay off the note when it fell due, the cosigner was responsible for the debt. Thomas Jefferson lost much of his fortune through cosigning a note for a friend undone by the financial collapse known as the Panic of 1819.

having been killed in Florida. Both her mother and her younger sister then came to Virginia where Tevis was flourishing as a schoolteacher.

Tevis made a decisive break with her social past when she became a Methodist. Her religious conversion brought her into contact with John Tevis, a young circuit rider, whom she married after a short courtship. Determined to have her own school, she talked her husband and father-in-law into letting her convert her father-in-law's gift house into a school. And so, in Shelbyville, Kentucky, young Julia Hieronymus Tevis started the Science Hill Academy for Young Women, which lasted into the twentieth century. Greatly admiring Emma Willard, the founder of the famous Troy Academy in New York, Tevis followed Willard's example and outfitted a laboratory so that her pupils might learn chemistry! Married in 1824, her first child arrived by the end of that year, just a few months before Science Hill opened. For the next fifty years she presided over her academy while bringing up seven children.

~ ζ ~

I HAVE arrived at that period of life from which I can look back with a calm and grateful heart upon the various and shifting scenes through which I have passed; and I now undertake to record, for the gratification of my family and immediate friends, the recollections so clearly and deeply impressed upon my memory. I begin the review under a profound sense of God's goodness, which has rendered every trial, thus far encountered in the journey of life, subservient to my everlasting welfare. . . .

I was born December 5, 1799, in Clarke County, Kentucky. My grand-parents, on both sides, were among the earliest emigrants from Virginia into this State. Their location in the vicinity of Boonesboro brought them into familiar intercourse and companionship with Daniel Boone; and my maternal grandfather, Ambrose Bush, with his four brothers, were among the most celebrated of the old "Indian fighters." Their numerous descendants were scattered over so large a portion of Clarke County as to give it the name of "Bush's Settlement." Thrifty and respectable farmers, they occupied a position in society both honorable and useful. The same may be said of my father's ancestors, who were Germans, as the name Hieronymus will suggest.

My paternal grandfather, with an elder brother, came to America before the Revolutionary War, and settled in the eastern part of Virginia. They were from Vienna, and thoroughly German in many respects; particularly in an obstinacy of character, which evinced itself in firmness of purpose and industrious habits. My grandmother was also of German descent, though born in America. . . .

My grand-parents, on my mother's side, were as English as those on the other side were German. My Grandmother Bush was a strictly pious Baptist; my Grandmother Hieronymus, a Methodist of the old school, a real Wesleyan, thoroughly and decidedly religious. . . .

I can even now see in the dim, shadowy distance, the tall, queenly form of my [maternal] grandmother, simply attired in a dove-colored dress and plain white kerchief, with a cap faultless in shape, and of snowy whiteness, setting off the most benevolent of features. I can hear her quick step, and sweet voice calling, "Jennie, Julia, Esther, Polly!"— her four daughters; for when she wanted one she never failed to call them all over before she could get the right name. And from habitual quickness of thought, word, and action, she often made a laughable pell-mell of words. When she called for her black mare to be saddled—for every body rode on horseback in those days, there being nothing more than bridle-paths—it was, "Warrick, run up the black mare, bring down the back-stairs, and put my saddle on it; quick, quick, for I must go to Sister Franky's right away." And how often have I ridden to the stone meeting-house behind her on that same black mare, and walked over and around the church-yard where now my beloved grand-parents lie buried, with many of their descendants! . . .

At the time that my grandfather, with his brothers and sister, came to Kentucky, many families traveled together for mutual safety and protection against the Indians, whose hunting-grounds extended to the border settlements of Virginia. On their way through the wilderness they encountered bears, buffaloes, wolves, wild-cats, and sometimes herds of deer. Thus they moved cautiously onward, in long lines, through a narrow bridle-path, so encumbered with brush and underwood as to impede their progress, and render it necessary that they should sometimes encamp for days, in order to rest their weary pack-horses and forage for themselves. . . .

One circumstance, often related to me, forcibly illustrates the keen instinct of the panther. My grandfather had been out on a hunt for many days. Weary eyes and anxious hearts were watching and waiting his return. It was midsummer, and the tall cane, with its gracefully waving leaves, excluded the view of every object not in the immediate vicinity of the lonely and scattered dwellings. About sunset, one lovely afternoon, my grandmother, with her faithful handmaiden, "Mourning," set out to fetch some water from the spring, which, though at no great distance from the house, was hidden from sight. Always in mortal fear of ambushed Indians, they were walking slowly along when startled by the familiar sound of the lost hunter's cry of "hoo-hoo," which was suppressed at intervals, as if listening for a response to assure him that he was in the neighborhood of home and loved ones. My grandmother answered, as she was wont to do, while her heart thrilled with the joyful anticipation of meeting her returning husband. "Hoo-hoo," in a loud voice, was again heard, and again responded to—each time seeming nearer and more distinct; when, just as they emerged from the thicket, and caught a glimpse of the shelving rock that over-arched the spring, they perceived something moving among the bushes above. At first they supposed it to be nothing more than a raccoon or an opossum, but it proved to be a panther. This animal, when stimulated by hunger, would assail whatever would provide him with a banquet of blood. Lo! there he stood, on the rock high above the spring, squatting on his hind-legs, in the attitude of preparing to leap—his glaring eyeballs fierce with expectation. His gray coat, extended claws, fiery eyes, and the cry which he at that moment uttered, rendered by its resemblance to the human voice peculiarly terrific, denoted him to be the most ferocious of his detested kind. My grandmother, whose presence of mind never forsook her, even under the most appalling circumstances, retreated slowly, keeping her eyes steadily fixed on the eyes of the monster, which seemed momentarily paralyzed by her gaze, until she and the negro girl could turn by a sudden angle into the woods, when, adding "wings to their speed," they soon reached the house, and barred the door behind them. . . .

Being the second child and oldest daughter, I was sent to a country school at a very early age. I think I was but four years old on that bright and happy morning when my mother, after filling our little school-

basket with a lunch to be eaten at play-time, sent my brother and me to
school. The dew was yet upon the grass, and the birds were caroling
their morning hymns as they fluttered among the branches of the trees
which shaded our pathway. Ah, well do I remember that lovely morning. How joyously I tripped along, playing bo-peep with the sun as his
golden beams glittered through a fretwork of green above my head, now
and then stopping to gather wild flowers that seemed too beautiful to be
left behind!

A little incident, though not amusing at the time, has afforded much
merriment since. My brother, two years my senior, carried our basket,
containing a square black bottle of milk, two or three nicely baked waf-
fles, two fried eggs, slices of ham, two apple-turnovers, and buttered
bread, rendered luscious by being thickly overspread with maple-sugar.
We had scarcely gone half our way—the school-house was two miles
distant from home—when it was proposed that we should rest awhile
under the shade of a magnificent tree, and peep into the basket. The
repast looked so inviting under the snowy covering that we were
tempted to eat a portion of the good things; after which my brother, to
whom the idea of school was not half so pleasing as to myself, begged
me to go back and ask permission to stay from school that day. I agreed
to it, and soon reached home and delivered my message; to which my
mother replied by taking my hand, and, gathering a switch, she silently
led me to the trysting-place where my brother awaited me; and after
applying the rod freely, to quicken his indolent faculties, accompanied
us to the log school-house, and handed us over to "the master," who
seated me beside one of the larger pupils, bidding her teach "the little
one" her A, B, C's from a board upon which they were pasted.

I recollect distinctly the house, and the school itself, which in its day
was a model. A square room, with a fireplace large enough to hold
nearly half a cord of wood; a puncheon floor, hard, rough, wooden
benches, without backs; an opening in the wall, of an oblong form, opposite the door, for a window, with crevices enough in every direction
to admit a free circulation of air! The furniture, consisting of a desk, at
which the teacher was placed, or rather perched, far above all the miserable little urchins; a ferule, a rod, and a pile of copy-books, complete the
picture.

At twelve, which was known by a mark on the door-sill—the primitive clock of our forefathers—the whole school was turned out for a two-

hours' recreation and dinner. Such shouts of merriment! such ringing laughter! So much outgushing happiness, with an abundance of fun and frolic, unrestrained by hoops and heels, or the fear of soiling delicate costumes!

Our dinner eaten, how heartily we romped, bent young saplings for riding-horses, made swings of the surrounding grape-vines, and anon rested on the green sward under the wide-spreading beech-trees, until we were not sorry to hear the stentorian voice of the master calling out, "Bo-o-ks! Bo-o-ks!". . .

I do not remember how long I continued under the instruction of Mr. Pettichord, my Clarke County teacher, but I know that I soon learned to read; and reading has been a passion with me all my life, a source of so great enjoyment as to be appreciated and understood by those who have enjoyed in like degree the pleasure and profit to be derived therefrom. My excellent parents, being educated in the very best manner that the times and circumstances by which they were surrounded afforded, highly appreciated the advantages of a superior education, and determined to seek for their children opportunities that Kentucky did not afford; for which purpose they removed to Virginia when I was but seven years of age.[1] Whilst my father was seeking a suitable location for a permanent residence—good schools being the principal object—we spent two years in Paris, a pretty little village at the foot of the Blue Ridge. . . .

I am not of those who are constantly bemoaning the "better times of the glorious old past;" and yet, I verily believe that the children of fifty years ago enjoyed life more, and were educated in a manner better suited to the development of their physical and mental energies, and to the fostering of that self-reliance so necessary for the life-struggle of mature age, than those of modern times. Our simple costume, unconfined by belt or girdle, and our bib-aprons, as distinctly separated the school girl from the young lady in society, as did the "*bulla* and *toga virilis*" separate childhood and manhood among the Romans.

With what pleasure, not unmingled with vanity, did I display my two school dresses for the Spring of 1812, both made of Virginia cotton

---

1. Tevis's father was unusual in that he gave as much attention to Julia's education as to that of her older brother, which is perhaps an indication of her scholastic aptitude.

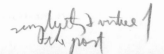

cloth, home spun and home woven—one a white ground with pink stripes running lengthwise; the other, a blue plaid, which was the admiration of all the unsophisticated girls in my class. . . .

I have said that we were mischievous; but never malicious, I am sure. Once I was induced by a fun-loving girl to put sugar in the inkstands, being assured that it would meet the approbation of our solemn writing-master. We gazed with admiration at the black, shining words of our beautiful copies, as we left them open on the desk while we were reciting in an adjoining room. It was Summer, and the flies were so busy during our absence that when the master came around there was not a legible word to be seen. "Who did this? Speak, instantly!" No reply; but agitation and alarm were so visible upon my face that, placing his heavy hand upon my brow, he stretched open my eyes to a painful extent, while he threatened to box my ears. My ludicrous appearance and terrified looks seemed to cool his anger almost to the laughing point, except that he *never* laughed. Thus he left me with a positive threat of severe punishment should it ever occur again. . . .

Previous to the declaration of war in 1812 there was intense excitement throughout the whole country. The political animosity existing between the two parties, Federalists and Democrats, was bitter beyond expression; even the children caught fire in the general conflagration. Some were Democrats, the war party; others Federalists, "whose voice was still for peace." It was not an unusual thing to see the girls of our school in battle array on the green common, during intermission, fighting like furies; and though, like Pompey's patrician soldiers, carefully avoiding scratched faces and broken noses, many a handful of hair was borne off as a trophy, many a neatly made dress torn into tatters; while a system of boxing was practiced, that would have done honor to a Grecian gymnasium. The war party, of course, were generally victorious, as they were not only more numerous but fiercer, and more demonstrative, and would not *stay* whipped. Nothing was effected, however, in these *melees;* the battles ended when we were tired of fighting. But it is a positive fact, that our dishevelled hair and torn garments increased our good humor to the highest pitch of merriment.

Among my most vivid recollections of the opening of the war was seeing a splendid body of cavalry passing through the streets of Winchester. It was a full regiment, handsomely equipped, bright new uniforms, a fine band of music, with all the "pomp and circumstance of glorious *war."* The spirited horses, and gallant bearing of the officers, with their flashing swords and waving plumes, rendered it an imposing sight. . . .

We removed to the District of Columbia in November, 1813, locating in Georgetown. Here I saw the first illumination I ever witnessed. The whole town, as well as Washington, was one blaze of light, in honor of General Harrison's victory over the British and Indians at the battle of the Thames, as well as the brilliant victory of Commodore Perry on Lake Erie, which just preceded it. Our little navy had crowned itself with laurels in its ocean fights, but Harrison's victory followed a succession of disasters by land. The death of Tecumseh in the battle of the Thames was also hailed with great joy by the nation, as it deeply depressed the Indians, who had become exceedingly fierce. Tecumseh was a host in himself; and had his lot been cast under favorable circumstances his powerful mind and heroic soul would have distinguished him, not only as a warrior, but as an orator and statesman. . . .

My education was continued in Georgetown under the care of two excellent teachers, Mr. and Mrs. Simpson. A considerable portion of my time was devoted to music, drawing, and French, with various kinds of embroidery. The girls in this school wrought the most elaborate samplers with a variety of stitches, and bordered them with pinks, roses, and morning-glories, and sometimes, when the canvas was large enough, with the name and age of every member of the family. We did not buy French-worked collars then, but embroidered them for ourselves, and some of them were exquisite specimens of the finest needlework; and the skirts of our white muslin dresses were wrought, frequently, half a yard in depth.

One interesting incident then, and pleasant to remember now, occurs to me. I was standing with a group of girls near a deep-toned piano, listening to some fine airs played by Mr. Simpson, when Miss Bowie, one of the grown pupils, stepped in with the "Star-spangled Banner" set to music. This was a charming advent to us, as we had heard of the piece, but had not before seen it. Every body's patriotism was at full tide then, as it was soon after the bombardment of Fort M'Henry and our successful repulse of the British at Baltimore.[2] Mr. Simpson was an en-

---

2. Francis Scott Key wrote "The Star Spangled Banner" during the British bombardment of Baltimore's Fort McHenry in September of 1814. It became the national anthem by law on March 3, 1931.

thusiast in both music and patriotism; and the chords vibrated under his touch, sending forth peals of harmony that made the welkin ring. He seemed inspired to the very ends of his fingers. A dozen girls soon struck in with their choral voices, making the whole house resound with the music. A crowd of little boys collected around the front door and at the window, and a scene presented itself such as one might have expected among the French with their "Marseillaise."

How true it is that the fire of patriotism is often stirred into a flame, even from the ashes of despondency, by national airs! The "Star-span-gled Banner" should be a consecrated song to every American heart, connected as it is with an event so thrilling in character—so marked among the honorable achievements of this nation, when the States of the Union stood up before the world, "distinct like the billow, but one like the sea"—when that bold, enterprising spirit that gave us a rank among the nations of the earth was abroad throughout the whole land. The powerful effect produced by this soul-stirring song was not owing to any particular merit in the composition, but to the recollection of something noble in the character of a young and heroic nation success-fully struggling against the invasion of a mighty people for life, freedom, and domestic happiness. . . .

It was during my residence in Georgetown that the fiercest conflicts of the war of 1812 occurred. An incident connected with this war im-pressed me deeply, and gave me a terrific idea of mobs. Every well read person is familiar with the history of the bloody drama enacted in Balti-more, when the brave General Lingan was killed by an infuriated mob, though he begged so piteously that his life might be spared for the sake of his wife and children. He besought them to remember how manfully he had fought for his country in the "old war;" but his voice was scarcely heard amid the roar of those wild beasts, who almost tore him to pieces. General Lee (Light Horse Harry) and several other Revolution-ary patriots were so injured by the same mob that they died soon after. They were opposed to the war.

Mrs. Lingan, with her family, was brought immediately by sympa-thizing friends to Georgetown. Never shall I forget the appearance of that mourning widow. Her tall, dignified form enveloped in sable gar-ments; her two daughters accompanying her, reminded me of Naomi returning sorrowfully to her own people, to hide her bowed head and stricken heart among friends, who vied in kindness to the untimely bereaved.

This event, like many others, is rendered deeply interesting by a glimpse into the mysterious long time ago. The circumstances attending the Baltimore mob having been so lightly touched upon by historians, it will, doubtless, be interesting to my readers to have a more particular account of the matter from one who was living so near the scene of action. War was declared on the 18th of June, 1812. The immediate effect of this measure was a violent exasperation of parties. The friends of the Government applauded the act as spirited and patriotic—the opposition condemned it as unnecessary, unjustifiable, and impolitic. In the New England States, particularly, where the "Revolutionary War" found ardent and active supporters, a decided opposition was manifested. They conceded that abundant provocation had been given, but denied the expediency, as the nation was not sufficiently prepared for the conflict. But in many of our large cities the news was received with extravagant demonstrations of joy. In Baltimore, especially, the popular voice was strongly in favor of it, and the first announcement created the wildest excitement. Two great parties convulsed the country at that time. They were so evenly balanced that it was difficult to determine the preponderant element. The Democrats were powerful, but the Federalists were determined. Distinguished congressmen pleaded in favor of the war; and among them stood conspicuous the talented young Kentuckian, Henry Clay, pledging, to the utmost of its ability, the support of his own State to the President. Orators harangued the people, and their burning eloquence increased the fervor of their shouts for "Free Trade and Sailor's Rights." Oh, these were thrilling times! To warm the life blood and fan the fires of patriotism was the broad road to distinction. The Democrats were denounced as reckless demagogues by the opposition, who dreaded the rekindling of the fires of the Revolution, which had just been extinguished by the blood of multiplied thousands; but there was no staying the surging waves of the popular voice. The Democratic Republicans triumphed, and rejoiced in their signal success. Many noble patriots of unimpeachable integrity, and brave officers who had served their country well and faithfully, were conscientious Federalists. One of these was Alexander Hanson, who edited a paper in Baltimore called the *Federal Republican*. He ventured to indulge in some severe strictures on the conduct of the Government. The consequence was, his printing-office was destroyed by the populace, and he obliged to fly the city. Hanson was a bold man, and determined not to be put down; he therefore returned to Baltimore with a party of friends who had volunteered to aid him in forcibly defending his house. General Henry Lee, who happened to be in the city when the riots commenced, was a personal friend of the editor, and, with characteristic impetuosity, offered his services against the mob. They prepared for an attack by arming themselves and barricading the house. The enraged mob attacked the building with great fury, and even brought a cannon to bear in the assault. The besieged defended themselves coolly and successfully. The result was that two of the assailants were killed and a number wounded, which so exasperated the crowd that but for the arrival of the city military Hanson and his friends would, in all probability, have been torn to pieces. . . .

Washington fifty years ago was a delightful retreat, full of bewildering loveliness. I loved to ramble over the grounds surrounding the magnificent old capitol and revel in its beauties—the beauty of lovely skies, luxuriant trees, rich herbage, and myriads of bright flowers. The hall windows of the quaint old building commanded an enchanting view of hill and plain, and at the end of an avenue of poplars a mile long could be seen the simple, noble mansion designed for the President of the United States—a fitting habitation for the executive of this great republic. In the distance, her feet laved in the gleaming waters of the Potomac, was the little city of Georgetown, her green hills crowned with groups of noble trees, some of them of ancient date, looking like the natural guardians of the charming country-seats scattered in the vicinity.

The Summer following the events just related was spent by our family in sweet seclusion, which united a loving household more closely together. It was the last I ever spent here, and it is rife with some of the sweetest recollections and tenderest associations of this early home of my heart. The crowd of strangers, office-seekers, and resident ministers, with their gray retinues, had gone. After the adjournment of Congress the city was exceedingly dull to these pleasure-seekers. A strange atmosphere of repose pervaded the place. There was opportunity to enjoy life's leisure in its fullest sense.

My father had gone to the far West on business, and my two older brothers being away, I was left to the constant companionship of my mother, which I had been deprived of by my long absence at school.

wordie rlyn

Even at this remote period my heart thrills at the recollection of this time—the quiet readings, the solemn Scripture teachings, which fell like the dews of heaven into my young heart, and I acknowledge with tearful thankfulness the sweet privilege then enjoyed.

The taking of Washington City in 1814 was marked by many interesting circumstances and unwritten incidents, affecting to the heart and worth remembering. August 24, 1814, was one of the sultriest of Summer days. The British, after a rapid march across the country, reached Bladensburg, eight miles from Washington, in the hottest part of the afternoon. A small number of hastily collected troops were prepared to meet the foe; yet, so exhausted were the way-worn British soldiers, that even these, few as they were, would have been sufficient to keep them out of Washington had there been any order or discipline. As it was, they were driven, fighting as they retreated, in great confusion to the capital. Their pursuers, however, were held at bay, for a short time, by the gallant General Winder, who, not being supported, was compelled to yield to the enemy, whose numbers more than quadrupled his own. The British commanders, flushed with success, drove the panic-stricken Americans before them, and entered the city amid the tumult and glitter of an army; with flying colors and beating drums. Dreading the mighty desolation which threatened them, the President and the Cabinet, with the principal citizens, fled precipitately through Georgetown and across the Potomac. Nothing was seen but people anxious to escape the dreaded catastrophe. Carriages, wagons, carts, vehicles of every description, crowded with women and children; servants hurrying in every direction, carrying away what goods and chattels they were able to bear; amid the wildest confusion of men on horseback and exhausted stragglers from the battle-field, made up a moving panorama for miles. It was a melancholy sight to behold, some wringing their hands and wailing, as if they were leaving behind all that made life valuable, and turning again and again to take a last glimpse of home; while others bitterly denounced their own selfish flight, forsaking friends who absolutely refused to leave.

The crowd swept on, wave after wave; but the most melancholy object among them was the President of the United States, whose delicate frame and feeble health might have rendered him an object of compassion, had he been an isolated man. Like poor David, when he fled from Jerusalem before his rebellious son, there were none to cry "God

incidents "affecting to the heart"

bless him." Yet Mr. Madison was worthy, for he had proved himself a patriot and an eminent statesman. . . .

Mrs. Madison distinguished herself during these troubles by her admirable firmness and superior womanly tact. Nature had lavished upon her more of the materials of happiness and greatness than are usually found in women who sway the fashionable world. She sustained herself nobly, and from her own quiet elevation of character watched calmly the disastrous rout, and sank not, for one moment, into despondency. Mr. Madison might have been overborne by the triumph of his enemies, had *she* not by her own self-possession inspired him with an energy that enabled him to rise superior to his misfortunes. I do not believe the executive office has ever been filled by a worthier man or a better statesman since the days of Washington than James Madison; nor was there ever a presiding genius in the White House more beloved, admired, and respected than his elegant and graceful wife. . . .

An incident occurred during this time illustrating the courage and patriotism of a woman who kept a variety shop. A british officer, entering her store, asked:

"Have you a husband or sons? If so, where are they?"

"I have a husband and two sons, who are trying to defend their country at the risk of their lives; and I hope you may meet them yet."

"Indeed! and you have here an instrument of war?" striking a drum which lay on the counter.

"And here is another," she replied, taking a loaded pistol from a shelf; "and if you dare take another article in this shop you shall receive its contents."

Her hand was on the trigger. The officer involuntarily stepped back, saying:

"Put aside your weapon, madam. If your men had manifested as much firmness you might have been spared the devastation we have accomplished in your country."

It is well known that the battle of New Orleans was fought after peace was ratified by our Commissioners at Ghent, the news of which did not reach the United States until after the eighth of January. The universal joy felt throughout the whole country was scarcely less than that realized at the close of the Revolution.

General Jackson and his wife made their advent at Washington soon after, and created quite a sensation among the *elite* of that day. Mrs.

Jackson, though uneducated, was an amiable Christian woman; and, while laughed at for her grammatical blunders, made herself loved for her kindness, and admired for her unsophisticated manners. The General, who even then bore the soubriquet of "Old Hickory," was cordially acknowledged as a noble, high-hearted man.

I had the pleasure of witnessing a theatrical entertainment, prepared in honor of these distinguished guests of the nation. Their entrance into the theater was announced by tremendous cheering. The General was tall, thin, and weather-beaten; but there was a Cassius-like firmness on his lip, and his brow was marked with the lines of thought and care. He was rather annoyed at being the observed of all observers, and oppressed by the attention that was paid him; while Mrs. Jackson, "fair, fat, and forty," with a good motherly look, seemed amused, and gazed with intense gratification at the display made in honor of him in whom her soul was centered. . . .

In 1815 I was placed under the charge of an English lady of deep piety and superior education. Her institution was in full view of the President's house—only a few squares from it. There were no regular streets at this time in this city of magnificent distances except Pennsylvania Avenue. They were laid out, it is true, but not built up. The school-house stood on a slight eminence near the Potomac, commanding a fine view of this noble river for a considerable distance. Unconfined by brick houses, we had a glorious breathing space, over which swept the sweet morning zephyrs, whispering through the foliage of magnificent trees; and the evening breeze from the Potomac fanned our glowing cheeks as we raced over the lawn, stretching almost to the water's edge, or sat on the doorstep watching the soft rosy clouds at day's decline. . . .

During the sitting of Congress the older girls were taken by Mrs. Stone once a week to hear the celebrated speakers, or listen to debates on interesting subjects. There were "giants in those days," and among the most conspicuous of the whole bright galaxy of intelligences that illuminated our legislative halls appeared Henry Clay, Speaker of the House of Representatives; John C. Calhoun, John Randolph, Sheffey, and others, who had been leaders of the war party, aspiring now to a place in the councils of the nation. Mr. Calhoun's features impressed me as being remarkably fine, and, though somewhat stern in repose, were yet capable of being molded to any meaning it was his will to express.

He always commanded the attention of the House as a character of that lofty cast which seems to rise above the ordinary wants and weaknesses of humanity.

John Randolph was another of the great speakers who made a deep impression upon my mind. One of the queerest and most wiry-looking men I ever saw, he was unmistakably a great man. His genius had angels' wings, but fed on the bitterest extracts from Mount Hymettus. Always on the side of the minority, difficulty seemed to possess a charm for him, because affording an opportunity for displaying the energies of his soul. His voice was weak and squeaking—thin, and sometimes harsh; yet his eloquence was irresistible. He wielded his weapons of wit and ridicule with conclusive power.

An authentic anecdote is related of his having effectually laid upon the table a bill, introduced after the adoption of the Federal Constitution, to have the seats of each delegation wrought with some device descriptive of the staples of their several States. Mr. Randolph arose, after listening to a long debate on the subject, and suggested the more elegant and impressive arrangement of a marble statue for each State. "North Carolina, for instance," he said, pointing his long bony finger, and shaking it in the most significant manner; "let her fill a conspicuous niche, leaning against a persimmon-tree, with an opossum at her feet, and a sweet potato in her hand." It brought down the house—and the plan, too.

In the Congress of the United States, at that time, no man occupied a more enviable position than did our own Henry Clay.

Mr. Clay could, by the magic of his amazing will and his irresistible self-assertion, lift a great audience to dizzy heights of enthusiasm, and stir unwonted throbbings in the heart.

When in his magnificent moments men saw him agitate the Senate into fury, and then, as born to command, play with the whirlwind and direct the storm, they felt in their inmost souls that he had Nature's patent for his oratorical tyranny.

Possessing that liquid melody of tone so fascinating by its variety of inflection and its ever-changing naturalness, Henry Clay could hold his audience enchained for hours without wearying them, and in a great speech move on through the whole oratorical voyage as gracefully as a noble ship, whose snowy sails flutter and quiver in storm and breeze by turns, but always majestic and swan-like in its movements. Mr. Clay's gestures naturally aided his eloquence. His pantomime was the perfect painting of his thoughts, and each discriminating gesture told its own story.

A man who was somewhat deaf, and could not get near enough to Mr. Clay in one of his finest efforts, remarked, "I did not hear a word he said; but, bless me! didn't he make his motions?". . .

I have said, that I was fond of reading, but what I read previous to the age of seventeen had not been well digested; it was rather a species of cramming, which a maturer judgment taught me to reject, and I now began to discriminate between healthy literature and the hot-bed productions with which the press teemed then as now: yet I did not eschew all fiction, and often, when reading an interesting novel, to which daylight could not be devoted, the moon lent her friendly aid.

My imprudence in thus straining my eyes, though it did not render me very nearsighted, prevented my being able to see things distinctly at a great distance common to good eyes. 'Tis a dangerous experiment to read by moonlight. My naturally strong gray eyes suffered less injury than weaker ones might have sustained.

I had traveled much into the dangerous realms of fancy, and frequently went beyond my depth; but not altogether without advantage. From the character of the innumerable heroines presented to my mind I formed an ideal of excellence; and many grains of wheat gathered from bushels of chaff were carefully stored in the treasure-house of memory.

As I advanced in years and stepped upon the threshold of womanhood, my mirror plainly told me that, though comely and symmetrical, I was not to depend upon my "face for my fortune;" or, in other words, I could never expect to be a "belle" on account of my beauty. I decided, therefore, that my attractions must be of the mind.

I read history, travels, biography, and general literature; learned much of the known world through the eyes of others; acquired a knowledge of Scotland and England through the writings of the "Great Unknown," which I read as they were issued from the press. It was a banquet of sweet things to my intellectual taste, never cloying. As far as I can judge, I retained the good without any of the evil. Certainly the reading of Scott's historical novels tended to purify my taste for fiction, and turned my attention more immediately to history.

At this critical period I began to acquire a taste for solid reading and useful information. A new world was open to me. I did not, however, lay down any plan for mental improvement, but tried to store my mind with the most useful knowledge. I have found reason, again and again, to be thankful that my thoughts were turned at this period into a channel which saved me from the desire of entering too early into society, and checked a career that might have been marked with the merest frivolities—resulting from a naturally gay disposition and exuberant spirits.

I spent one of my Summer vacations in Mrs. Stone's house, that I might profit by the instruction and conversation of our French governess, who alone, of all the teachers, remained during the holidays. We walked, talked, and read together; and as Mademoiselle was my sole companion, and spoke English too imperfectly to make it a pleasure to converse with her in that language, I was compelled to use the French, though she was as anxious to learn English as I was to learn her language. . . .

The first Winter I spent at home was crowded with so many incidents that it seemed extended over a longer time than usual. My father's residence was near the Capitol; and several members of Congress, with their families, boarded with us, forming what was familiarly called "a mess," the family constituting a part of it. This afforded me an opportunity of becoming well acquainted with some of the most distinguished statesmen of the day; among whom were Henry Clay, Judge Poindexter, Dr. Floyd, Mr. Calhoun, and others. One of my most agreeable friends was an old gentleman—General Stevens, of Revolutionary memory—who had taken part in the destruction of the tea in Boston Harbor, and to whom I was ever a willing listener. When he spoke of the Revolution, he kindled a fire of patriotism in my heart that made me almost wish I had lived in those stirring times. . . .

Our Congress, which ought to have been a model of wisdom, did not, even in its youthful vigor, always show the dignity expected in the councils of a great nation. Statesmen of prestige, and of the highest ability, plunged into an excess of dissipation that would have disgraced heathendom. Some of our Senators, it is true, were grave and reverend, and among our Representatives were found men of great integrity and supereminent virtue; but even to the eye of the uninitiated many of our legislators were utterly unfit to be intrusted with the important duties that devolved upon them. How often I have felt shocked to hear of the recklessness exhibited by men high in power, and in whose hands were placed the dearest rights of the people, suggesting the thought, "If such things are done in the green tree, what may be expected in the dry!". . .

Novice as I then was in every thing that related to political affairs, I felt troubled for our newly formed government. The idea of men legislating for millions of people, after spending the live-long night at the gambling-table, besotted with wine and strong drink—one shudders to think of it!

James Monroe, the fifth President of the United States, I had the pleasure of seeing often. A plain, unostentatious, honest man, diligent in business, he worked hard to secure the highest interest of his country, though not then known to be the great statesman which time has since proved him. Mrs. Monroe was a perfect contrast to Mrs. Madison. The latter was a woman of superior elegance, devoted to society, and yet possessed of a clear head and an accurate judgment. She was said to be not only the better but the wiser half of Mr. Madison; and while she could play with a lap-dog or grace a dining party, or be the cynosure of all eyes in a ball-room, she could preside in council, write out state documents, and give the finishing touch to the President's Message.

Mrs. Monroe's domestic habits unfitted her for the eternal round of receptions required in her position, and she very soon retired with disgust from the artificial surroundings of her station, abolished the weekly levees, and scarcely appeared, even on "New-Year's Day," to receive the greetings of the people. Yet she was admired; for, like Cornelia, she placed most value upon the jewels of her own household. A married daughter took her place in society, and gloried in the prestige of the Presidential Mansion. . . .

The current of my life flowed smoothly until I entered my twentieth year,—then came a tide of misfortunes which well nigh sank our family into despair. Poverty, sudden and unexpected, came by one of those not uncommon catastrophes expressed in these bitter words, "Taken for security debts." My father was a generous man, liberal to profusion, and had never learned to manage dollars and cents economically. He could not say "nay" to a friend who wished to borrow. In an evil hour he indorsed to a large amount for one who proved a traitor to the best of friends. The integrity of my truly excellent father forbade his taking any advantage by that evasion so often practiced under such circumstances, and which amounts to downright swindling. He placed all his property at the disposal of the creditors, not reserving even the smallest amount of personal property.

There was no hiding away of silver spoons or valuable plate,—even my paintings were sold at auction; but what grieved me most was the loss of my piano—one of superior tone and quality, knocked off under the hammer for thirty-five dollars. Then came the pinchings of close economy, which, notwithstanding the industry of my mother and the untiring energy of my father, failed to place us in comfortable circumstances again; and it was found so exceedingly difficult to live in Washington that my father resolved to seek a home in St. Louis, where he had friends and relatives who were willing to aid him in procuring some lucrative business.

Before he left I had sought and obtained a situation as a teacher in the interior of Virginia. In this I was aided by the influence of some kind friends in high places, who, being persuaded of my fitness for the position, soon procured me ample patronage. But, alas! the place selected for my new home was at the distance of three hundred miles, which I was to travel by stage in the dreary month of December, and over the worst of roads, three weeks being the time required to accomplish it.

I was placed under the care of a respectable old gentleman who lived at Wytheville, whither I was going to try my fortune as a school-ma'am. The afternoon upon which I left my home can never be effaced from my memory. Ours was a silent meal, as we surrounded for the last time the family board together. My tears flowed fast, and every mouthful of food that I attempted to swallow seemed as if it would choke me. Though my own heart was breaking, I tried to smile, that my dearly loved father and mother might the better bear my departure. The scene that followed that meal is indescribable. I left the house clinging to my father's arm, without daring to look behind me; and he handed me into the stage-coach after one more convulsive pressure in his arms. I closed my eyes for a moment in agony,—and when I opened them again he was gone. I never saw him more. I can not now, after the lapse of nearly fifty years, dwell upon this without anguish—'tis never to be forgotten "while life or being" lasts. . . .

The principal object of interest in Richmond was the Monumental Church, founded on the very spot where the theater was burned. This melancholy and startling event marked the close of the year 1811. During the representation of a popular tragedy, "The Bleeding Nun," the stage scenery caught fire from the lamps. It was at first thought to be a slight affair, as the fire was promptly arrested, and supposed to be entirely extinguished; but, in less than five minutes after, the exciting cry of fire! fire! was heard from behind the scenes, and the actors came rushing across the stage in the greatest confusion; some on fire, others striving to pull down the burning curtains. The terrific scene that followed was beyond description. There was but one mode of egress from the theater, and the flames were spreading with unexampled rapidity; the passage was so crowded in a few minutes that many were trampled to death; some sprang from the upper windows, and others tried to escape across the stage, though it was enveloped in flames. Seventy-two persons lost their lives in the conflagration; among them the Governor of Virginia. The inhabitants, while the flood-gates of grief were open in their hearts, and sorrow a living object before them, planned this church as a memorial of the dead buried under the ruins of the old theater. They poured out their money like water. Art, taste, and genius lent their aid, and the work went on rapidly for a while; but more and more slowly, as the awful scene faded from their memory, and the building in 1819 was yet unfinished, though another theater had been erected in another part of the city, as if to show how narrowly joy may be partitioned off from sorrow. . . .

Wytheville was noted for a total indifference to religion. There was not a church or any place of worship in the town. The only preacher in the vicinity was of the Dutch Reformed Church. His example was of the worst kind—carousing, drinking, cock-fighting, and playing cards during the week, with an occasional sermon on the Sabbath to a sleepy, ungodly congregation, that seemed to know as little about the truths of the Gospel, as if our Savior had never made his advent into the world. Strange to tell, however, there was much refinement among the better class; for this we do not generally expect where there are no godly ministers and no churches. Politeness, kindness, and true Virginia hospitality reigned pre-eminently.

My first introduction into their midst was at the wedding before mentioned. . . .

We were then ushered into the ball-room, the bride and bridegroom occupying the first place in a "Virginia reel." The "new school-teacher," who had previously received an introduction to nearly every body present, was taken out and placed third in the set.

I was passionately fond of dancing, but would have preferred being a spectator on that evening had I not been afraid of giving offense. Some amusing mistakes were made in the various attempts to speak correctly the unpronounceable name of "Hieronymus." My first partner asked the pleasure of dancing in the reel with "Miss Roundabuss;" the next, a lad about seventeen, very pompously called me "Miss Hippopotamus." Afterwards came a young disciple of Æsculapius, who had recently put up his Galen's-head in the town, and whose family I knew in Winchester. He thought he had the name precisely when he called me "Heterogeneous;" others called me "Hatrogenous;" but all agreed that it was far easier to call me "Miss Julia Anne," and this was almost universally adopted. . . .

True, I had left a home to which in all probability I was never to return,—never again to meet in the home circle father, mother, brothers, and sisters. I was now to stand alone, and must necessarily rely upon myself. The broad highways of the world were now before me, and I must emancipate myself from all customary indulgence, take my place among the thronging multitude, and commence life's struggle in earnest.

Oh, how my solitary spirit yearned to see once more those whom I had left behind! No more sweet girl friendships, no more pleasant walks and drives along the banks of the lovely Potomac—a name that even now touches the tenderest chord in my heart, and stirs up the life-blood in my old veins! A long and weary way, the difficulties of which I shuddered to think of, separated me from those I had loved and cherished from the first dawn of life. Oh, how much anguish is often crowded into our hearts, battling with bitter memories! But in the midst of all this darkness the trembling star of Hope still faintly shone, and ere the rosy light of morning came my soul felt stronger, and with the natural elasticity of a cheerful disposition I commenced immediately to prepare for my new vocation. I soon learned that the life of a faithful teacher must be one of toil and unremitting care. All my fairy visions of romance faded into stern reality as my responsibility for others increased. . . .

But to return to my school. I rented a large upper room in a house contiguous to General Smyth's. The kindness of my patrons relieved me from all trouble and expense as regarded desks, benches, etc. My schoolroom was neatly fitted up for the accommodation of thirty or forty pupils. All the little misses in the village attended—some grown girls—and a few little boys. A few of the girls were larger and considerably taller than the teacher. One, I remember, stood over six feet in her shoes, and had seen but sixteen Summers. This, however, was an exception.

The first day, with all its petty vexations, passed off smoothly, though I retired at night with an aching heart, burdened with a painful interest for my pupils. I was rather doubtful whether, with my inexperience and want of tact, our association would be for weal or woe. I began again the next morning with renewed vigor, classing and arranging my pupils so as to give me as little trouble as possible; and then commenced my course of instruction with the elementary principles. By the end of the first week I had learned an important lesson myself, which can not be too deeply impressed upon a teacher's mind. A person who has not the patience to communicate knowledge, drop by drop, should never undertake the instruction of ignorant children, since it is impossible to pour into their minds by copious streams. The heart, too, must be deeply interested in the work, or there will be no success. That teacher, who feels no conviction of the importance of the cause, and no solicitude about the issue, should give up the office. . . .

My first serious difficulty was with a little girl about ten years of age, the youngest child of a large family, who had been badly spoiled at home. She was noisy, indolent, and impatient under restraint. Continually teasing and annoying others, this little nettle-top went on from bad to worse, until endurance was no longer a virtue. I was anxious to keep her in school, as I had five from the same family, and it was quite to my interest to get along pleasantly with her. But it could not be. One afternoon her resistance to my authority reached its climax; so I quietly removed her from the school-room to an adjoining apartment and gave her the well-merited punishment with my slipper, the first she had ever had in her life. Her screams were terrific. There was an awful silence in the school-room, and you might have heard a pin drop, as I led her back, and, placing her bonnet on her head, ordered her to go home and never return. I then quietly resumed my seat, and the lessons proceeded as usual until the hour of dismissal.

I remained alone until nearly night, weeping, praying, and struggling to conquer what I thought my own ungovernable temper. I began to think that teaching was not my vocation. I understand it all now. I was well pleased so far as the dictatorial part was concerned. In the control

I had hitherto exercised over my sisters while at school, I had never been contradicted; and, notwithstanding the constantly recurring petty trials in early life, I had not learned how to be calm and unmoved when my will was opposed. Every possible pain had been taken to secure for me the best education. I had been the idol of my father's heart, and the object of my mother's tenderest solicitude; but, while the love of knowledge was carefully instilled into my mind, I had failed to learn that modest diffidence in reference to my attainments, which presents an effectual barrier to disagreeable parade and pedantry. Every thing I did at home was excellent, and no opportunity was lost to parade my attainments to friends and visitors. The shock I sustained in being obliged to devote my talents to the dull routine of a school-room, instead of making a display in society, was terrible; but a sense of duty to God and to my parents sustained me. I knew I could teach, and I determined I would not be an inferior teacher. But let me here remark that young persons should cultivate a humility with regard to themselves, which is the life and soul of youthful exertion.

After this contest with my little pupil, I retired to my room with a violent headache, deeply humbled, but perfectly determined to sustain my dignity at all hazards. The first voice that I heard in the morning uttered this expression with deep feeling: "She will drive away all her pupils; people will not submit to such correction." "I hope not," was the gentle reply, "and I'm sure she had better commence in the right way, and let them know what is due from the pupil to the teacher." This I heard as I descended the stairs which opened into the breakfast-room. General Smyth was there, looking cold and reserved. Frances ventured one kind glance from her sunny blue eyes, but Nancy, her younger sister, sat trembling, with her face flushed to an unusual redness, and my sweet little Nannie Henderson, the granddaughter, a child six years of age, seemed fluttered and amazed at my presence. Mrs. Smyth bade me good morning with her usual cordiality. No one spoke during the breakfast except by way of courtesy.

I went immediately after this silent meal to my school-room. It was early, but most of the girls were already assembled, some conversing in an undertone, others studying diligently. I spoke pleasantly to them, and gave kindly answers to the few timid questions asked about their lessons, though my heart was oppressed in reference to the possibility of my losing five pupils instead of one. I would not, however, have taken a step backward if I had lost my whole school. But, lo! I had scarcely finished calling the roll, when in walked my refractory pupil, followed by the other four. The little girl walked rather irresolutely to my desk and placed a note in my hand. She stood with downcast eyes while I read it. The contents were somewhat in this style: "Please receive my penitent little girl again, with the positive assurance that every thing shall be done to prevent future trouble; and we will aid you in subduing and punishing any disobedience on her part. We are satisfied that you will do every thing in your power to promote her highest interest, and are willing to leave the matter in your hands."

The struggle was over. She remained with me as long as I was in Wytheville, first an obedient, afterward an affectionate pupil. . . .

My mother soon procured a dwelling, comfortable and sufficiently spacious to admit of one large room being fitted up for my sister's prospective day-school.[3] This was in a short time filled with young girls, among whom were half a dozen music scholars. Mrs. Smith, from the "Meadows," the name of Captain Smith's place, came as soon as she knew of my arrival to take me to her home. This home was but a short walk from my mother's, yet I had the convenience of a carriage to go and come as I pleased. My kind and excellent patrons manifested so much interest in those I loved best in the world, that my heart was completely won. My dear mother had a great passion for gardening, was particularly fond of the cultivation of flowers, and had here ample space to indulge herself in the sweetness and beauty of the fairy creations she cherished. . . .

About this time I became acquainted with that excellent but eccentric old lady, Mrs. Russell, through the medium of General Frank Preston's family. . . .

Mrs. Russell was in every way an extraordinary woman. The sister of Patrick Henry, she possessed some of his characteristics. Her second husband, General Russell, was quite as distinguished as the first for worth and bravery. Both she and General Russell were faithful members of the Methodist Church. They were converted in the good old-fashioned way, when nobody objected to shouting, if it came from an overflowing

---

3. Tevis soon undertook to offer both drawing and piano classes, attracting enough students to provide work for her sister, who came to Virginia the next year accompanied by their mother.

heart filled with the love of God. The old General walked worthy of his vocation until he was taken home to a better world, leaving his excellent widow a true type of Wesleyan Methodism. "Madam Russell," as she was generally called, was a "mother in Israel;" and the Methodist preachers in those days esteemed her next to Bishop Asbury. She lived for a while in Abingdon, but as the gay society of that place, particularly among her own relatives, was uncongenial to her, she withdrew to a retired spot near the "Camp-ground," in the vicinity of the sulphur springs. . . .

She dressed in the style of '76—full skirts, with an over-garment, long, flowing, open in front and confined at the waist by a girdle, and made of a material called Bath coating. In this girdle were tucked two or three pocket-handkerchiefs. The sleeves of her dress came just below the elbows—the lower part of the arm being covered with long, half-handed gloves. She wore a kerchief of linen lawn, white as snow, and sometimes an apron of the same material; and on her head a very plain cap, above which was usually placed a broad-brimmed hat given her by Bishop Asbury in days long gone by, and worn by the old lady with probably the same feeling that Elisha wore Elijah's mantle. She was erect as in the meridian of life though she must have been seventy years old when I first saw her. A magnificent-looking woman, "she walked every inch a queen," reminding me of one of the old-fashioned pictures of Vandyke. She never shook the hand of a poor Methodist preacher in parting without leaving in it a liberal donation; she knew the Gospel was free, but she also knew that "the laborer was worthy of his hire.". . .

My nature was essentially unfitted for fashionable society. I went into it because it was easier to go than to refuse the kindness that forced on me those uncongenial amusements. I had often prayed to be saved from temptation without, perhaps, forming any resolution to resist it. From early childhood I had desired to be a Christian. Could I expect that God would do all this for me when I had never even formed a determination to *resist* evil? Did I really desire to serve God? *To serve God,* what a thought! Now, for the first time, I realized its import. If I do serve God I can not serve the world. What is it to serve the world, and what will be its reward? Is it to follow its fashions, to love its spirit of levity and vanity, to seek its pleasures, and forgetting God, be the ungrateful recipient of all his mercies? The reward will only be "the pleasures of sin for a season," and then the future, the dark, unending future. . . .

Mrs. Smith had much to tell me about the quarterly meeting, and the interesting religious persons with whom she had become acquainted. The presiding elder had tarried with them during the meeting. . . .

We were sitting one evening conversing upon the subject of the great revival that had occurred in the Methodist Church during the last two years, and the changed aspect of things, when Mrs. Smith, after praising enthusiastically the new presiding elder from Kentucky, who had been a guest in their house during the Christmas meeting, and who seemed to have inspired her with a degree of reverence that left her scarcely anything else to talk of, exclaimed—

"I wish you could see him and hear him pray."

"How does he look?" I asked.

"Tall, dignified, fine looking, but by no means handsome; yet there is so much character, so much real worth expressed in his face, that you would never remark his prominent nose and wide mouth, except as indicative of intellect."

"But he must look odd in one of those *Methodist coats?*"

"No, he does not; every thing he wears is becoming; it could not be otherwise, with a man upon whose brow is written the simplicity of a Christian."

"Well, I hope I shall have an opportunity of seeing this paragon of yours, but I warn you, I almost feel prejudiced against him, when I remember the Scripture declaration, 'Wo unto those of whom *all* men speak well.' "

"I do not know that every body does speak well of him—I am sure that sinners must feel exceedingly uncomfortable under his searching sermons. I am told that quite a number thought the first sermon he preached at the Court-house powerfully severe, unveiling as he did the iniquity of the age with firm hand, and making them see themselves as God sees them."

We were interrupted by the entrance of Captain Smith, just from town, who exclaimed—

"Polly, have another roll of blankets put on Tevis's bed; he will be here to-night after preaching."

"Indeed! I am truly glad; we were just speaking of him, and I am gratified at so soon having an opportunity of introducing him to our young friend. This is his rest week; he will spend it with us, I hope."

94

I was conscious of a desire to see the man whose wonder-working energy and pious efforts had been crowned with almost unexampled success throughout the district over which he had for two years presided. . . .

The week passed away, and the wayfaring man of God had gone; but not so the remembrance of his fervent prayers and pious conversation. Mrs. Smith had often expressed her fears that living out of the Church, as she did, was not in keeping with her duty to herself and her family, though she had always been a strict attendant on the services of the Presbyterian Church, in which she had been brought up. She had lived in the world without partaking much of its spirit, and now she was almost persuaded to become a Methodist. Her husband opposed it steadily, but not violently. The law of rigid simplicity, which reigned at this time so pre-eminently among the Methodists, was not according to his taste; and he feared the influence of religion in earnest, and that a change in his household arrangements, superinduced by these rigid people who were turning the world upside down, might cast a shadow over his daughter's entrance into the gay world, and throw her too much out of its dress-circle. Thus he ridiculed the precision of its members and their particular exclusiveness, which did in reality make a dividing line between them and other religious sects, as well as the outer world.

I had expected to remain at "The Meadows" until Mary's education should be completed, and this was ardently desired by all concerned; but the period was rapidly approaching which was to make an important change in my future. In the latter part of September, Mr. Tevis tarried a few days at Captain Smith's, on his way to his Kentucky home, where he was accustomed to spend a week at the close of each conference year. Having had frequent opportunities of learning the true elevation of soul which characterized this self-sacrificing, noble-minded Christian, and contrasting the true value and lofty worth of the things of God and eternity with the vanities and follies of the world, it was very natural that I should esteem and honor one so thoroughly a missionary of the cross, one in whom goodness seemed personified. His prayer for the family, on the morning of his departure, was more than usually fervent, and characterized by a simple and lofty eloquence that kindled a devotional spirit in every heart; and when he bade us farewell, a glow of holy feeling beamed on his face, as if it were to be his last meeting with us on earth. Almost involuntarily, I walked to the window to watch his receding form as he passed rapidly down the lawn through the gate-way and mounted his horse and quickly disappeared. I was conscious then of a deeper interest in Mrs. Smith's model preacher than I was willing to acknowledge even to myself.

Scarce two weeks had elapsed when I received a pastoral letter from him, post-marked Knoxville, Tennessee, requesting a reply at Shelby-ville, Kentucky. Not a single expression in his letter evinced a deeper interest in me than he might have felt and expressed for others of his numerous charge. I readily accepted the opportunity of corresponding with one whose pious advice might aid me in my onward efforts through the new and almost untried path before me. A truly religious friendship, imbued with the spirit of the Gospel, is one of the greatest of earthly blessings. My reply found him at his father's home, near Shelbyville. Our correspondence was continued without the slightest allusion to the prospect of a more intimate relationship, though we both afterward ac-knowledged to an occasional glimpse, somewhat vague, it is true, of a more united interest thereafter for time and for eternity.

The usual Christmas quarterly-meeting brought him back to Abing-don, but he tarried in town with a brother Will. On New Year's Eve a long letter, written closely and with great care, was handed me. This contained a plain, matter-of-fact proposal of marriage, but sufficiently tender for a dignified minister of the Gospel. He requested my earnest and prayerful consideration of the matter, previous to a personal inter-view, which he desired might take place on the morrow. Early on the first day of January we quietly talked the whole subject over, as we sat in Mrs. Smith's dining-room, one on each side of the fire-place. We were not young enough for romance, he being thirty-two years of age and I twenty-four; and we were both too serious for affectation or trifling. Thus after settling some difficulties which appeared to me insuperable, relating to a continued provision for the comfort and support of my mother and family, all of which were obviated, as soon as presented, by this liberal-minded Christian, who cheerfully promised to aid me in all that I might be required to do for them, an engagement was agreed upon. We felt assured that the blessing of God would follow a union so entered into; and that, bound together by the most sacred of earthly ties, we might toil and weep and pray and rejoice together in this fallen world and meet as friends in the Celestial Paradise, where there are greetings such as only angelic hearts can know.

Captain Smith, though thoroughly vexed at the derangement of his own plans, entered heartily into ours. He could not forbear exclaiming, however, "Well, I'll never invite another Methodist preacher into my house unless he be ugly, old, and disagreeable." The day of our marriage was fixed for Tuesday, March 9, 1824, in honor of the birth-day of my future father-in-law. During the interim our regular duties were not interrupted. The presiding elder did not ride a mile less, nor did he omit the preaching of a single sermon. My books and pupils occupied my attention as completely as ever, though at intervals I plied diligently the swift, shining needle, for I was still my own mantua-maker.

For the benefit of my lady readers, and especially to satisfy the curiosity of my pupils, I will merely advert to my trousseau. My wedding-dress was an India muslin robe, made in the prevailing style, only three widths in the skirt, and severely plain in every respect; no chaplet of orange flowers gleaming with pearls; no rich laces, no ornaments of any kind, not even a bridal veil. I did expect to take a trip, but I should need neither a traveling dress nor a large trunk. A pair of common saddle-bags would carry all I wanted. The only expensive dress that I had was a black Canton crape robe, purchased at what I considered at the time to be an enormous price, twelve dollars.

The eventful day at last arrived. It was cloudy and drizzling, cold and cheerless, with only occasional glimpses of sunshine. Mr. Tevis spent the day in his own room, having donned his wedding-suit when he first arose, to the complete astonishment of those who met him at the breakfast-table. I have said that the day was unpleasant; leaden clouds hung low on the misty horizon; but no gloomy doubts pressed upon my mind. Late in the afternoon the clouds in the West broke away, and the sun, sinking into night, threw his parting beams upon the earth.

No cards of invitation had been issued, but some twenty or thirty of our mutual friends were made acquainted with the day and the hour. Thus, soon after early candle-light, the wedding-guests came dropping in until the parlor was comfortably filled. The ceremony, performed by the Rev. W. P. Kendrick, was long and impressive; and as we knelt down in solemn prayer, offered up at the close, the whole company knelt with us. Then came the usual congratulations, warm greetings, and the social interchange of sentiment and feeling. A sumptuous and costly banquet followed, where brilliant repartee and well-timed compliment lost nothing from the exhilarating influence of happy hearts. No pains had been spared to render the evening agreeable, and the effort was not only fully appreciated, but eminently successful. Even Mr. Tevis, always serious as eternity, and whom I had never known to laugh, was compelled to smile frequently at the sallies of our ever-mirthful friend, Captain Smith, who was, on that memorable evening, as gleeful as a school-boy. . . .

We talked of our future plans; I promising never to interrupt his itinerant course, while it was agreed that I should continue my vocation as a teacher, by locating in the beautiful village of Shelbyville, within two miles of the home of his aged parents.[4] All these plans were carried out. I do not think he ever preached a sermon less, and, thank God! there was never any impediment in his having, as St. Paul would say, "a wife to lead about." We were happy then in arranging these plans; happier, under God's blessing, in being able to carry them out. How fully we realized the sweet promise, "Seek first the kingdom of God, and all these things shall be added unto you," will be seen in the course of my biography.

On Monday we returned to our usual vocations—he to his district appointments, and I to my school-room. "The Meadows" was now, by cordial invitation, a home for both of us; yet Mr. Tevis could be there only at long intervals, as his district, comprising nine hundred square miles, required not only celerity of movement, but constant work. A presiding elder in those days preached usually one and sometimes two sermons every day, besides attending quarterly-meetings; whereas now the districts are so much smaller that the presiding elder is only required to attend his quarterly-meetings, and seldom has an appointment during the week, giving him an opportunity of resting ten or twelve days at a time. . . .

Monday, March 25, 1825, our school opened with eighteen or twenty pupils. We did not expect a larger number because we had taken

4. The newly married couple returned to Shelbyville, Kentucky, where John Tevis's family lived. Expecting the young couple to live with them, the elder Tevises had given them a house to rent out to supplement the meager income of a Methodist circuit rider. Julia talked both her husband and father-in-law into letting her start a girls' school in the house instead. Because it was perched on a slight elevation, she named it the "Science Hill Academy" to indicate the seriousness of the education it offered the young women of the South.

no pains to advertise in any way, consequently it was not known abroad.

I had four boarders to commence with. . . .

Few of my pupils had been subjected to the wholesome discipline of a well-regulated school,—thus they required to be taught the simplest rudiments of knowledge. Some had been properly instructed, but so irregularly, and by so many different teachers, that I found it necessary to tear down a portion of the superstructure and lay the corner-stone more firmly—preparatory to the cultivation of thorough intellectual habits.

There was not a positively disagreeable girl among my limited number of boarders, the first year; and my day scholars were docile, and placed so entirely under my control by their sensible parents that I passed many pleasant hours in the school-room,—and the fruits of my efforts in their behalf soon became apparent. Amid all my anxiety for their mental improvement, one object I kept steadily in view—the cultivation of the affections and giving them right views of the claims of God upon their hearts; and I cherish the hope that at the day of final account it may appear that my labor was "not in vain in the Lord."

We were so situated that, unembarrassed by other considerations, I could so lay plans and make arrangements that I felt myself at liberty to give undivided attention to the business of teaching, with the perfect assurance that minor affairs would be promptly and effectively rendered subservient to this our settled vocation. I had spent so much of my life in boarding-schools, taking notes all the time, that I was anxious, while adopting with them the regular routine and the salutary discipline necessary for success, to avoid the many objectionable features. . . .

I began my reform by excluding the girls from their bed-chambers after they left them in the morning. They made their own beds, swept and dusted their rooms, and put every thing in order before the school hour. As soon as the school-bell rang in the morning, and after the rooms had been inspected by a careful eye, the doors were locked, and the keys placed in the hands of a careful person appointed for that purpose, only giving the girls the privilege, when necessary, of getting the key and returning it as soon as the errand was performed,—thus making them thoughtful as to what they might want during the day. This proved an excellent arrangement. If there were several girls in a room, the duty devolving upon each in turn, of keeping the room in order, made them cautious in throwing articles of clothing about, knowing the penalty would be a demerit mark, a dictionary lesson, or several pages of extra writing.

I grew fonder of teaching as days and months rolled on, and moved steadily onward with my daily duties, courageously encountering difficulties, looking full in the face whatever was before me, and taking most conscientious care that my pupils should never be neglected, nor the duties of to-day left for to-morrow. Consequently, it was not an uncommon thing for night to find me still at my post, too weary even to sigh. Yet I was never gloomy, never desponding; and amid all my perplexities prayer and the Word of God had the living power to stir my heart to its very depths and prevent that stupor and apathy which sometimes settles on the soul. In the darkest hours of doubt and foreboding I rested strongly upon the abiding faith of my beloved husband as a treasure of our common life. Trust flowed into his heart as rivers enter the sea; his soul was like a well-watered garden planted by the river's side. . . .

Ours was the first Protestant female academy founded in the Mississippi Valley, except that of the Rev. Mr. Fall, situated in Nashville, which antedates it a few years. . . .

Much care was exercised in regulating our terms so as to leave an open door for those in moderate circumstances; and we endeavored always to promote a prudent economy in our arrangements, while we left no means untried and spared no expense to promote the highest interests of education. Our ambition was not to accumulate wealth, though we wished remuneration, but to render the school a blessing to the rising generation,—and certainly we have not been altogether disappointed.

Teaching should be considered as a profession, and the loftiest calling except that of preaching the Gospel. To communicate moral and religious truth is the very noblest employment of an intelligent being. Teachers, as well as preachers, should never sigh for that ease which some think so "friendly to life's decline."

During the first ten or fifteen years of my teaching in Shelbyville girls cared much less for personal adornment, and studied with a more hearty good-will, than at any time since; whilst I took the greatest pains possible to cultivate as much taste for dress as was compatible with the highest intellectual improvement. I remember but few girls during the period referred to that gave me much trouble on this score. Those with the most limited wardrobes were the best students, as well as the neatest in dress.

A well-cultivated mind scorns tawdry finery, and teaches us the refining truth that cleanliness is next to godliness.

Much annoyance was felt the first few years by invitations through the medium of the post-office to parties and balls—a custom prevalent in all the little towns of Kentucky, but fatal to good scholarship, making fashionable young ladies of children from the ages of ten to fifteen. They were, in fact, the society of the place. Married women, no matter how young, were never invited to places of amusement, and a girl of eighteen or twenty was quite *passé*. I tried to change the custom as far as my school was concerned, by returning the billets unopened. . . . My kind but positive manner had the desired effect; and I would take this opportunity to say, for the benefit of those who preside over female institutions, where there are also male schools and colleges, that a candid, open course pursued towards both boys and girls will generally break up any clandestine communications. This will cultivate a high moral sense of personal responsibility, and, under strict surveillance, give a security not obtained by any other means. Let there be no mystery and as little suspicion as possible. . . .

I have said there must be but one supreme controlling head in every school, thus preventing jealousy among teachers and insubordination among pupils. But in a large school, where there are several teachers, each should be the supreme ruler in his or her department; there should be no appeal to the principal except for consultation. A meeting of the teachers is desirable now and then to compare notes. A perfect unanimity should exist; one single jarring string destroys the harmony and clogs the onward progress of the pupils.

Children love to work, and nothing charms them more than to be made to feel their importance. I have often endeared a young girl to me by asking her assistance, and many an idle one have I made industrious by finding her something to do for others, when she was unwilling to work for herself. A personal attachment of the warmest kind may thus be awakened between teacher and pupil. We must be careful, however, while asking the assistance of some and showing an honest gratification for the assistance rendered, not to awaken the jealousy of others. I have seen the happiest results attending judicious measures of this kind. The time is well spent, even if the regular course of study be interrupted, when we can induce our pupils to act in concert with us, and make them feel how much pleasanter it is to co-operate than to thwart and oppose;

[handwritten marginalia: Teacher as throned monarch]

yet whenever reproof or correction is necessary, the teacher must be a throned monarch; look on the favorable side as far as is consistent with duty, but be ever ready with an efficient hand to arrest evil.

I have had very many excellent assistant teachers of both sexes, superior in tact and successful in their vocation, yet I do not hesitate to give it as my decided opinion that women are the best, the most patient, and the most successful teachers save, perhaps, in the higher and more abstruse sciences, which belong to the learned professions. They are certainly better fitted to govern a female school. . . .

January 8, 1870. Just fifty years ago I began my career as a teacher, and have continued with but little interruption,—no rest from duties save in the vacations.

When the light of the sun grows dim upon my fading eyes, when the fountains of life are low, when the frosts of age descend upon my feeble frame, then through the halls of memory, like the "still, sweet strains of music far away," will come tender recollections of the happy throngs that have hearkened to my instructions. The grateful remembrance of those for whom I have patiently and zealously toiled casts a halo of light over life's decline, soothes the infirmities of age and kindles upon the altar of my heart a purer love for the human race. Each pupil, whom by advice or encouragement I prompted to nobler aims or urged to higher attainments, is a gem in my casket of more worth than the treasures of the deep blue sea.

[handwritten marginalia: Pupils of true, successful teacher]

Charles Ball

1 7 8 5 [?] – 1 8 3 7

 I T H a superb gift for recall, Charles Ball recounted to an anonymous scribe his memories of over forty years spent as an enslaved person in Maryland, South Carolina, and Georgia. "The design of the writer who is no more than the record of the facts detailed to him by another," the preface explains, "has been to render the narrative as simple, and the style of the story as plain, as the laws of the language would permit." Obviously published as part of an abolitionist campaign against slavery, Ball's autobiography, which appeared in three different editions within a year, depicts the daily cruelties of the slave system in a peculiarly forceful way.

Ball's autobiography begins with the poignant scene of Ball being separated from his mother and siblings when they are sold after the death of their master. Yet a young child, Ball remained in Maryland, where he had the chance still to visit his father as well as his grandfather, a native of Africa. The Constitution gave Congress the power to outlaw the foreign slave trade in 1808. After that date, the domestic slave trade flourished, because the high prices given for labor in the new cotton lands of South Carolina, Georgia, Alabama, and Mississippi created a powerful incentive among slave owners in the Upper South to sell their slaves. Indeed, by 1860 the slave population of Delaware, Maryland, Kentucky, and Missouri had gone from twenty to ten percent of the total population.

The breakup of slave families, as Ball's story demonstrates, was most likely to occur at the time of a master's death, when estates were liquidated in order to make bequests. A young man when his turn came, Ball was literally driven South in chains, one of more than fifty men and women gathered into a coffle. Once on a South Carolina plantation, Ball's knowledge of fishing, gained in his youth on the waters of the Chesapeake, proved to be his passport out of the drudgery of the cotton fields. His new master asked him to set up a seine fishery on the river abutting the plantation. Ball made the most of his chance, creating a profitable side business for his master while bargaining in the illicit river traffic to obtain better food for himself and his workers.

Extraordinarily reflective, Ball enlivened his narrative with shrewd comments on Southern mores, African traits, the class system of the white people, and contrasts between the Deep South and the border states. Ruminating on the attitudes of his fellow workers, Ball stated that he had never known "a slave who believed, that he violated any rule of morality, by appropriating to himself any thing that belonged to his master, if it was necessary to his comfort."[1]

When another master's death delivered him into the hands of a cruel mistress, Ball began an epic flight back to Maryland, hiding by day and hiking by night for several fearful months. As with Chauncey Jerome and Alfred Lorrain, the War of 1812 played a role in the life of Charles Ball; the urgent need for seamen earned him a job safe from the scrutiny of slave catchers. From this vantage point, Ball witnessed the destruction wrought by the British in the Chesapeake Bay, including the large number of enslaved persons captured by the British. "These were the first black people whom I had known to desert to the British, although the practice was afterwards so common," Ball reports, adding that "in the course of this summer, and the summer of 1814, several thousand black people deserted from their masters and mistresses, and escaped to the

---

1. Charles Ball, *Slavery in the United States: A Narrative of the Life and Adventures of Charles Ball, a Black Man* (Lewistown, Pa., 1836), p. 231. This memoir has also been published as *Fifty Years in Chains, or, The Life of an American Slave* (New York, 1836).

British fleet." "None of these people were ever regained by their own-ers," he explains, because "the British naval officers treated them as free people."[2] After his discharge, Ball assumed the life of a free man in Baltimore, but his adventures were far from over, for he was recaptured and sent South—only to escape once more and settle in Philadelphia, where he ended his days. He never found his wife and children.

~ 𝑒 ~

*M*Y story is a true one, and I shall tell it in a simple style. It will be merely a recital of my life as a slave in the Southern States of the Union—a description of negro slavery in the "model Republic."

the contradiction

My grandfather was brought from Africa and sold as a slave in Cal-vert county, in Maryland. I never understood the name of the ship in which he was imported, nor the name of the planter who bought him on his arrival, but at the time I knew him he was a slave in a family called Maud, who resided near Leonardtown. My father was a slave in a family named Hauty, living near the same place. My mother was the slave of a tobacco planter, who died when I was about four years old.[1] My mother had several children, and they were sold upon master's death to separate purchasers. She was sold, my father told me, to a Georgia trader. I, of all her children, was the only one left in Maryland. When sold I was naked, never having had on clothes in my life, but my new master gave me a child's frock, belonging to one of his own children. After he had purchased me, he dressed me in this garment, took me before him on his horse, and started home; but my poor mother, when she saw me leaving her for the last time, ran after me, took me down from the horse, clasped me in her arms, and wept loudly and bitterly over me. My mas-ter seemed to pity her, and endeavored to soothe her distress by telling her that he would be a good master to me, and that I should not want anything. She then, still holding me in her arms, walked along the road beside the horse as he moved slowly, and earnestly and imploringly besought my master to buy her and the rest of her children, and not permit them to be carried away by the negro buyers; but whilst thus entreating him to save her and her family, the slave-driver, who had first

---

2. Ball, *Slavery in the United States*, p. 363.
1. Judging from internal evidence, Ball was born in 1785.

How of Ball's mother's life

bought her, came running in pursuit of her with a raw-hide in his hand. When he overtook us, he told her he was her master now, and ordered her to give that little negro to its owner, and come back with him.

My mother then turned to him and cried, "Oh, master, do not take me from my child!" Without making any reply, he gave her two or three heavy blows on the shoulders with his raw-hide, snatched me from her arms, handed me to my master, and seizing her by one arm, dragged her back towards the place of sale. My master then quickened the pace of his horse; and as we advanced, the cries of my poor parent became more and more indistinct—at length they died away in the distance, and I never again heard the voice of my poor mother. Young as I was, the horrors of that day sank deeply into my heart, and even at this time, though half a century has elapsed, the terrors of the scene return with painful vividness upon my memory. Frightened at the sight of the cruelties inflicted upon my poor mother, I forgot my own sorrows at parting from her and clung to my new master, as an angel and a saviour, when compared with the hardened fiend into whose power she had fallen. . . .

My father never recovered from the effects of the shock, which this sudden and overwhelming ruin of his family gave him. He had formerly been of a gay, social temper, and when he came to see us on a Saturday night, he always brought us some little present, such as the means of a poor slave would allow—apples, melons, sweet potatoes, or, if he could procure nothing else, a little parched corn, which tasted better in our cabin, because he had brought it. . . .

He became gloomy and morose in his temper, to all but me; and spent nearly all his leisure time with my grandfather, who claimed kindred with some royal family in Africa, and had been a great warrior in his native country. . . .

The name of the man who purchased me at the vendue, and became my master, was John Cox; but he was generally called Jack Cox. He was a man of kindly feelings towards his family, and treated his slaves, of whom he had several besides me, with humanity. He permitted my grandfather to visit me as often as he pleased, and allowed him sometimes to carry me to his own cabin, which stood in a lonely place, at the head of a deep hollow. . . .

When I was about twelve years old, my master, Jack Cox, died of a disease which had long confined him to the house. I was sorry for the death of my master, who had always been kind to me; and I soon discovered that I had good cause to regret his departure from this world. He had several children at the time of his death, who were all young; the oldest being about my own age. The father of my late master, who was still living, became administrator of his estate, and took possession of his property, and amongst the rest, of myself. This old gentleman treated me with the greatest severity, and compelled me to work very hard on his plantation for several years, until I suppose I must have been near or quite twenty years of age. As I was always very obedient, and ready to execute all his orders, I did not receive much whipping, but suffered greatly for want of sufficient and proper food. . . .

Some short time after my wife became chambermaid to her mistress, it was my misfortune to change masters once more. . . .

My change of masters realized all the evil apprehensions which I had entertained. I found Mr. Ballard sullen and crabbed in his temper, and always prone to find fault with my conduct—no matter how hard I had labored, or how careful I was to fulfil all his orders, and obey his most unreasonable commands. Yet, it so happened, that he never beat me, for which, I was altogether indebted to the good character, for industry, sobriety and humility, which I had established in the neighborhood. I think he was ashamed to abuse me, lest he should suffer in the good opinion of the public; for he often fell into the most violent fits of anger against me, and overwhelmed me with coarse and abusive language. He did not give me clothes enough to keep me warm in winter, and compelled me to work in the woods, when there was deep snow on the ground, by which I suffered very much. I had determined at last to speak to him to sell me to some person in the neighborhood, so that I might still be near my wife and children—but a different fate awaited me. . . .

This man [a stranger] came up to me, and, seizing me by the collar, shook me violently, saying I was his property, and must go with him to Georgia. At the sound of these words, the thoughts of my wife and children rushed across my mind, and my heart beat away within me. I saw and knew that my case was hopeless, and that resistance was vain, as there were near twenty persons present, all of whom were ready to assist the man by whom I was kidnapped. I felt incapable of weeping or speaking, and in my despair I laughed loudly. My purchaser ordered me to cross my hands behind, which were quickly bound with a strong cord;

and he then told me that we must set out that very day for the South. I asked if I could not be allowed to go to see my wife and children, or if this could not be permitted, if they might not have leave to come to see me; but was told that I would be able to get another wife in Georgia.

My new master, whose name I did not hear, took me that same day across the Patuxent, where I joined fifty-one other slaves, whom he had bought in Maryland. Thirty-two of these were men, and nineteen were women. The women were merely tied together with a rope, about the size of a bed-cord, which was tied like a halter round the neck of each; but the men, of whom I was the stoutest and strongest, were very differently caparisoned. A strong iron collar was closely fitted by means of a padlock round each of our necks. A chain of iron, about a hundred feet in length, was passed through the hasp of each padlock, except at the two ends, where the hasps of the padlock passed through a link of the chain. In addition to this, we were handcuffed in pairs, with iron staples and bolts, with a short chain, about a foot long, uniting the handcuffs and their wearers in pairs. In this manner we were chained alternately by the right and left hand; and the poor man to whom I was thus ironed, wept like an infant when the blacksmith, with his heavy hammer, fastened the ends of the bolts that kept the staples from slipping from our arms. For my own part, I felt indifferent to my fate. It appeared to me that the worst had come that could come, and that no change of fortune could harm me. . . .

I was now a slave in South Carolina, and had no hope of ever again seeing my wife and children. I had at times serious thoughts of suicide so great was my anguish. If I could have got a rope I should have hanged myself at Lancaster. The thought of my wife and children I had been torn from in Maryland, and the dreadful undefined future which was before me, came near driving me mad. . . .

The landlord assured my master that at this time slaves were much in demand, both in Columbia and Augusta; that purchasers were numerous and prices good; and that the best plan of effecting good sales would be to put up each *nigger* separately, at auction, after giving a few days' notice, by an advertisement, in the neighboring country. Cotton, he said, had not been higher for many years, and as a great many persons, especially young men, were moving off to the new purchase in Georgia, prime hands were in high demand, for the purpose of clearing the land in the new country. . . .

It was manifest that I was now in a country where the life of a black man was no more regarded than that of an ox, except as far as the man was worth the more money in the market. On all the plantations that we passed, there was a want of live stock of every description, except slaves, and they were deplorably abundant.

The fields were destitute of everything that deserved the name of grass, and not a spear of clover was anywhere visible. The few cattle that existed, were browsing on the boughs of the trees, in the woods. Everything betrayed a scarcity of the means of supplying the slaves, who cultivated the vast cotton-fields, with a sufficiency of food. . . .

By the laws of the United States I am still a slave; and though I am now growing old, I might even yet be deemed of sufficient value to be worth pursuing as far as my present residence, if those to whom the law gives the right of dominion over my person and life, knew where to find me. For these reasons I have been advised, by those whom I believe to be my friends, not to disclose the true names of any of those families in which I was a slave, in Carolina or Georgia, lest this narrative should meet their eyes, and in some way lead them to a discovery of my retreat.

I was now the slave of one of the most wealthy planters in Carolina, who planted cotton, rice, indigo, corn, and potatoes; and was the master of two hundred and sixty slaves.

The description of one great cotton plantation will give a correct idea of all the others; and I shall here present an outline of that of my master's.

He lived about two miles from Caugaree river, which bordered his estate on one side, and in the swamps of which were his rice fields. The country hereabout is very flat, the banks of the river are low, and in wet seasons large tracts of country are flooded by the super-abundant water of the river. There are no springs, and the only means of procuring water on the plantations is from wells, which must be sunk in general about twenty feet deep, before a constant supply of water can be obtained. My master had two of these wells on his plantation—one at the mansion house, and one at the quarter.

My master's house was of brick (brick houses are by no means common among the planters, whose residences are generally built of frame work, weather boarded with pine boards, and covered with shingles of the white cedar or juniper cypress) and contained two large parlors, and a spacious hall or entry on the ground floor. The main building was two stories high, and attached to this was a smaller building, one story and a half high, with a large room, where the family generally took breakfast, with a kitchen at the farther extremity from the main building.

There was a spacious garden behind the house, containing, I believe, about five acres, well cultivated, and handsomely laid out. In this garden grew a great variety of vegetables; some of which I have never seen in the market of Philadelphia. . . .

It is impossible to reconcile the mind of the native slave to the idea of living in a state of perfect equality, and boundless affection, with the white people. Heaven will be no heaven to him, if he is not to be avenged of his enemies. I know, from experience, that these are the fundamental rules of his religious creed; because I learned them in the religious meetings of the slaves themselves. A favorite and kind master or mistress, may now and then be admitted into heaven, but this rather as a matter of favor, to the intercession of some slave, than as [a] matter of strict justice to the whites, who will, by no means, be of an equal rank with those who shall be raised from the depths of misery, in this world.

The idea of a revolution in the conditions of the whites and the blacks, is the corner-stone of the religion of the latter; and indeed, it seems to me, at least, to be quite natural, if not in strict accordance with the precepts of the Bible; for in that book I find it every where laid down, that those who have possessed an inordinate portion of the good things of this world, and have lived in ease and luxury, at the expense of their fellow men will surely have to render an account of their stewardship, and be punished, for having withheld from others the participation of those blessings, which they themselves enjoyed. . . .

Christmas approached, and we all expected two or three holidays— but we were disappointed, as only one was all that was allotted to us.

I went to the field and picked cotton all day, for which I was paid by the overseer, and at night I had a good dinner of stewed pork and sweet potatoes. Such were the beginning and end of my first Christmas on a cotton plantation. We went to work as usual the next morning, and continued our labor through the week, as if Christmas had been stricken from the calendar. . . .

It may well be supposed, that in our society, although we were all slaves, and all nominally in a condition of the most perfect equality, yet

110

there was in fact a very great difference in the manner of living, in the several families. Indeed, I doubt if there is as great a diversity in the modes of life, in the several families of any white village in New York or Pennsylvania, containing a population of three hundred persons, as there was in the several households of our quarter. This may be illustrated by the following circumstance: Before I came to reside in the family with whom I lived at this time, they seldom tasted animal food, or even fish, except on meat-days, as they were called; that is, when meat was given to the people by the overseer, under the orders of our master. The head of the family was a very quiet, worthy man; but slothful and inactive in his habits. When he had come from the field at night, he seldom thought of leaving the cabin again before morning. He would, and did, make baskets and mats, and earned some money by these means; he also did his regular day's work on Sunday; but all his acquirements were not sufficient to enable him to provide any kind of meat for his family. All that his wife and children could do, was to provide him with work at his baskets and mats; and they lived even then better than some of their neighbors. After I came among them and had acquired some knowledge of the surrounding country, I made as many baskets and mats as he did, and took time to go twice a week to look at all my traps.

As the winter passed away and spring approached, the proceeds of my hunting began to diminish. The game became scarce, and both rackoons and opossums grew poor and worthless. It was necessary for me to discover some new mode of improving the allowance allotted to me by the overseer. I had all my life been accustomed to fishing in Maryland, and I now resolved to resort to the water for a living; the land having failed to furnish me a comfortable subsistence. With these views, I set out one Sunday morning, early in February, and went to the river at a distance of three miles from home. From the appearance of the stream I felt confident that it must contain many fish; and I went immediately to work to make a weir. With the help of an axe that I had with me, I had finished before night the frame-work of a weir of pine sticks, lashed together with white oak splits. I had no canoe, but made a raft of dry logs, upon which I went to a suitable place in the river and set my weir. I afterwards made a small net of twine that I bought at the store; and on next Thursday night I took as many fish from my weir as filled a half bushel measure. This was a real treasure—it was the most fortunate circumstance that had happened with me since I came to the country.

I was enabled to show my generosity, but, like all mankind, even in my liberality, I kept myself in mind. I gave a large fish to the overseer, and took three more to the great house. These were the first fresh fish that had been in the family this season; and I was much praised by my master and young mistresses, for my skill and success in fishing; but this was all the advantage I received from this effort to court the favor of the great:—I did not even get a dram. . . . I went away from the house not only disappointed but chagrined, and thought with myself that if my master and young mistresses had nothing but words to give me for my fish, we should not carry on a very large traffic.

On next Sunday morning, a black boy came from the house, and told me that our master wished to see me. This summons was not to be disobeyed. When I returned to the mansion, I went round to the kitchen, and sent word by one of the house-slaves that I had come. The servant returned and told me, that I was to stay in the kitchen and get my breakfast; and after that to come into the house. A very good breakfast was sent to me from my master's table, after the family had finished their morning meal; and when I had done with my repast I went into the parlor. I was received with great affability by my master, who told me he had sent for me to know if I had been accustomed to fish in the place I had come from. I informed him that I had been employed at a fishery on the Patuxent, every spring, for several years; and that I thought I understood fishing with a seine, as well as most people. He then asked me if I could knit a seine, to which I replied in the affirmative. After some other questions, he told me that as the picking of cotton was nearly over for this season, and the fields must soon be ploughed up for a new crop, he had a thought of having a seine made, and of placing me at the head of a fishing party, for the purpose of trying to take a supply of fish for his hands. No communication could have been more unexpected than this was, and it was almost as pleasing to me as it was unexpected by me. I now began to hope that there would be some respite from the labors of the cotton field, and that I should not be doomed to drag out a dull and monotonous existence, within the confines of the enclosures of the plantation. . . .

The native Africans are revengeful, and unforgiving in their tempers, easily provoked, and cruel in their designs. They generally place little, or even no value, upon the fine houses, and superb furniture of their masters; and discover no beauty in the fair complexions and delicate forms of their mistresses. They feel indignant at the servitude that is imposed upon them, and only want power to inflict the most cruel retribution upon their oppressors; but they desire only the means of subsistence, and temporary gratification in this country, during their abode here.

They are universally of the opinion, and this opinion is founded in their religion, that after death they shall return to their own country, and rejoin their former companions and friends, in some happy region, in which they will be provided with plenty of food, and beautiful women, from the lovely daughters of their own native land.

The case is different with the American negro, who knows nothing of Africa, her religion, or customs, and who has borrowed all his ideas of present and future happiness, from the opinions and intercourse of white people, and of Christians. He is, perhaps, not so impatient of slavery, and excessive labour, as the native of Congo; but his mind is bent upon other pursuits, and his discontent works out for itself other schemes, than those which agitate the brain of the imported negro. His heart pants for no heaven beyond the waves of the ocean; and he dreams of no delights in the arms of sable beauties, in groves of immortality, on the banks of the Niger, or the Gambia; nor does he often solace himself with the reflection, that the day will arrive when all men will receive the awards of immutable justice, and live together in eternal bliss, without any other distinctions than those of superior virtue, and exalted mercy. Circumstances oppose great obstacles in the way of these opinions.

The slaves who are natives of the country, (I now speak of the mass of those on the cotton plantations, as I knew them,) like all other people who suffer wrong in this world, are exceedingly prone to console themselves with the delights of a future state, when the evil that has been endured in this life, will not only be abolished, and all injuries be compensated by proper rewards, bestowed upon the sufferers, but, as they have learned that wickedness is to be punished, as well as goodness compensated, they do not stop at the point of their own enjoyments and pleasures, but believe that those who have tormented them here, will most surely be tormented in their turn hereafter. . . .

In my opinion, there is no order of men in any part of the United States, with which I have any acquaintance, who are in a more debased and humiliated state of moral servitude, than are those white people who inhabit that part of the southern country, where the landed property is all, or nearly all, held by the great planters. Many of those white people live in wretched cabins, not half so good as the houses which judicious planters provide for their slaves. Some of these cabins of the white men are made of mere sticks, or small poles notched, or rather thatched together, and filled in with mud, mixed with the leaves, or *shats*, as they are termed, of the pine tree. Some fix their residence far in the pine forest, and gain a scanty subsistence by notching the trees and gathering the turpentine; others are seated upon some poor, and worthless point of land, near the margin of a river, or creek, and draw a precarious livelihood from the water, and the badly cultivated garden that surrounds, or adjoins the dwelling.

These people do not occupy the place held in the north by the respectable and useful class of day labourers, who constitute so considerable a portion of the numerical population of the country.

In the south, these white cottagers are never employed to work on the plantations for wages. Two things forbid this. The white man, however poor and necessitous he may be, is too proud to go to work in the same field with the negro slaves by his side; and the owner of the slaves is not willing to permit white men, of the lowest order to come amongst them, lest the morals of the negroes should be corrupted, and illicit traffic should be carried on, to the detriment of the master.

The slaves generally believe, that however miserable they may be, in their servile station, it is nevertheless preferable to the degraded existence of these poor white people. This sentiment is cherished by the slaves, and encouraged by their masters, who fancy that they subserve their own interests in promoting an opinion amongst the negroes, that they are better off in the world than are many white persons, who are free, and have to submit to the burthen of taking care of, and providing for themselves.

I never could learn nor understand how, or by what means, these poor cottagers came to be settled in Carolina. They are a separate and distinct race of men from the planters, and appear to have nothing in common with them. If it were possible for any people to occupy a grade in human society below that of the slaves, on the cotton plantations, certainly the station would be filled by these white families, who cannot be said to possess any thing in the shape of property. The contempt in which they are held, and the contumely with which they are treated, by the great planters, to be comprehended, must be seen. . . .

I shall now return to my narrative. Early in March, or perhaps on one of the last days of February, my seine being now completed, my master told me I must take with me three other black men, and go to the river to clear cut a fishery. This task of clearing out a fishery, was a very disagreeable job; for it was nothing less than dragging out of the river, all the old trees and brush that had sunk to the bottom, within the limits of our intended fishing ground. My master's eldest son had been down the river, and had purchased two boats, to be used at the fishery; but when I saw them I declared them to be totally unfit for the purpose. They were old batteaux, and so leaky, that they would not have supported the weight of a wet seine, and the men necessary to lay it out. I advised the building of two good canoes, from some of the large yellow pines, in the woods. My advice was accepted, and together with five other hands, I went to work at the canoes, which we completed in less than a week.

So far things went pretty well, and I flattered myself that I should become the head man at this new fishery, and have the command of the other hands. I also expected that I should be able to gain some advantage to myself, by disposing of a part of the small fish that might be taken at the fishery. . . . Of the common fish, such as pike, perch, suckers, and others, we had the liberty of keeping as many as we could eat; but the misfortune was, that we had no pork, or fat of any kind, to fry them with; and for several days we contented ourselves with broiling them on the coals, and eating them with our corn bread, and sweet potatoes. We could have lived well, if we had been permitted to broil the shad on the coals, and eat them; for a fat shad will dress itself in being broiled, and is very good, without any oily substance added to it.

All the shad that we caught, were carefully taken away by a black man, who came three times every day to the fishery, with a cart.

The master of the fishery had a family that lived several miles up the river. In the summer time, he fished with hooks, and small nets, when not engaged in running turpentine, in the pine woods. In the winter he went back into the pine forest and made tar of the dead pine trees; but returned to the river at the opening of the spring, to take advantage of the shad fishery. He was supposed to be one of the most skilful fishermen on the Congaree river, and my master employed him to superintend his new fishery, under an expectation, I presume, that as he was to get a tenth part of all the fish that might be caught, he would make the most of his situation. My master had not calculated with accuracy the force of habit, nor the difficulty which men experience, in conducting very simple affairs, of which they have no practical knowledge.

The fish-master did very well for the interest of his employer, for a few days; compelling us to work, in hauling the seine, night and day, and scarcely permitting us to take rest enough to obtain necessary sleep. We were compelled to work full sixteen hours every day, including Sunday; for in the fishing season, no respect is paid to Sunday by fishermen, anywhere. We had our usual quantity of bread and potatoes, with plenty of common fish; but no shad came to our lot; nor had we any thing to fry our fish with. A broiled fresh-water fish is not very good, at best, without salt or oil; and after we have eaten them every day, for a week, we cared very little for them.

By this time, our fish-master began to relax in his discipline; not that he became more kind to us, or required us to do less work; but to compel us to work all night, it was necessary for him to sit up all night and watch us. This was a degree of toil and privation to which he could not long submit; and one evening soon after dark, he called me to him and told me that he intended to make me overseer of the fishery that night; and he had no doubt, I would keep the hands at work, and attend to the business as well without him as with him. He then went into his cabin, and went to bed; whilst I went and laid out the seine, and made a very good haul. We took more than two hundred shad at this draught; and followed up our work with great industry all night, only taking time to eat our accustomed meal at midnight. . . .

We worked hard all night, the first night of my superintendence, and when the sun rose the next morning, the master had not risen from his bed. As it was now the usual time of dividing the fish, I called to him to come and see this business fairly done; but he did not come down immediately to the landing, I proceeded to make the division myself, in as equitable a manner as I could: given, however, a full share of large fish to the master. When he came down to us, and overlooked both the piles of fish—his own and that of my master—he was so well satisfied with what I had done, that he said, if he had known that I would do so well for him, he would not have risen. I was glad to hear this, as it led me to hope, that I should be able to induce him to stay in his cabin during the greater part of the time; to do which, I was well assured, he felt disposed.

When the night came, the master again told me he should go to bed, not being well; and desired me to do as I had done the night before. This night we cooked as many shad as we could all eat; but were careful to carry, far out into the river, the scales and entrails of the stolen fish. In the morning I made a division of the fish before I called the master, and then went and asked him to come and see what I had done. He was again well pleased, and now proposed to us all, that if we would not let the affair be known to our master, he would leave us to manage the fishery at night according to our discretion. To this proposal, we all readily agreed, and I received authority to keep the other hands at work, until the master would go and get his breakfast. I had now accomplished the object that I had held very near my heart, ever since we began to fish at this place.

From this time, to the end of the fishing season, we all lived well, and did not perform more work than we were able to bear. I was in no fear of being punished by the fish-master; for he was now at least as much in my power, as I was in his; for if my master had known the agreement, that he had made with us, for the purpose of enabling himself to sleep all night in his cabin, he would have been deprived of his situation, and all the profits of his share of the fishery. . . .

Since my arrival in Carolina I had never enjoyed a full meal of bacon; and now determined, if possible, to procure such a supply of that luxury, as would enable me and all my fellow-slaves at the fishery to regale ourselves at pleasure. At this season of the year, boats frequently passed up the river, laden with merchandise and goods of various kinds, amongst which were generally large quantities of salt, intended for curing fish, and for other purposes on the plantations. These boats also carried bacon and salted pork up the river, for sale; but as they never moved at night, confining their navigation to daylight, and as none of them had hitherto stopped near our landing, we had not met with an opportunity of entering into a traffic with any of the boat masters. . . .

Upon inquiring of the captain if he had any bacon that he would exchange for shad, he said, he had a little; but, as the risk he would run in dealing with a slave was great, I must expect to pay him more than the usual price. He at length proposed to give me a hundred pounds of bacon for three hundred shad. This was at least twice as much as the bacon was worth; but we did not bargain as men generally do, where half of the bargain is on each side; for here the captain of the keel-boat settled the terms for both parties. However, he ran the hazard of being prosecuted for dealing with slaves, which is a very high offence in Carolina; and I was selling that which, in point of law, did not belong to me; but to which, nevertheless, I felt in my conscience that I had a better right than any other person. . . .

Notwithstanding the privation of our potatoes, we at the fishery lived sumptuously; although our master certainly believed, that our fare consisted of corn bread and river fish, cooked without lard or butter. It was necessary to be exceedingly cautious in the use of our bacon. . . .

In the fall of this year I went with my master to the Indian country, to purchase and bring to the settlement cattle and Indian horses. We travelled a hundred miles from the residence of my master, nearly west, before we came to any Indian village.

The country where the Indians lived was similar in soil and productions to that in which my master had settled; and I saw several fields of corn amongst the Indians of excellent quality, and well enclosed with substantial fences. I also saw amongst these people several log-houses, with square hewn logs. Some cotton was growing in small patches in the fields, but this plant was not extensively cultivated. Large herds of cattle were ranging in the woods, and cost their owners nothing for their keeping, except a small quantity of salt. These cattle were of the Spanish breed, generally speckled, but often of a dun or mouse colour, and sometimes of a leaden gray. They universally had long horns, and dark muzzles, and stood high on their legs, with elevated and bold fronts. When ranging in droves in the woods, they were the finest cattle in appearance that I ever saw. They make excellent working oxen, but their quarters are not so heavy and fleshy as those of the English cattle. The cows do not give large quantities of milk.

The Indian horses run at large in the woods like the cattle, and receive no feed from their owners, unless on some very extraordinary occasion. They are small, but very handsome little horses. I do not know that I ever saw one of these horses more than fourteen hands high; but they are very strong and active, and when brought upon the plantation, and broken to work, they are hardy and docile, and keep fat on very little food. The prevailing colour of these horses is black; but many of them are beautiful grays, with flowing manes and tails, and, of their size, are fine horses. . . .

Ever since I had been in the southern country, vast numbers of African negroes had been yearly imported; but this year the business ceased altogether, and I did not see any African who was landed in the United States after this date.

I shall here submit to the reader, the results of the observations I have made on the regulations of southern society. It is my opinion, that the white people in general, are not nearly so well informed in the southern states, as they are in those lying farther north. The cause of this may not be obvious to strangers; but to a man who has resided amongst the cotton plantations, it is quite plain.

There is a great scarcity of schools, throughout all the cotton country, that I have seen; because the white population is so thinly scattered over the country, and the families live so far apart, that it is not easy to get a sufficient number of children together to constitute a school. The young men of the country, who have received educations proper to qualify them for the profession of teachers, are too proud to submit to this kind of occupation; and strangers, who come from the north, will not engage in a service that is held in contempt, unless they can procure large salaries from individuals, or get a great number of pupils to attend their instructions, whose united contributions may amount, in the aggregate, to a large sum.

Great numbers of the young men of fortune are sent abroad to be educated: but thousands of the sons of land and slave-holders receive very little education, and pass their lives in ignorant idleness. The poor white children are not educated at all. It is my opinion, that the women are not better educated than the men. . . .

It is a mistake to suppose that the southern planters could ever retain their property, or live amongst their slaves, if those slaves were not kept in terror of the punishment that would follow acts of violence and disorder. There is no difference between the feelings of the different races of men, so far as their personal rights are concerned. The black man is as anxious to possess and to enjoy liberty as the white one would be, were he deprived of this inestimable blessing. It is not for me to say that the one is as well qualified for the enjoyment of liberty as the other. Low ignorance, moral degradation of character, and mental depravity, are

education the
key to
improvement

inseparable companions; and in the breast of an ignorant man, the passions of envy and revenge hold unbridled dominion.

It was in the month of April that I witnessed the painful spectacle of two fellow-creatures being launched into the abyss of eternity, and a third, being tortured beyond the sufferings of mere death, not for his crimes, but as a terror to others; and this, not to deter others from the commission of crimes, but to stimulate them to a more active and devoted performance of their duties to their owners. My spirits had not recovered from the depression produced by that scene, in which my feelings had been awakened in the cause of others, when I was called to a nearer and more immediate apprehension of sufferings, which, I now too clearly saw, were in preparation for myself. . . .

My master died in the month of May, and I followed him to his grave with a heavy heart, for I felt that I had lost the only friend I had in the world, who possessed at once the power and the inclination to protect me against the tyranny and oppression to which slaves on a cotton plantation are subject.

Had he lived, I should have remained with him, and never have left him, for he had promised to purchase the residue of my time of my owners in Carolina; but when he was gone, I felt the parting of the last tie that bound me to the place where I then was, and my heart yearned for my wife and children, from whom I had now been separated more than four years.

I held my life in small estimation, if it was to be worn out under the dominion of my mistress and her brothers, though since the death of my master she had greatly meliorated my condition by giving me frequent allowances of meat and other necessaries. I believe she entertained some vague apprehensions that I might run away, and betake myself to the woods for a living, perhaps go to the Indians; but I do not think she ever suspected that I would hazard the untried undertaking of attempting to make my way back to Maryland. My purpose was fixed, and now nothing could shake it. I only waited for a proper season of the year to commence my toilsome and dangerous journey. . . .

I furnished myself with a fire-box, as it is called, that is, a tin case containing flints, steel, and tinder, this I considered indispensable. I took the great coat that my master had given me, and with a coarse needle and thread quilted a scabbard of old cloth in one side of it, in which I could put my sword and carry it with safety. I also procured a small bag of linen that held more than a peck. This bag I filled with the meal of parched corn, grinding the corn after it was parched in the woods where I worked at the mill at night. These operations, except the grinding of the corn, I carried on in a small conical cabin that I had built in the woods. The boots that my master gave me, I had repaired by a Spaniard who lived in the neighbourhood, and followed the business of a cobbler.

Before the first of August I had all my preparations completed, and had matured them with so much secrecy, that no one in the country, white or black, suspected me of entertaining any extraordinary design. I only waited for the corn to be ripe, and fit to be roasted, which time I had fixed as the period of my departure. I watched the progress of the corn daily, and on the eighth of August I perceived, on examining my mistress' field, that nearly half of the ears were so far grown, that by roasting them, a man could easily subsist himself. . . .

I now took to the forest, keeping, as nearly as I could, a north course all the afternoon. Night overtook me, before I reached any watercourse, or any other object worthy of being noticed; and I lay down and slept soundly, without kindling a fire, or eating any thing. I was awake before day, and as soon as there was light enough to enable me to see my way, I resumed my journey and walked on, until about eight o'clock, when I came to a river, which I knew must be the Appalachie. I sat down on the bank of the river, opened my bag of meal, and made my breakfast of a part of its contents. I used my meal very sparingly, it being the most valuable treasure that I now possessed; though I had in my pocket three Spanish dollars; but in my situation, this money could not avail me any thing, as I was resolved not to show myself to any person, either white or black. After taking my breakfast, I prepared to cross the river, which was here about a hundred yards wide, with a sluggish and deep current. The morning was sultry, and the thickets along the margin of the river teemed with insects and reptiles. By sounding the river with a pole, I found the stream too deep to be waded, and I therefore prepared to swim it. For this purpose, I stripped myself, and bound my clothes on the top of my knapsack, and my bag of meal on the top of my clothes; then drawing my knapsack close up to my head, I threw myself into the river. In my youth I had learned to swim in the Patuxent, and have seldom met with any person who was more at ease in deep water than myself. I kept a straight line from the place of my entrance into the Appalachie, to the opposite side, and when I had reached it, stepped on the margin of the land, and turned round to view the place from which I had set out on my aquatic passage; but my eye was arrested by an object nearer to me than the opposite shore. Within twenty feet of me, in the very line that I had pursued in crossing the river, a large alligator was moving in full pursuit of me, with his nose just above the surface, in the position that creature takes when he gives chase to his intended prey in the water. The alligator can swim more than twice as fast as a man, for he can overtake young ducks on the water; and had I been ten seconds longer in the river, I should have been dragged to the bottom, and never again been heard of. . . .

When the sun had been up two or three hours, I saw an appearance of blue sky at a distance, through the trees, which proved that the forest had been removed from a spot somewhere before me, and at no great distance from me; and, as I cautiously advanced, I heard the voices of people in loud conversation. Sitting down amongst the palmetto plants, that grew around me in great numbers, I soon perceived that the people whose conversation I heard, were coming nearer to me. I now heard the sound of horses' feet, and immediately afterwards, saw two men on horseback, with rifles on their shoulders, riding through the woods, and moving on a line that led them past me, at a distance of about fifty or sixty yards. Perceiving that these men were equipped as hunters, I remained almost breathless, for the purpose of hearing their conversation. . . .

Notwithstanding they were gone, I remained in the water full a quarter of an hour, until I was certain that no other persons were moving along the road near me. These were the same gentlemen who had passed me, early in the night, and from whom I learned the distance to the river. From these people I had gained intelligence, which I considered of much value to me. It was now certain, that the whole country had been advised of my flight; but it was equally certain that no one had any knowledge of the course I had taken, nor of the point I was endeavouring to reach. To prevent any one from acquiring a knowledge of my route, was a primary object with me; and I determined from this moment, so to regulate my movements, as to wrap my very existence, in a veil of impenetrable secrecy. . . .

I lay still by the side of the log for a long time after the horses, dogs, and men, had ceased to trouble the woods with their noise; if it can be said that a man lies still, who is trembling in every joint, nerve, and muscle, like a dog lying upon a cake of ice; and when I arose and turned round, I found myself so completely bereft of understanding, that I could not tell south from north, nor east from west. I could not even distinguish the thicket of bushes, from which I had removed to come to this place, from the other bushes in the woods. I remained here all day, and at night it appeared to me, that the sun set in the south-east. After sundown, the moon appeared to my distempered judgment, to stand due north from me; and all the stars were out of their places. Fortunately I had sense enough remaining to know, that it would not be safe for me to attempt to travel, until my brain had been restored to its ordinary stability; which did not take place until the third morning after my fright. The three days that I passed in this place, I reckon the most unhappy of my life; for surely it is the height of human misery, to be oppressed with alienation of mind, and to be conscious of the affliction. . . .

It was now, by my computation, the month of November, and I was yet in the state of South Carolina. I began to consider with myself, whether I had gained or lost, by attempting to travel on the roads; and, after revolving in my mind all the disasters that had befallen me, determined to abandon the roads altogether, for two reasons:—the first of which was, that on the highways, I was constantly liable to meet persons, or to be overtaken by them; and a second, no less powerful, was, that as I did not know what roads to pursue, I was oftener travelling on the wrong route than on the right one.

Setting my face once more for the north-star, I advanced with a steady, though slow pace, for four or five nights, when I was again delayed by dark weather, and forced to remain in idleness nearly two weeks; and when the weather again became clear, I was arrested, on the second night, by a broad and rapid river, that appeared so formidable, that I did not dare to attempt its passage, until after examining it in daylight. On the succeeding night, however, I crossed it by swimming— resting at some large rocks near the middle. After gaining the north side of this river, which I believed to be the Catawba, I considered myself in North Carolina, and again steered towards the north. . . .

Judging by the aspect of the country, I believed myself to be at this time in Virginia; and was now reduced to the utmost extremity, for want of provisions. The corn that I had parched at the barn, and brought with me, was nearly exhausted, and no more was to be obtained in the fields, at this season of the year. For three or four days I allowed myself only my two hands full of parched corn per day; and after this I travelled three days without tasting food of any kind; but being nearly exhausted with hunger, I one night entered an old stack-yard, hoping that I might fall in with pigs, or poultry of some kind. I found, instead of these, a stack of oats, which had not been threshed. From this stack I took as much oats in the sheaf, as I could carry, and going on a few miles, stopped in a pine forest, made a large fire, and parched at least half a gallon of oats, after rubbing the grain from the straw. After the grain was parched, I again rubbed it in my hands, to separate it from the husks, and spent the night in feasting on parched oats. . . .

Before day I reached the Matapony river, and crossed it by wading; but knowing that I was not far from Maryland, I fell into a great indiscretion, and forgot the wariness and caution that had enabled me to overcome obstacles apparently insurmountable. Anxious to get forward, I neglected to conceal myself before day; but travelled until day-break before I sought a place of concealment, and unfortunately, when I looked for a hiding place, none was at hand. This compelled me to keep on the road, until gray twilight, for the purpose of reaching a wood that was in view before me; but to gain this wood I was obliged to pass a house, that stood at the road side, and when only about fifty yards beyond the house, a white man opened the door, and seeing me in the road, called to me to stop. As this order was not obeyed, he set his dog upon me. The dog was quickly vanquished by my stick, and setting off to run at full speed, I at the same moment heard the report of a gun, and received its contents in my legs, chiefly about, and in my hams. I fell on the road, and was soon surrounded by several persons, who it appeared were a party of patrollers, who had gathered together in this house. They ordered me to cross my hands, which order not being immediately obeyed, they beat me with sticks and stones until I was almost senseless, and entirely unable to make resistance. They then bound me with cords, and dragged me by the feet back to the house, and threw me into the kitchen, like a dead dog. One of my eyes was almost beaten out, and the blood was running from my mouth, nose and ears; but in this condition they refused to wash the blood from my face, or even to give me a drink of water.

In a short time, a justice of the peace arrived, and when he looked at me, ordered me to be unbound, and to have water to wash myself, and also some bread to eat. This man's heart appeared not to be altogether void of sensibility, for he reprimanded, in harsh terms, those who had beaten me; told them that their conduct was brutal, and that it would have been more humane to kill me outright, than to bruise and mangle me in the manner they had done.

He then interrogated me as to my name, place of abode, and place of destination, and afterwards demanded the name of my master. To all these inquiries I made no reply, except that I was going to Maryland, where I lived. The justice told me it was his duty under the law, to send me to jail; and I was immediately put into a cart, and carried to a small village called Bowling Green, which I reached before ten o'clock.

There I was locked up in the jail, and a doctor came to examine my legs, and extract the shot from my wounds. In the course of the operation he took out thirty-four duck shot, and after dressing my legs left me to my own reflections. No fever followed in the train of my disasters, which I attributed to the reduced state of my blood, by long fasting, and the fatigues I had undergone. . . .

For several days I was not able to stand, and in this period found great difficulty in performing the ordinary offices of life for myself, no one coming to give me any aid; but I did not suffer for want of food, the daily allowance of the jailer being quite sufficient to appease the cravings of hunger. After I grew better, and was able to walk in the jail, the jailer frequently called to see me, and endeavoured to prevail on me to tell where I had come from; but in this undertaking, he was no more successful than the justice had been in the same business.

I remained in the jail more than a month, and in this time became quite fat and strong, but saw no way by which I could escape. The jail was of brick, the floors were of solid oak boards, and the door, of the same material, was secured by iron bolts, let into its posts, and connected together by a strong band of iron, reaching from the one to the other. . . .

When I had been in prison thirty-nine days, and had quite recovered from the wounds that I had received, the jailer was late in coming to me with my breakfast, and going to the door I began to beat against it with my fist, for the purpose of making a noise. After beating some time against the door I happened, by mere accident, to strike my fist against one of the posts, which, to my surprise, I discovered by its sound, to be a mere hollow shell, encrusted with a thin coat of sound timber, and as I struck it, the rotten wood crumbled to pieces within. On a more careful examination of this post, I became satisfied that I could easily split it to pieces, by the aid of the iron bolt that confined my feet. The jailer came with my breakfast, and reprimanded me for making a noise. This day appeared as long to me, as a week had done heretofore; but night came at length, and as soon as the room in which I was confined, had become quite dark, I disentangled myself from the irons with which I was bound, and with the aid of the long bolt, easily wrenched from its place, the large staple that held one end of the bar, that lay across the door. The hasps that held the lock in its place, were drawn away almost without force, and the door swung open of its own weight.

I now walked out into the jail-yard, and found that all was quiet, and that only a few lights were burning in the village windows. At first I walked slowly along the road, but soon quickened my pace, and ran along the high-way, until I was more than a mile from the jail, then taking to the woods, I travelled all night, in a northern direction. At the approach of day I concealed myself in a cedar thicket, where I lay until the next evening, without any thing to eat.

On the second night after my escape, I crossed the Potomac, at Hoe's ferry, in a small boat that I found tied at the side of the ferry flat; and on the night following crossed the Patuxent [to home], in a canoe, which I found chained at the shore. . . .

When on my journey I thought of nothing but getting home, and never reflected, that when at home, I might still be in danger; but now that my toils were ended, I began to consider with myself how I could appear in safety in Calvert county, where everybody must know that I was a runaway slave. With my heart thrilling with joy, when I looked upon my wife and children, who had not hoped ever to behold me again; yet fearful of the coming of daylight, which must expose me to be arrested as a fugitive slave, I passed the night between the happiness of the present and the dread of the future. In all the toils, dangers, and sufferings of my long journey, my courage had never forsaken me. The hope of again seeing my wife and little ones, had borne me triumphantly through perils, that even now I reflect upon as upon some extravagant dream; but when I found myself at rest under the roof of my wife, the object of my labours attained, and no motive to arouse my energies, or give them the least impulse, that firmness of resolution which had so long sustained me, suddenly vanished from my bosom; and I passed the night, with my children around me, oppressed by a melancholy foreboding of my future destiny. The idea that I was utterly unable to afford protection and safeguard to my own family, and was myself even more helpless than they, tormented my bosom with alternate throbs of affection and fear, until the dawn broke in the east, and summoned me to decide upon my future conduct.

When morning came, I went to the great house, and showed myself to my wife's master and mistress who treated me with great kindness, and gave me a good breakfast. Mr. Symmes at first advised me to conceal myself, but soon afterwards told me to go to work in the neighbourhood for wages. I continued to hire myself about among the farmers, until after the war broke out; and until Commodore Barney came into the Patuxent with his flotilla, when I enlisted on board one of his barges, and was employed sometimes in the capacity of a seaman, and sometimes as cook of the barge. . . .[2]

When we reached Bladensburg, and the flotilla men were drawn up in line, to work at their cannon, armed with their cutlasses, I volunteered to assist in working the cannon, that occupied the first place, on the left of the Commodore. We had a full and perfect view of the British army, as it advanced along the road, leading to the bridge over the East Branch; and I could not but admire the handsome manner in which the British officers led on their fatigued and worn-out soldiers. I thought then, and think yet, that General Ross was one of the finest looking men that I ever saw on horseback.

I stood at my gun, until the Commodore was shot down, when he ordered us to retreat, as I was told by the officer who commanded our gun. If the militia regiments, that lay upon our right and left, could have been brought to charge the British, in close fight, as they crossed the bridge, we should have killed or taken the whole of them in a short time; but the militia ran like sheep chased by dogs.

My readers will not, perhaps, condemn me if I here make a short digression from my main narrative, to give some account of the part that I took in the war, on the shores of the Chesapeake, and the Patuxent. I did not enlist with Commodore Barney until the month of December, 1813; but as I resided in Calvert county, in the summer of 1813, I had an

---

2. This is the War of 1812.

opportunity of witnessing many of the evils that followed in the train of war, before I assumed the profession of arms myself.

In the spring of the year 1813, the British fleet came into the bay, and from this time, the origin of the troubles and distresses of the people of the Western Shore, may be dated. I had been employed at a fishery, near the mouth of the Patuxent, from early in March, until the latter part of May, when a British vessel of war came off the mouth of the river, and sent her boats up to drive us away from our fishing ground. There was but little property at the fishery that could be destroyed; but the enemy cut the seines to pieces, and burned the sheds belonging to the place. They then marched up two miles into the country, burned the house of a planter, and brought away with them several cattle, that were found in his fields. They also carried off more than twenty slaves, which were never again restored to their owner; although, on the following day, he went on board the ship, with a flag of truce, and offered a large ransom for these slaves.

These were the first black people whom I had known to desert to the British, although the practice was afterwards so common. In the course of this summer, and the summer of 1814, several thousand black people deserted from their masters and mistresses, and escaped to the British fleet. None of these people were ever regained by their owners, as the British naval officers treated them as free people, and placed them on the footing of military deserters. . . .

I continued with the army after the sack of Washington, and assisted in the defence of Baltimore; but in the fall of 1814, I procured my discharge from the army, and went to work in Baltimore, as a free black man. From this time, until the year 1820, I worked in various places in Maryland, as a free man; sometimes in Baltimore, sometimes in Annapolis, and frequently in Washington. My wife died in the year 1816, and from that time I was not often in Calvert county. I was fortunate in the enjoyment of good health; and by constant economy I found myself in possession, in the year 1820, of three hundred and fifty dollars in money, the proceeds of my labour.

I now removed to the neighbourhood of Baltimore, and purchased a lot of twelve acres of ground, upon which I erected a small house, and became a farmer on my own account, and upon my own property. I purchased a yoke of oxen and two cows, and became a regular attendant of the Baltimore market, where I sold the products of my own farm and dairy. In the course of two or three years, I had brought my little farm into very good culture, and had increased my stock of cattle to four cows and several younger animals. I now lived very happily, and had an abundance of all the necessaries of life around me. I had married a second wife, who bore me four children, and I now looked forward to an old age of comfort, if not of ease; But I was soon to be awakened from this dream. . . .[3]

This intelligence almost deprived me of life; it was the most dreadful of all the misfortunes that I had ever suffered. It was now clear that some slave-dealer had come in my absence, and seized my wife and children as slaves, and sold them to such men as I had served in the south. They had now passed into hopeless bondage, and were gone forever beyond my reach. I myself was advertised as a fugitive slave, and was liable to be arrested at each moment, and dragged back to Georgia. I rushed out of my own house in despair and returned to Pennsylvania with a broken heart.

For the last few years, I have resided about fifty miles from Philadelphia, where I expect to pass the evening of my life, in working hard for my subsistence, without the least hope of ever again seeing my wife and children:—fearful, at this day, to let my place of residence be known, lest even yet it may be supposed, that as an article of property, I am of sufficient value to be worth pursuing in my old age.

---

3. He is captured, reenslaved and returned to Georgia, but again escapes. Returning to his home in Baltimore, he learns that his property had been confiscated and his wife and children sold into slavery.

CHESTER HARDING

1792-1866

HE title of Chester Harding's memoirs, *My Egotistography*, suggests that he viewed himself as an idiosyncratic person. In truth, his life was as remarkable as can be imagined. Growing up in an artisanal family in rural Massachusetts, he went west, to Pennsylvania, to find his fortune in 1810 and, after a variety of ventures, discovered that he had a talent for drawing portraits. His talent was so exceptional and popular that within a dozen years of his first portrait-painting, Harding had a studio in London and was painting members of the royal family, including the Prince of Wales! Indeed, so phenomenal had been his success in Boston that the great painter Gilbert Stuart was wont to ask friends, "How wages the Harding fever?"

His father being an improvident inventor striving to create a perpetual-motion machine, Harding was born into poverty and was hired out at age twelve. Two years later, he left with his family for the New York frontier, where he became familiar with "that great civilizer," the ax. Musically talented, Harding served as a drummer in the War of 1812, an experience which left him with a fund of wry stories. Unlike Alfred Lorrain, who recalls serving alongside upright men, Harding remembers the thievery of his hungry comrades in arms. Falling behind the troops one day, he stopped at a farmhouse to ask which way they had gone. "Oh!" said the woman he spoke to, "you have only to follow the feathers." Apt to interweave his memories with recollections of music, Harding relates that when sickness began to thin the soldiers' ranks, the song "Away

Goes the Merryman Home to His Grave," which signaled the return from a burial, became their constant musical companion.[1]

After the war, Harding successively went into cabinetmaking with his brother, worked as an itinerant salesman, ran up debts, got married, tried his hand at tavern-keeping, and eventually fled to Pittsburgh when he feared that he would be imprisoned for his debts. In Pittsburgh, having set himself up as a sign painter, Harding encountered a portrait painter who both helped him and ridiculed his efforts to become a portraitist himself. From old age, Harding could still recall the thrill of doing the first painting of his wife. When he heard from his brother, who had established himself as a chair-maker in Kentucky, that good portrait painters in Lexington got fifty dollars a head, Harding, by now a father, shared with one Jarvis in the purchase of a large skiff to take their families and possessions down the Ohio. Both Jarvis and Harding played the clarinet, and the two men made music as the two families floated down the river.

In Paris, Kentucky, Harding launched himself as a portrait painter, doing almost a hundred portraits at twenty-five dollars a head in six months. From there he went to Philadelphia to study art, and on to Cincinnati, St. Louis, and Boston, all the while getting subjects to paint. In Kentucky he sought out the ninety-year-old Daniel Boone and the Territorial Governor and Revolutionary hero William Clarke for sittings.

Harding's success was closely tied to the prosperity and urban tastes emerging in the United States in the first decades of the nineteenth century, but the old-timers found the indulgence of buying portraits alarming. When Harding tried to impress his grandfather with the savings he had returned home with, the old man told him witheringly that it was "very little better than swindling to charge forty dollars for one of those effigies."[2] Eager to clear his name, Harding also paid off the debt he had fled from.

Harding recounts his life in a picaresque manner which offers a witty

---

1. Chester Harding, *My Egotistography* (Cambridge, 1866), pp. 7–8.
2. Harding, *My Egotistography*, p. 31.

contrast to the more pious accounts left by his contemporaries. Life in retrospect was something of a lark for him, enlivened by early success and instructive with its painful lessons. He had left his family in America when he went off to Europe in 1823, but when he learned that his family would not be accepted in the social circles that he had mixed in as a single artist, he returned to the United States and eventually settled in Springfield, Massachusetts. The National Portrait Gallery recently held a retrospective exhibit of Harding's work.

*O*F my ancestors I know nothing beyond my grandparents. My paternal grandfather was a substantial farmer in Deerfield, Mass. He lived in a two-story house, which to my youthful imagination was a palace; filled many offices of profit and trust in the town, lived to a good old age, and was gathered to his fathers with the universal respect of his neighbors.

On the maternal side, I can go no further back. My grandfather Smith was a farmer, who lived to a ripe old age, and died much respected. For many years he held the office of deacon, in the town of Whately, where he resided. I was born in the adjoining town of Conway, on the 1st of September, 1792.

My parents were poor; and, of course, I was brought up like all other poor children of that period. My first recollection is of our moving from Conway to Hatfield. I well remember the brook that ran close by the house we lived in there, and the amusement I had in catching the little fishes with a pin-hook. As I grew older, I began to fish with a real hook, and to catch trout. Like most boys of my age, I thought more of "going a-fishing" than all other indulgences. Indeed it amounted almost to a passion with me. I would go miles on an errand, or do any amount of service, for a penny or two, that I might be able to buy my fish-hooks.

From the age of eight to ten, I lived in Bernardston, with an aunt. Here again I had a brook that constantly enticed me from my daily duties, which consisted chiefly of the care of a flock of young geese. I played truant nearly every day, and as often was whipped by my aunt. I returned home at the end of two years. We were very poor, and were often in need of the necessaries of life. My father was a good man, of unexceptionable habits; but he was not thrifty, and did little towards the support of the family. He had a great inventive genius, and turned all his powers towards the discovery of perpetual motion. At the time of his death, his attic was full of machines, the making of which had occupied a large part of his life. But this brought no bread and butter to his hungry children.

One hard winter he went to Northfield, Mass., to get work, where my mother supposed he was earning something for the maintenance of the family. While there, he had the small-pox; and all the work he did was to make the body of a very large bass-viol. Imagine the disappointment of his family when they found that this monster skeleton was all he had brought home to them!

My mother was a noble woman. In all the trials of poverty, she managed to keep her children decently dressed, that they might go to meeting on Sunday, and make a respectable appearance among other boys. It is true our more prosperous cousins rather turned up their noses at us now and then, much to our mortification.

At the age of twelve, I was hired out at six dollars a month, to a Mr. Graves, in Hatfield. He was a good and religious man. I lived with him two years. I went to school in the winter, and learned to read enough to read the Bible. I partook largely of the religious sentiment that pervaded the family. I said my prayers night and morning, and was deemed a model boy. At the age of fourteen, my father moved to the western part of New-York State, into Madison County, then an unbroken wilderness. Now began my hard work and harder fare. Our first business was to build a log-house, and to clear a patch of ground, and fit it for seed. I had two brothers older than myself, the oldest of whom was a chair-maker by trade, and made common flag-bottomed chairs for the neighbors. By this means we could get an occasional piece of pork, some flour and potatoes; whilst my father and his other boys wielded the axe,—that great civilizer.

We finished the house, and in the spring we had a few acres felled and ready for burning. We planted corn and potatoes amongst the blackened stumps; fortunately, the crop needed no labor beyond that of planting. Before the season was far spent, we were all down with chills and fever. We managed somehow to live through that year, which was the hardest we had ever seen. I grew strong, and was distinguished for my skill in using the axe. I could lift a larger log than any one else, and, in short, at eighteen was considered a prodigy of strength. Our means for intellectual development were very scant. Our parents would sometimes read the Bible to us, the only book we had in the house; and occasionally we were blessed with a visit from some itinerant preacher, when the whole forest settlement would meet in some large building, either the schoolhouse or a barn, and listen to his divine teachings. At nineteen I changed my mode of life. I began to think there might be an easier way of getting a living than by cutting down and clearing up the heavily timbered forest, and worked one winter with my brother at turning stuff for chairs.

About this time, war was declared between the United States and Great Britain. A military spirit was aroused throughout the whole of Western New York, and I imbibed as much of it as any one. I had become a distinguished drummer, and had drummed for pay, until I was obliged to do military duty. My brother, next younger than myself, was one of the first to enlist in the service for one year. The troops were soon called to active service at Oswego. After six months he was anxious to return home. I offered myself, and was accepted as a substitute. As he was a drummer, I could easily fill his place.

Nothing of importance broke in upon the monotony of camp-life until mid-winter, when we were ordered to prepare three days' provisions, and to march next morning for Sacket's Harbor. The snow was very deep, and the weather cold; yet the days of our march were holidays, when compared to camp-life. We committed many depredations on our way, such as stealing chickens, or, on rare occasions, a pig. I was on the rear section of the column one day, and with another soldier had fallen so far behind, that we had lost sight of the troops. Being uncertain which of two roads to take, we applied at a house which was near, for directions. "Oh!" said the woman, "you have only to follow the feathers."

Sacket's Harbor was threatened with an attack by the British. They had a considerable force in Canada, nearly opposite; and the lake at that point was completely frozen over. We were constantly drilled, and kept in readiness for an attack. We had several alarms, and were often drummed out at midnight to face the foe; but he was only found in the imagination of the frightened sentinel.

Sickness now began to thin our ranks. Every hour in the day, some poor fellow would be followed to Briarfield; and the tune, "Away goes the merryman home to his grave," played on returning from the burial, was too often heard to leave listeners indifferent to its notes. . . .

I suffered intensely on my way home. I was thinly clad, without overcoat or gloves. I started from camp with a lad who was taking back a horse that an officer had ridden to Sacket's Harbor: he was warmly clothed and of a very robust make. We travelled on, until I began to feel a good deal fatigued. We at last came to house where we had been told we could find accommodation. We arrived there just at dusk; and, to our dismay, were told by the master of the house, that he could not keep us, and that he had nothing on hand for either man or beast to eat. It was six miles to the next house, and the road lay on the beach of the lake, exposed to the piercing winds which blew over it. We started off, I on foot as before, while the boy was mounted. I had to run to keep warm. At length we came in sight of a light; but what was our dismay to find an open river between us and it! I shouted to the utmost capacity of my lungs, but could get no response. What was to be done? Nothing, but to return to the shelter we had left an hour and a half before. I started back at the same speed I came; but, before we had gone half the distance, my strength gave out, leaving me no other alternative but to mount the horse with the boy. I soon found myself getting very cold, and a strong desire to go to sleep came over me. I looked at the thick clumps of evergreen that stood by our path, and thought seriously of lying down under one of them to wait until daylight. The boy was crying, and begged me to keep on, saying, "If you lie down there, you will freeze to death," which would indeed have been inevitable. I yielded to his entreaties, and we finally reached the house we had left three hours before. The boy was not much frozen, but I was badly bitten. My face, hands, and thighs were stiff. After a good deal of rapping and hallooing, the door was opened. The man of the house had been used to such scenes, and knew well what to do. He put my feet into cold water, at the same time making applications to my face, ears, and legs. Mortal never suffered more acute pain than I did through that sleepless night. I experienced the truth of our host's statement with regard to provisions. The next day at noon, we started again on our perilous journey, having been assured that we were mistaken about the river being open. Travelling more leisurely than we had done the previous night, we reached the river again; and, owing to the intense cold, it was covered with a thin coat of ice, but not thick enough to bear a man in an upright position. I got a long pole, and, by putting myself in a swimming posture, reached the opposite shore in safety, though it was frightful to feel the ice, not much thicker than a pane of window-glass, bending under me. At the house, I was told that the crossing was half a mile back. I recrossed the river; and, retracing our steps a mile, we found a blind road leading over the bluff, which soon took us in safety to a comfortable house, where we found enough to eat for ourselves and our horse. The next day I started for my home, where my sufferings were soon forgotten. I speedily recovered, and went to work with my brother. We had a contract for drum-making from the United States, which gave us employment all the following summer.

Early in the fall of this year, I embarked in a new business. A mechanic had invented and patented a spinning-head, which was thought to be a great improvement upon the old plan. I accepted an offer he made me to sell the patent in the State of Connecticut. The only thing in the way of my making a fortune was the want of capital. However, "where there's a will, there's a way." I soon contrived to get a horse and wagon, and five or six dollars in money, besides a quantity of essences, such as peppermint, tanzy, winter-green, &c. With this fit-out I launched forth into the wide world in pursuit of fortune. There is no period in the history of a young man which awakens so many of the finer feelings of his nature as that when he leaves his home, and for the first time assumes the position and responsibility of an independent man. All the joyful recollections of that home he is about to leave, no matter how humble it is, rush with overwhelming force upon his susceptible heart. I started with all the firmness and resolution I could call to my aid; yet, if my mother could have looked into my eyes, she would have seen them filled with big tears. I jumped into my wagon, whipped up my horse, and was soon out of sight of what, at that moment, seemed all the world to me. . . .

At this juncture, I happened to meet with Caroline Woodruff, a lovely girl of twenty, with handsome, dark eyes, fine brunette complexion, and of an amiable disposition. I fell in love with her at first sight. I can remember the dress she wore at our first meeting as well as I do those beautiful eyes. It was a dark crimson, woollen dress, with a neat little frill about the neck. I saw but little of her; for the family soon moved to a distance of forty or fifty miles. Though she was absent, however, her image was implanted too deeply in my heart to be forgotten. It haunted me day and night. At length I took the resolution to go to see her; which was at once carried out. I set out on foot, found her and proposed, and was bid to wait a while for my answer. I went again, in the same way, and this time had the happiness to be accepted; and, three weeks after, she became my wife, and accompanied me to my home. We had hardly reached it before I was sued for a small debt, which I could not meet: in short, business was not very flourishing, and we were much embarrassed.

To relieve myself, I went into an entirely new business—that of tavern-keeping. Here I paid off some old debts by making new ones. Matters, however, did not improve: on the contrary, creditors grew more clamorous and threatening. Nothing could strike me with more horror than the thought of being shut up in Batavia Jail. At that time the barbarous practice of imprisonment for debt was in full force. My mind was made up. On Saturday night, I took leave of my wife and child, and left for the head waters of the Alleghany River. As soon as the river opened, I took passage on a raft, and worked my way down to Pittsburg. Here I was at a loss what to do. Times were hard; and, besides, I was not a good enough mechanic to get employment at the only trade I knew any thing of. I finally got a job at house-painting; but I felt lonely and unhappy. As soon as I had saved a few dollars, I started for my wife and child. I walked over mountains, and through wild forests, with no guide but the blazed trees. Bears, wolves, deer, and turkeys I met so often, that I would hardly turn around to look at them. At last I reached the settlement within a few miles of Caledonia. Here I halted till night, thinking it safer to travel by moonlight than in broad day. As it grew dark, I started, tired and foot-sore. I saw a horse grazing in the road, and the thought struck me that he could ease my weary limbs. I succeeded in catching and mounting him; and, by means of my staff or walking-stick, I steered him to the street of Caledonia. I then turned him on his way home, and bade him good-night. I remained in close concealment three or four days, and when all was ready, started again for the head waters of the Alleghany, but not alone: this time my wife and child were with me. We experienced many hardships on our way, but nothing of particular interest occurred. At Orleans Point we embarked upon a raft, with a comfortable shanty on board, and in a week floated down the river to Pittsburg. Before I had left Pittsburg, I had rented a ten-footer, with two rooms in it; so we went directly there. All our availables consisted of one bed, and a chest of clothing, and some cooking utensils; so that we had little labor in getting settled down.

But now all my money was gone, and how to get more was the question. I could find no work as a house-painter, and what to do I did not know. I would walk about the town, and return to find my wife in tears,—though she always had a smile for me. I went into the market the next morning, though for what purpose I could hardly tell; for I had not one cent of money. At last I ventured to ask the price of a beefsteak. I had the impudence to say to the man, that I should like that piece very much, but that I had no change with me. To my great surprise, he said I could take it, and pay for it the next time I came. As I had made the acquaintance of Mr. Sands, a barber who occupied the twin part of the house I was in, I went to his wife, and asked her to loan me half a loaf of bread, which she did cheerfully. If we went hungry that day, it was not because we had not enough to eat, and that, too, with an honest appetite.

There was an opening just now for a sign-painter. I had talked with Neighbor Sands upon the subject of my becoming one. He approved the plan, and was the means of my getting an order. A Mr. W. H. Wetherell wanted a sign painted in gold letters on both sides, so as to project it into the street. I agreed to do it; but where was the stock of gold paint and board to come from? I went into Neighbor Sands' half a dozen times, for the purpose of asking him to lend me the money to procure the materials, and as often my heart failed me. At last I made a grand effort, and said, "Neighbor Sands, I wish you would lend me twenty dollars for a few days, as I have no money by me that is current."—"Certainly, with pleasure." I could hardly believe it real. I took the money, and hurried into my room, and threw it into my wife's lap. She was frightened, fearing I had obtained it by some unlawful means. The first use I made of it was to go to the market, and to pay the credulous butcher; and to buy some vegetables, tea, sugar, and some other little luxuries. I got my sign-board made, bought my gold leaf, paints, &c.; went to a printer, and got some very large impressions of the alphabet; and, having in my chair-making experience learned the art of gilding, I soon had my sign finished, and paid back my neighbor his money. He never knew that I was not flush of money; but his kindness I never forgot. I was at once established as a sign-painter, and followed that trade for a year.

About this time, I fell in with a portrait-painter by the name of Nelson,—one of the primitive sort. He was a sign, ornamental, and portrait painter. He had for his sign a copy of the "Infant Artists" of Sir Joshua Reynolds, with this inscription, "Sign, Ornamental, and Portrait Painting executed on the shortest notice, with neatness and despatch." It was in his sanctum that I first conceived the idea of painting heads. I saw his portraits, and was enamored at once. I got him to paint me and my wife, and thought the pictures perfection. He would not let me see him paint, nor would he give me the least idea how the thing was done. I took the pictures home, and pondered on them, and wondered how it was possible for a man to produce such wonders of art. At length my admiration began to yield to an ambition to do the same thing. I thought of it by day, and dreamed of it by night, until I was stimulated to make an attempt at painting myself. I got a board; and, with such colors as I had for use in my trade, I began a portrait of my wife. I made a thing that looked like her. The moment I saw the likeness, I became frantic with delight: it was like the discovery of a new sense; I could think of nothing else. From that time, sign-painting became odious, and was much neglected.

I next painted a razeed portrait of an Englishman who was a journeyman baker, for which I received five dollars. He sent it to his mother in London. I also painted portraits of the man and his wife with whom I boarded, and for which I received, on account, twelve dollars each. This was in the winter season: the river was closed, and there was but little to be done in sign-painting. . . .

Up to this time, I had never read any book but the Bible, and could only read that with difficulty. My wife, who had received a comparatively good education, and had once taught school, borrowed of one of the neighbors "The Children of the Abbey," a popular novel of that day. I was rather opposed to her reading it, as I had been taught to believe by my mother, that cards and novels were the chief instruments of the Devil in seducing mortals from the paths of virtue. However, her desire to read it was too strong to be overcome by any objections I could raise, so I had to yield; but I insisted upon her reading it aloud. One dark and rainy day, she commenced the reading. She read on till bed-time, and then proposed to leave the rest of the story until the next day; but I was altogether too eager to hear how the next chapter ended to consent to that. She was persuaded to read the next chapter, and the next, and the next. In short, I kept her reading all night, and gave her no rest until the novel was finished. The first novel I ever read myself was "Rob Roy." I could only read it understandingly by reading it aloud, and to this day I often find myself whispering the words in the daily newspaper.

My brother Horace, the chair-maker, was established in Paris, Ky. He wrote to me that he was painting portraits, and that there was a painter in Lexington who was receiving fifty dollars a head. This price seemed fabulous to me; but I began to think seriously of trying my fortune in Kentucky. I soon settled upon the idea, and acted at once. Winding up my affairs in Pittsburg, I found that I had just money enough to take me down the river. I knew a barber, by the name of Jarvis, who was going to Lexington; and I proposed to join him in the purchase of a large skiff. He agreed to it; and we fitted it up with a sort of awning or tent, and embarked, with our wives and children. Sometimes we rowed our craft; but oftener we let her float as she pleased, while we gave ourselves up to music. He, as well as I, played the clarionet; and we had much enjoyment on our voyage. We arrived in Paris with funds rather low; but, as my brother was well known there, I found no difficulty on that score.

Here I began my career as a professional artist. I took a room, and painted the portrait of a very popular young man, and made a decided hit. In six months from that time, I had painted nearly one hundred portraits, at twenty-five dollars a head. The first twenty-five I took rather disturbed the equanimity of my conscience. It did not seem to me that the portrait was intrinsically worth that money; now, I know it was not. . . .

In June of this year, I made a trip of one hundred miles for the purpose of painting the portrait of old Colonel Daniel Boone. I had much trouble in finding him. He was living, some miles from the main road, in one of the cabins of an old block-house, which was built for the protection of the settlers against the incursions of the Indians. I found that the nearer I got to his dwelling, the less was known of him. When within two miles of his house, I asked a man to tell me where Colonel Boone lived. He said he did not know any such man. "Why, yes, you do," said his wife. "It is that white-headed old man who lives on the bottom, near the river." A good illustration of the proverb, that a prophet is not without honor save in his own country.

I found the object of my search engaged in cooking his dinner. He was lying in his bunk, near the fire, and had a long strip of venison wound around his ramrod, and was busy turning it before a brisk blaze, and using salt and pepper to season his meat. I at once told him the object of my visit. I found that he hardly knew what I meant. I explained the matter to him, and he agreed to sit. He was ninety years old, and rather infirm; his memory of passing events was much impaired, yet he would amuse me every day by his anecdotes of his earlier life. I asked him one day, just after his description of one of his long hunts, if he never got lost, having no compass. "No," said he, "I can't say as ever I was lost, but I was *bewildered* once for three days."

He was much astonished at seeing the likeness. He had a very large progeny; one grand-daughter had eighteen children, all at home near the old man's cabin: *they* were even more astonished at the picture than was the old man himself.

I will mention in this connection the fact of my painting one of the Osage chiefs. There was a deputation from this tribe on a visit to Governor Clarke. I asked some of them to go to my room, and there showed them the portrait of Governor Clarke, at the sight of which they gave several significant grunts. They were not satisfied with merely looking, but went close to the picture, rubbed their fingers across the face, looked behind it, and showed great wonder. The old chief was a fine-looking man, of great dignity of manner. I asked him to sit for his portrait. He did so; and, after giving evident signs of pleasure at seeing himself reproduced on canvas, he said that I was a god (a great spirit), and, if I would go home with him, I should be a brave, and have two wives. . . .

My ambition in my profession now began to take a higher flight, and I determined to go to Europe. I had accumulated over a thousand dollars in cash, and had bought a carriage and pair of horses. With these I started with my family for Western New York, where my parents were still living and by whom we were warmly welcomed.

My success in painting, and especially the amount of money I had saved, was the wonder of the whole neighborhood. My grandfather Smith, at an advanced age, had followed his children to the West, and was living in the same place with my father. He had, as yet, said nothing congratulatory upon my success: but one day he began, "Chester, I want to speak to you about your present mode of life. I think it is very little better than swindling to charge forty dollars for one of those effigies.

Now, I want you to give up this course of living, and settle down on a farm, and become a respectable man." . . .

And now, at last, I took my departure for a foreign land, leaving wife, children, and friends,—all indeed that I had sympathy with,—to cast in my lot, for a time, with strangers in a strange land. My heart was full of conflicting emotions. Scores of my patrons in Boston had tried to dissuade me from taking this step, some urging as a reason, that I already had such a press of business that I could lay up a considerable sum of money yearly; while others insisted that I need not go abroad, for I already painted better pictures than any artist in this country, and probably better than any in Europe. My self-esteem was not large enough, however, to listen to all this, and my desire for study and improvement was too great to be overpowered by flatter. In spite of all advice to the contrary, I sailed for England, in the good packet ship "Canada," on the first day of August, 1823.

After a favorable passage of eighteen days, we arrived safely in port, at Liverpool; and I remember feeling so ridiculously happy at setting foot on shore again, that I laughed heartily without knowing why.

During the two years of separation from my family which ensued, I kept a journal to send to my wife. . . .

I now began my career again in Boston; not as I did on my first appearance in that city, for then I was entirely self-taught, and little could be expected of one from the backwoods; but now I came fresh from the schools of Europe, and with some reputation. I felt keenly how much more would be required of me now to fill the expectations of the connoisseurs and patrons of art.

My first picture was of Emily Marshall, then the reigning beauty of Boston. No artist's skill could be put to a severer test; for her beauty depended much upon the expression of her animated face, which, when lighted up in conversation, was bewitchingly lovely. I did not succeed to my own satisfaction, though others seemed well pleased.

Much interest was shown in my paintings, and I soon had enough to do; though, of the eighty applicants on my list when I left Boston, not one came to renew his engagement. Many whom I had painted previously wanted their pictures altered, either because the dress was out of fashion, or the expression did not please them; but I found it would never do to begin to alter the old pictures. So I adopted for a rule, that I would paint a new picture in the place of the old one, and deduct the price of the latter. I now charged one hundred dollars for a head: my former price was fifty dollars. . . .

During my stay in Washington, alluded to above, I painted many of the distinguished men of the day, such as Mr. Adams, Mr. Wirt, all the judges of the Supreme Court, &c. Among them was a full length portrait of Judge Marshall, for the Athenaeum. I consider it a good picture. I had great pleasure in painting *the whole* of such a man. . . .

I again met Judge Marshall in Richmond, whither I went during the sitting of the convention for amending the Constitution. He was a leading member of a quoit club, which I was invited to attend. The battleground was about a mile from the city, in a beautiful grove. I went early, with a friend, just as the party were beginning to arrive. I watched for the coming of the old chief. He soon approached with his coat on his arm, and his hat in his hand, which he was using as a fan. He walked directly up to a large bowl of mint-julep, which had been prepared, and drank off a tumbler full of the liquid, smacked his lips, and then turned to the company, with a cheerful "How are you, gentlemen?" He was looked upon as the best pitcher in the party, and could throw heavier quoits than any other member of the club. They game began with great animation. There were several ties; and, before long, I saw the great chief justice of the Supreme Court of the United States, down on his knees, measuring the contested distance with a straw, with as much earnestness as if it had been a point of law; and, if he proved to be in the right, the woods would ring with his triumphant shout. What would the dignitaries of the highest court of England have thought, if they had been present? . . .

I was again in Washington in the winter of 1830–31, when I painted the portrait of John C. Calhoun. During the sittings, he invited me to come up to the Senate, as there was to be an interesting debate. Mr. Hayne was to speak on the subject of "Foote's Resolutions," in reply to a short speech of Mr. Webster. I accepted the invitation, and Mr. Calhoun admitted me as one of the many favored ones.

Mr. Hayne was most eloquent, and exceedingly bitter in his remarks upon Mr. Webster's speech; and so scathing in his denunciations of New England and her policy, that I felt his sarcasms were unanswerable. I think all the friends of Mr. Webster thought so too. The South side of the Senate were vociferous in their applause. At night, I went to see the fallen great man, as I considered him. My daughter was visiting Mr. Webster's daughter at the time. To my surprise, I found him cheerful, even playful. He had the two girls upon his knees. I told him I expected to find him in another room, pointing to his library. "Time enough for that in the morning," said he.

Mr. Calhoun gave me another sitting the next morning. He seemed to think the great champion of the North was annihilated. He said it was a pity he had laid himself open at so many points.

I needed no invitation to go to the Senate that morning. I went early to the gallery, and secured a seat among the reporters. As Mr. Webster entered the Senate, all eyes were turned upon him. He was elegantly dressed, and apparently less excited than any of his friends. I felt towards Mr. Webster as I imagine a criminal might feel who looks to his counsel to save him from punishment for some crime he is charged with. He soon, however, put me at my ease. As he proceeded with his speech, all his friends felt satisfied that victory was his.[1] I need make no further allusion to this splendid effort, as it is as familiar to all as household words.

The next morning, I asked Mr. Calhoun what he thought of Webster's reply. He said simply, but with great emphasis, "Mr. Webster is a *strong man*, sir, a *very strong man*."

In the latter part of the summer of 1830, I had taken my family to Springfield, Mass., to spend a portion of the warm weather. We were all so well pleased with the place, that I exchanged my house in Beacon Street for one in Springfield, which has been our home ever since.

Little of interest occurred in my life for several years. Its monotony was varied only by several professional trips to the West and South.

In 1845 I met with a sore bereavement in the death of my wife. She died on the 27th of August, after an illness of but three days.

---

1. This forensic duel between Senators Daniel Webster and Robert Young Hayne over the nature of the Union acquired fame in American history as the Webster-Hayne debate, which many a nineteenth-century school child committed to memory.

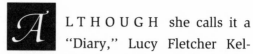

LUCY FLETCHER KELLOGG

1793–1878

*A*LTHOUGH she calls it a "Diary," Lucy Fletcher Kellogg left eighteen typescript pages of memoirs, which she had not begun to write until she was eighty-six years old.[1] Her autobiography is not as full an account of a life as others in this collection, but is noteworthy, considering the relative rarity in the early Republic of women writing their life stories at all. Yet more arresting is the fact that Kellogg and her sons and daughters were involved in one of the then most radical educational experiments in America—that of Oberlin College, with its path-breaking admission of women and African Americans in the 1830s; even so, Oberlin figures in Kellogg's memoirs primarily as the site of family events.

Born Lucy Fletcher, Kellogg grew up in New England, moving from place to place because, as she notes of her family, "In accordance with the instincts of New England people, they must sell their farm and move to New Hampshire or some other new place."[2] Her father alternately farmed, traded goods, ran a brickyard, and kept a tavern. Prosperous enough to send his daughter to dancing classes and a boarding school, he still welcomed her effort to earn some money herself, which she and

---

1. "The Diary of Lucy Fletcher Kellogg," a typescript in the manuscript collection of the American Antiquarian Society, Worcester, Massachusetts. Published here by the permission of Barbara J. F. Wyman, a descendent of Lucy Fletcher Kellogg.
2. Kellogg, "Diary," p. 1.

her sisters did by braiding straw for hats and weaving fine gingham shirting and bed ticking.

Kellogg's frontier experience—so common for those reaching maturity after the War of 1812—came when she accompanied her married sister to Chautauqua County, New York, making what to her was a romantic journey in a large covered wagon pulled by a yoke of oxen. Traveling twenty miles a day, they finished their 500-mile trip in less than a month. Kellogg found a school-teaching job which paid $1.25 a week plus room and board. Lodging in the same home was a man "of good deportment and steady habits" from Vermont, Titus Kellogg, whom she married when she was twenty-five years old.

Like her father, Lucy Fletcher's husband farmed, turned his hand to merchandising, and ran an ashery where he bought the potash from local farmers' timber burning to process into pearl ash. Like so many other ventures in the ebullient American economy, his failed, and he began a search for a new frontier, which took him to Louisiana and Texas. In Louisiana Titus Kellogg bought soldiers' bounty land warrants for many thousands of acres, only twelve hundred of which he took possession of. Congress in the early nineteenth century voted to give soldiers warrants to land, which the soldiers often sold for ready cash. Veterans of the War of 1812, for instance, received bounties of 160 acres between the Illinois and Mississippi Rivers. For many years there was a brisk business in soldiers' patents.

The Kelloggs were attracted to Oberlin College because it offered students a chance to mix manual labor with schooling, and they sent their two eldest children and a younger son there. For their daughter Mary, Oberlin became a permanent home when she married a fellow student, James Harris Fairchild, who was also a native of Massachusetts. After graduating in 1831, Fairchild served his alma mater for the next fifty-seven years, twenty-three of which as president.

At this juncture, having left the two eldest children at Oberlin, the Kellogg family moved to Louisiana, where Kellogg's husband had bought a farm in Claiborne Parish. Traveling through the month of August, they departed from Cincinnati in a covered wagon, camping along the way with their remaining children. Despite their Northern background and Oberlin associations, the Kelloggs had six adult slaves, each with families. Kellogg makes no mention of slavery as an institution in her autobiography and makes only the most oblique references to slaves, in order to distinguish them from her "white family." In Louisiana, a dear sister lived nearby and the emerging careers of her children gave Kellogg pleasure, but bad luck struck again in the forms of a cotton crop lost to the boll weevil and the death of her husband. Having, as she reports, "never been very well contented in Louisiana," Kellogg returned to the North, where she made her home with two children in Keokuk, Iowa.

~ ? ~

I A M nearly eighty-six years old, and not finding much to do, and to busy myself, I thought I would write down some events of my life which are impressed upon my memory.

I am the third child of my parents. My father's name was Ebenezer Fletcher. My mother's name was Mary Goldthwait.

My father had a small farm left him by his father, in the town of Sutton, Mass., where they, my parents, moved nine years after they first married. Their three first children were born there.

In accordance with the instincts of New England people, they must sell their farm and move to New Hampshire or some other new place. They did so, and removed to Croydon, New Hampshire. My father engaged in merchandizing, and remaining there five years, returned to Massachusetts and bought a farm in the town of Worcester. We had a family of five children. We lived there about eighteen years, having left New Hampshire in the year 1800. I was then six years old, but I remember the place we left in New Hampshire well, and of going to school and many of my playmates, and the journey back to Massachusetts.

I also remember when Washington died, which occurred when we were living in Croydon in 1799 when I was in my seventh year. My father at the time was lieutenant in a militia company. I remember how he was dressed: with long blue coat, metal buttons and yellow facings, with small clothes and vest of same color, with long white stockings and cocked hat, with a long black ribbon tied on his left arm as a badge of mourning for Washington. Some time afterward, at school, we repeated in concert these lines—

> "General George Washington is no more,
> Who shall now defend our coasts,
> Guide our councils, lead our hosts,
> Heaven propitious, hear our cry,
> Send us help when danger's nigh."

Worcester is the town where I spent my youth. We had good common school advantages. My father lived in a large house and kept a tavern. When I was twelve years old, I attended a dancing school, with my two brothers and two sisters, which I enjoyed much. . . .

When I was sixteen I went to a boarding school at Sutton, Mass. The teacher's name was Miss Thayer, where I learned some things not taught in the common schools in those days, such as geography with the use of maps, needlework, drawing and painting in watercolors, and I was much interested in studying them. Of my work in the latter I had two pieces framed. One was Dr. Stern's "Maria", and the other was a bunch of the beautiful Moss Roses.

Before my boarding school experience, when I was thirteen, my sister Fanny and myself went into a town adjoining Worcester, to learn the art of braiding straw. After that we could earn our own clothes. New England people in those days were very industrious. My father owned a small farm, and a nice home, but had not sufficient income to supply his daughters with all their wants. But the war of 1812 coming on, the straw business failed, and we changed our business. We got a couple of looms and set them up in our east room, and we took cotton yarn from the factories, which were beginning to spread in Massachusetts, and wove fine shirtings, gingham, and bed tickings, for the factories, and for ourselves, as English goods were not to be had. Of No. 20 yarns we made fine gingham dresses of light and dark colors, which were good enough in time of war. We continued our business of weaving four or five years.

While our brothers Eleazer and Adolphus lived at home, my father had a brickyard and my oldest brother, Eleazer, went into the brickmaking business, and brother Adolphus went into town into the office of

Isaiah Thomas, the renowned printer of the "Massachusetts Spy". I think it was in 1812 that he, Adolphus, commenced learning this trade. My oldest brother, Eleazer, joined an independent company of light infantry in Worcester; the Captain's name was Levi Lincoln.

The governor of Massachusetts called troops to go to Boston to guard the town, and that company volunteered to go. I remember it was quite a trial to us to fix him off, but he came safely back after a time.

About this time my sister Fanny was married to Jas. McClellan, of Sutton. They lived in Sutton near his father's till 1817, when they made up their minds to move to the far west, to Chautauqua County, N. Y. He, McC., not having been fortunate in some factory investments, my sister being delicate, my mother consented to my going with them. This was a romantic journey to me. My oldest brother had gone the year before, and had bought mills, there, and had invited me to come, telling me their country justice of the peace was single.

But this long and exciting journey I began to tell about: we had a large covered wagon, a large yoke of oxen, and a large strong horse, just what we should want when we got there. I well remember the morning we started from father McClellan's hospitable mansion, having made our adieus and seated ourselves in the wagon. My brother-in-law, with his ox whip in hand, was to walk. As he started up his team, his little daughter, two years old, called out in high glee, "Cornelia, do ride", which was noticed and repeated by the dear family whom we were leaving. The journey we had commenced was 500 miles. If no mishap prevented, we traveled about twenty miles per day. The first day riding in the covered wagon, I got dreadfully seasick, but I got better and started on the next morning.

The third day we arrived in Springfield, sixty miles from Sutton. It was the largest town we had seen after leaving Worcester. It was a grief to me to leave Massachusetts without having seen Boston or the Ocean; Springfield was remarkable for its bridge across the Connecticut river, and the arsenal. The bridge was long and covered. We trudged on until we arrived in Albany, N. Y. This was the largest place I had ever seen. There we crossed the Hudson on a horse boat, which was a great curiosity to me. In those days there were no steamboats, canals, nor railroads, but a large public road, called the great western turnpike, with toll gates and taverns in plenty. It was a flat country of three hundred miles between Albany and Buffalo, and we could look straight ahead as far as the eye could reach and discern several tavern signs ahead of us as we proceeded onwards.

When we arrived in Buffalo, a town at the foot of Lake Erie, as we found the roads very bad, my brother-in-law took the heaviest of his goods from the wagon, and his family and shipped them on board a little sloop called the "Buffalo Packet". His family consisted of his wife, myself, and two children, James, aged nearly four years, and Cornelia, two years, and he went on with his team on the lake shore, through the mud, sixty miles, arriving in due time at Portland Harbor, the place where he expected to meet his family. There he waited several days. The night after we started, there came up a storm and drove us back to Buffalo, but we could not get in, and had to cast anchor two miles out, in sight of the town, where we laid tossing two days and nights. As soon as possible the people of Buffalo sent out a boat and took the passengers, sixteen in number, in safety back to a public house, where we stayed until the storm was over, when we went aboard again, and arrived at last at our desired haven, Portland Harbor, where we took the stage or wagon to Mayville, a little town at the head of Chautauqua Lake. We traveled on, near the shore of that lake, about twenty miles to a clearing, where my brother-in-law had located, having been on the road about six weeks. It was a romantic little place in the thick woods. A few years before, Reuben Slayton had built a saw and grist mill and a log house, which had grown to be a large dwelling as the family increased, and now having plenty of boards, had built on bed rooms and galleries on all sides. It looked like an oasis in the wilderness, which we were rejoiced to find ready for our use and we named it the "Old Abbey".

We were all in good health, and we went to work contentedly in the little log cabin, though we had left handsome and spacious dwellings in Massachusetts. My sister Fanny and I enjoyed the new country well. I continued to live with my sister till the next winter, when I had an application to teach a small school in the neighborhood. It was my first attempt at school keeping, but the school was small, and my wages were also small, namely $1.25 per week and boarded. I got through with my term at last, and was glad to get back to my home with my sister. The summer following I engaged in another school; here I enjoyed myself better, the school was some larger and more young people my own age. My wages were $1.50 per week and boarded, as before. Boarding in the family where I lived was a young man from Burlington, Vt., by the name of Titus Kellogg, of good deportment and steady habits, to whom I became engaged in a short time, and was married the next winter. It was on February 7, 1819, that that event took place and I was twenty-five years old.

My husband was industrious and energetic, and he bought some land near to the settlements of my brothers, and to the village afterwards called Ashville, and built a house and barn. But clearing that heavy timbered land soon told injuriously upon his constitution, and he was obliged to change. He went into merchandising, and in that business he was more successful. He built an ashery and bought from the farmers their pot ashes, and manufactured them into pearl ashes, which he could exchange for goods. He built a store and a dwelling in Ashville, and continued in that business six or eight years, or until 1830, when wishing to increase his business, he sold out his prosperous business and property in Ashville, and removed to the larger town of Jamestown. There he went heavily into business, with two partners, and in about three years failed and lost all he had gained in the preceeding ten years.

We continued to live in Jamestown until 1838. —My husband striving courageously to regain his former easy circumstances, with varying success, but on the whole, failed to do so, though quite able to provide a decent living for his family. In that year my husband, whose health had become impaired with long troubles, determined to change his residence to a southern climate. The preceding winter he had traveled south in company with a family by the name of Russell, in search of health, and on his part, also in search of business opportunities. They took a sea voyage from New Orleans Texasward, and landed at the port of Matagorda, at the mouth of the Colorado, and spent the winter there. Having taken from New Orleans a small stock of goods, he went into trade, where he was reasonably successful in business, and increased his means. Among other transactions he bought many soldiers' bounty land warrants, many thousand acres, but from want of proper care and attention, the lands and warrants were scattered and lost in after years. Nevertheless, the deed and protected title to twelve hundred acres of this land, in Brown County, is still in our family.

My husband returned to Jamestown the following season, and set to work to settle his affairs with the view to take his family south.

Up to this time I have not mentioned a word about our children, three daughters and three sons, and it was our pleasant duty to care for them.

Three years before this time, there came to us at Jamestown, a report of a famous school, a manual labor school at Oberlin in Ohio, where young people could acquire an education and learn to work and help to support themselves. As we had little now to depend on, we made up our minds to send our two oldest, Mary and Augustus, to Oberlin. They were pretty well advanced in the common branches, having attended the academy in Jamestown. The school at Oberlin had prospered and become a college. Mary, my daughter, has lived there ever since, except two years spent in the south. She became engaged to a student there, Jas. H. Fairchild, who afterwards became a professor in the college, about 1840. . . .

Our son Augustus, remained in the school about two years, having entered college there about 1837, soon after which it became necessary for lack of money in those hard times, that he should return home.

But I was going to tell about moving south. We gathered up our household effects, embarked on a flat boat, Capt. Benham, at Jamestown, and continued on her down the river as far as Cincinnati. My husband being already gone on in advance, to look after the business he had already established in Texas. Our children were all with us then, as also my niece, Martha Fletcher. The season was much advanced towards winter, and we concluded to pass the winter at Cincinnati, where we remained until August of the following year 1839. Mary and Augustus went to teaching in the common schools of the city. We kept house altogether there, and not unpleasantly, while my husband was preparing a home for us at the south. In about a year or less he returned for us, having closed up his Texas venture, and had located at Minden, Claiborne Parish, Louisiana. It was in the month of August, 1839, the weather was warm, and we all thought it would be pleasant to journey southward in our own conveyance and camp out. So my husband bought three good horses, one larger and stronger, for the barouche, in which I and my younger children were to ride. The other two horses to draw a covered wagon, which contained our trunks, camp equipage and other baggage, and the two boys were to drive that. He said he could sell the horses, etc. on our arrival at Minden, for as much as they had cost. We started from Cincinnati, crossed the Ohio River and entered the State of Kentucky, taking a southwesterly course, on the first of August 1839, and never had a rainy day, or any bad weather, for the six weeks we were on the road, until we reached within about fifty miles of our journey's end, when we all got a wetting in a severe storm, which caused three of our family severe attacks of fever, which required careful nursing some time after our arrival at home, to cure and overcome. On the whole, we had a very delightful and successful journey. We went on very leisurely, and did not *suffer* from heat. We had a tent, and would buy our provisions on the road, both for ourselves and horses; cooked for ourselves, slept on good beds under our tent, and stopped on the grassy banks of a stream for regular washdays and for rest when needed.

I could relate some anecdotes of remarkable providences and hair-breadth escapes we experienced during our protracted journey. My husband had selected, by the side of the road, a charming grove of high trees for our camping ground, one still summer evening just about sundown, and the Katydids were making the grove ring. They were the first I had ever heard. We were preparing for the night, pitching the tent and getting ready for our picnic supper. Mary was sitting under a tree bathing her feet, when we began to hear a crackling sound, and soon one of the big trees fell with a thundering crash; some of the small limbs fell on Mary's dress as she sat there, but it did not hurt any of us.

Our children were all with us then. We had three sons and three daughters, and Mary was the oldest. This was in Kentucky, the first night, I think, after crossing the river at Cincinnati. We were taking a southwestern course, and in a few days we were in the neighborhood of the Mammoth Cave. We stopped to examine a cave we found contiguous—we had halted at a place by the side of the road; it was not a public place. There were some women there; they told us we could go in, and my two boys, Augustus and Edwin, eighteen and sixteen years old, eager to see the cave, had taken the two lamps from the barouche and gone in at the opening without any guide and we felt not a little fearful. The rest of us were waiting around the outside until we thought it high time they should return, and my husband called them but no answer. He raised his voice to loudest pitch, when we became frightened and screamed with all our might, but never made them hear. Then came a few minutes of agony. I thought my precious boys were gone forever, but soon, perhaps ten minutes, the light began to glimmer, and they came back safely to our arms. We were afterwards informed that sound would not circulate or penetrate far into caves where there were many short turns. So we cheerily pursued our journey.

By some accident my little boy, George, lost his pretty straw hat that I had bought for him in Cincinnati. For pastime and pleasure I gathered straw from the bundles of oats we bought for our horses and made him another. I braided and sewed it as we rode along in our pretty barouche. As we were traveling along one day, our pet, baby Lucy, fell out between the wheels. In agony I looked out just in time to see the wheel grazing her legs as she lifted them on the outside of the wheel. She escaped without a scratch. So we were enabled by a kind providence assisting, to proceed on our journey.

I will tell another little story, a snake story. We had camped on the Cumberland river, on a pleasant rocky bluff, and had supped. My husband took the little tin bucket containing our butter to a safe place by the side of a spring, when he saw two rattlesnakes; it was in the twilight, and we could not change our location then. So, with a tender father's care, he never told us about the snakes, but made up his mind to watch by the side of the tent, all night, which he did, but saw no more of the snakes.

We stopped one day to wash. We had lost our reckoning; thought it was Saturday and it proved to be Sunday. We washed all that day, and did not find it out till Monday morning, when we saw all the people going about their work. But our horses got a day of rest, if we did not.

We came to the Mississippi river at Memphis, where we crossed the river on a ferry boat. I remember how hard it was getting up the bank on the other side. Now we had to cross the great Mississippi swamp bottom. It was a dry season, and my husband thought it a favorable time to make the crossing, but we found plenty of black mud to go through. Our pretty barouche was sadly disfigured. We had to walk a good part of the way. My two daughters, finding they could get along better barefooted, took off their shoes and stockings. I remember how their little white feet contrasted with the black mud. We traveled on two or three days through this swamp.

After further journeying through a more elevated region we reached the city of Little Rock, in Arkansas, and found an old friend there. We kept on our course, southwest from Little Rock, through a pine woods hilly country, with light sandy soil. When we had reached within some seventy-five miles of our destination, we were overtaken by the storm before mentioned. It rained harder and faster than I had ever seen it do before. We were in an unsettled wilderness; there was no shelter whatever, and we had to take it, and were all thoroughly drenched, which was followed by the fever in three of our number, with the consequences before mentioned.

It was noticable that Mary and Augustus who had already experienced some malarial influences, in Ohio, were two who escaped this attack of fever at this time. It was my husband, Edwin and Marcia that were sick.

At last we arrived in Minden, found Joel Rathburn in charge of the store of goods my husband had left in his hands, a duty that he had faithfully discharged. We took board for a time with Mr. Cleveland, where our sick met the care and kindly treatment so necessary to us all, especially our sick ones.

Our next change was to go on a plantation, which I gladly complied with.

My husband had traded for a good improvement two or three miles from Minden, and thither we went with good courage. We had three men, Richard, Ackrell and Joe, and three women, Peggy, Jane and Mary. Peggy's children were Chloe, Maria, Cinderella, Henry and Joe; Jane's children were Cornelia and Hatty. We remained at this first plantation but about two years, when we sold that place and removed to another place purchased down on Lake Bistineau, some fifteen miles away, and in a better planting country, and only a short distance from my dear sister Lovisa, who had, with her husband, Joshua Alden, and their children, settled in this region many years before, and whose presence there had been the cause of my husband's first visiting this remote part of the country, and influenced us strongly in favor of settlement in Louisiana, and reconciled us in a measure to the necessary deprivations which were inseparable from a residence there.

This last removal took place in the year, I think of 1843 or 1844.

Our white family at this time consisted of my husband and myself, and Lucy, then eleven or twelve years old. My oldest daughter, Mary, as before stated, had been married to Prof. Fairchild, in 1841, and returned to Oberlin, taking with her my youngest son, George, for the privilege of education at Oberlin. Marcia had shortly after married, and was settled in the north. Augustus, about this time, after being engaged for some time as a steamboat clerk, was established as a clerk in a commercial house in New Orleans. Edwin, having been elected county clerk at the age of twenty-one years, went to the county seat, Bellevue, of the new parish lately formed from Claiborne, called Bossier.

Our new plantation was situated in the southern part of this parish, near to Lake Bistineau. Sister Alden, with her interesting and good children, was situated on their little prairie farm, only two miles from us. Her being there was an unspeakable comfort and consolation to me. We met very frequently and could and did greatly encourage each other. We had about two hundred acres of land under fence and improvement, all cultivated, say one hundred acres in corn, and one hundred acres in cotton. The soil was so rich and mellow that it was wonderful to see how thriftily and easily everything would grow. We had a garden paled in, where vegetables grew in abundance.

Our fruits were chiefly peaches and figs, and some wild varieties, but we had no apples. About this time, my husband built a gin house, for the ginning of cotton. While raising it, it fell, but very fortunately no one was injured. The builder, however, put it up again directly, and more securely.

One year our crop of cotton was totally destroyed by the cotton worm. Apparently the worms went through the fields inside of three days, eating up every green leaf or tender twig or boll. The fields looked as though ravaged by fire, leaving a reddish black desolation.

We had plenty of cows, horses and hogs, and did not *suffer* for the necessaries of life, but had to forego many of the conveniences, and most of the luxuries. I tried to be contented through all my tribulations while my husband lived. About this time my dear mother died at sister Fanny's, in Illinois, where they had been established since the year 1835.

My husband had commenced the work of the year vigorously, had got in a large and good crop, which was near maturity, when in the month of August, there came a fatal disease, the congestive chill, which carried him off very suddenly and unexpected. I had, myself, during the same summer, suffered much from fever, and my husband nursed me. Now, he was taken and I was left.

And, now my husband being gone, and Augustus, my oldest son, being in New Orleans, I had never been very well contented in Louisiana, it did not take long to make up our minds to sell out our plantation and other effects. Considering our neighbors, the Bryans, were able and willing to buy all our property, so we sold out to them, and left Bossier for New Orleans, and thought we would make a home in New Orleans, and board Augustus. We rented and furnished a house very pleasantly, and lived there about two months. However, it was the year the cholera was so bad in New Orleans, and upon a nearer view of this repulsive and dangerous disease, we got frightened, and no doubt with good reason, we packed up our goods, such as we thought best to take, got on a steamer, and never stopped until we reached our final refuge among friends and relatives, in the goodly and Christian town of Oberlin, Ohio, where we arrived on the tenth of April, 1849, just about ten years after our departure for the south, from Cincinnati.

We lived in James' and Mary's family for one year, when we bought a house in Oberlin and occasionally kept some student boarders. Also, my sister, Lovisa Alden and Emma, came from Jamestown, to live with us, and Emma and Lucy attended the college school. Edwin obtained employment in a store, and was soon to go into that business where he continued many years. My son George, who had graduated before from Oberlin College, commenced the study of the medical profession at Cleveland.

My sister, Lovisa, and I continued housekeeping with some boarders, for a year or two, when Edwin's health becoming somewhat impaired, and having a good chance to sell, we sold our house to Mr. Johnson, and I and my family went back to board with James and Mary, which always felt to us as a home.

Soon afterwards my son Edwin went into business in merchandising with Mr. Isaac Johnson, and not long after, about 1853, was married to Miss Julia Birge, with whom [he] has lived happily unto this day. Her sister, Esther Birge, who was married to Reuben Fairchild, on the same day with Julia, died in, I believe, 1855, leaving a little boy eleven months old, whom Julia took, and has brought up and educated, now the promising young man, E. K. Fairchild.

My sister Alden, not far from this time, I think in the fall of 1853, was married to Mr. William Maxwell, of Mansfield, Ohio, with whom she lived in peace and contentment until his decease at Mansfield, a few years ago, and where I have been a guest, and passed many pleasant weeks through the intervening long years, always finding sympathy and an open-armed and sisterly welcome.

My oldest son, Augustus, after helping us off in 1849, to seek a place of safety, went back to his business in New Orleans, where he continued from the time his beginning there, say about 1844, until 1857, some thirteen years, when he dissolved his New Orleans business connection, and, with his savings, established himself in Keokuk, Iowa, just in time to escape some of the bad effects of the great financial revulsions and misfortunes that prevailed in the United States before the close of that year.

Mr. Charles P. Birge had become engaged to my daughter Lucy since 1855 or '56. In the fall of that year, 1856, in association with my son, Augustus, he came to Keokuk, Iowa, and commenced business which has been continued with much success until this day. Augustus and Edwin, one or both of them being associated therewith throughout the entire period. Mr. Birge came to Oberlin in the fall of 1857, and was married to Lucy in December of that year, and with her removed to Keokuk immediately, and was soon established in housekeeping.

As one after another my daughters have been married and left me, I have naturally felt as though the youngest most needed such aid and assistance as I could give. And I have made my home ever since, shortly after her marriage, with her in Keokuk, where she and her young family have shared my care—and all that I could do for their benefit. My daughter Lucy, has always been a good and affectionate daughter, and her house has furnished me a fit and very happy home and refuge in my old age. My son Augustus, has also been, during the whole of this period, except for the four years he was in Europe, my constant friend and associate, and under the same roof.

CHAUNCEY JEROME

1793–1868

*I*T is quite fitting that Chauncey Jerome should have entitled his autobiography *History of the American Clock Business,* for, as he announces in his preface, he could not write his life without having much to say about the "Yankee clocks" that had made the small state of Connecticut a world manufacturing center. Claiming for himself a remarkable memory, Jerome promises his readers a minute account of "every important transaction of my whole life," which amounts to the story of the technological development of timepieces. As Jerome boasts, his name could be seen on millions of clocks around the world. While they were the pride of his life, it was enough, he says, for the American people "to know that their country supplies the whole world with its most useful time-keepers."[1]

Jerome's father had been a blacksmith and nail-maker whose death, when Jerome was eleven, precipitated the breakup of the family and Jerome's being put out to work. As Jerome explains to his readership of the 1860s, "There being no manufacturing of any account in the country, the poor boys were obliged to let themselves to the farmers, and it was extremely difficult to find a place to live where they would treat a poor boy like a human being. Never shall I forget," he continues with unabashed sentiment, "the Monday morning that I took my little bundle

---

1. Chauncey Jerome, *History of the American Clock Business for the Past Sixty Years, and Life of Chauncey Jerome, written by himself* (New Haven, 1860), preface.

of clothes, and with a bursting heart bid my poor mother good-bye. I knew that the rest of the family had got to leave soon, and I perhaps never to see any of them again."[2]

When he landed a job making dials for clocks, Jerome discovered a vocational passion, despite the admonition of Jerome's "guardian, a good old man," who told him that "there was so many clocks then making, that the country would soon be filled with them, and the business would be good for nothing in two or three years." In fact, Jerome became part of a revolution in clock making when he went to work for the remarkable Eli Terry.[3] In 1810 Terry was both clock-maker and clock-seller, regularly lashing two or three tall, wooden grandfather clocks on his horse and setting out for nearby villages to look for customers. Over the next few years, by redesigning and scaling down his clocks by replacing wooden parts with brass ones, Terry turned Litchfield County, Connecticut, into the clock-making center of the world. By 1816, Chauncey had his own shop and was both shipping clocks to South Carolina and selling to local peddlers.

When others of Terry's former workers set themselves up like Jerome in nearby workshops, they provided the inventive stimulus and competition for a succession of stunning improvements in clock mechanisms. Driving the price of a clock down to five dollars by increasing the volume of production, the clock-makers then had to come up with some imaginative marketing. Jerome got the idea of shipping his clocks to Great Britain. At the time, British customs officials were enjoined to confiscate any imports that they suspected of being priced under their cost of production; as the world's great dumpers, the British were not going to allow anyone else to dump on them. Jerome had to send three shipments before the customs officials became convinced that his prices actually reflected his production costs.

Jerome also records the small-town boy's amazement at first visiting New York City, where, he recalls, he stood at the corner of Chatham and

2. Jerome, *History of the American Clock Business*, pp. 5 ff.
3. Jerome, *History of the American Clock Business*, pp. 16–18.

Pearl streets for an hour watching the bustle. Jerome visited the city at a time when workers were finishing the interior of the City Hall. His visit also coincided with the outbreak of the War of 1812. In the harbor stood the British ship *Macedonian,* which had been brought in as an American prize. "Brain and blood" from the fight was still scattered across its decks. Stephen Decatur's capture of the *Macedonian* thrilled Americans, who had suffered through the recent surrender of Detroit by General William Hull. Decatur was remembered for saying: "Our country . . . may she always be in the right; but our country, right or wrong."

Back home the governor raised a couple of regiments of state troops to defend Connecticut from invasion, and Jerome signed up. "In the afternoon we attended church in a body, wearing our uniforms," he recalls, "to the wonder and astonishment of boys, but terrible to the old people." In fact, he hated army life and bristled when civilians would treat "us all [as] a low set of fellows." His discharge came after guarding New London, Connecticut, for forty-five days.

At war's end Jerome married Salome Smith, a daughter of Captain Theophilus Smith, "one of the last of the Puritanical families there was in the town." Jerome does claim for his thirty-nine-year marriage a union of great happiness; yet his life story remains unabashedly a paean to American industry. Not even the failure of his Jerome Manufacturing Company in 1855 could dampen his ardor for the progress he had witnessed, for he concludes, "I cannot now believe that there will ever be in the same space of future time so many improvements and inventions as those of the past half century."

~ ¿ ~

I WAS born in the town of Canaan, Litchfield County, in the State of Connecticut, on the 10th day of June, 1793. My parents were poor but respectable and industrious. My father was a blacksmith and wrought-nail maker by trade, and the father of six children: four sons and two daughters. I was the fourth child.

In January, 1797, he moved from Canaan to the town Plymouth, in the same County, and in the following spring built a blacksmith shop, which was large enough for three or four men to work at the nail-making business, besides carrying on the blacksmithing. At the time all the nails used in the country were hammered by hand out of iron rods, which practice has almost entirely been done away by the introduction of cut nails.

My advantages for education were very poor. When large enough to handle a hoe, or a bundle of rye, I was kept at work on the farm. The only opportunity I had for attending school was in the winter season, and then only about three months in the year, and at a very poor school. When I was nine years old, my father took me into the shop to work, where I soon learned to make nails, and worked with him in this way until his death, which occurred on the fifth of October, 1804. For two or three days before he died, he suffered the most excruciating pains from the disease known as the black colic. The day of his death was a sad one to me, for I knew that I should lose my happy home, and be obliged to leave it to seek work for my support. There being no manufacturing of any account in the country, the poor boys were obliged to let themselves to the farmers, and it was extremely difficult to find a place to live where they would treat a poor boy like a human being. Never shall I forget the Monday morning that I took my little bundle of clothes, and with a bursting heart bid my poor mother good-bye. I knew that the rest of the family had got to leave soon, and I perhaps never to see any of them again. Being but a boy and naturally very sympathizing, it really seemed as if my heart would break to think of leaving my dear old home for good, but stern necessity compelled me, and I was forced to obey.

The first year after leaving home I was at work on a farm, and almost every day when alone in the fields would burst into tears—not because I had to work, but because my father was dead whom I loved, and our happy family separated and broken up never to live together again. In my new place I was kept at work very hard, and at the age of fourteen did almost the work of a man. It was a very lonely place where we lived, and nothing to interest a child of my age. The people I lived with seemed to me as very old, though they were probably not more than thirty-six years of age, and felt no particular interest in me, more than to keep me constantly at work, early and late, in all kinds of weather, of which I never complained. I have many times worked all day in the woods, chopping down trees, with my shoes filled with snow; never had a pair of boots till I was more than twenty years old. Once in two weeks I was allowed to go to church, which opportunity I always improved. I liked to attend church, for I could see so many folks, and the habit which I then acquired has never to this day left me, and my love for it dates back to this time in my youth, though the attractions now are different.

I shall never forget how frightened I was at the great eclipse which took place on the 16th of June, 1806, and which so terrified the good people in every part of the land. They were more ignorant about such operations of the sun fifty-four years ago than at the present time. I had heard something about eclipses but had not the faintest idea what it could be. I was hoeing corn that day in a by-place three miles from town, and thought it certainly was the day of judgment. I watched the sun steadily disappearing with a trembling heart, and not till it again appeared bright and shining as before, did I regain my breath and courage sufficient to whistle.

The winter before I was fifteen years old, I went to live with a house carpenter to learn the trade, and was bound to him by my guardian till I was twenty-one years old, and was to have my board and clothes for my services. I learned the business very readily, and during the last three years of my apprenticeship could do the work of a man.

It was a very pleasant family that I lived with while learning my trade. In the year 1809 my "boss" took a job in Torringford, and I went with him. After being absent several months from home, I felt very anxious to see my poor mother who lived about two miles from Plymouth. She lived alone—with the exception of my youngest brother about nine years old. I made up my mind that I would go down and see her one night. In this way I could satisfy my boss by not losing any time. It was about twenty miles, and I only sixteen years old. I was really sorry after I had started, but was not the boy to back out. It took me till nearly morning to get there, tramping through the woods half of the way; every noise I heard I thought was a bear or something that would kill me, and the frightful notes of the whippoorwill made my hair stand on end. The dogs were after me at every house I passed. I have never forgotten that night. The boys of to-day do not see such times as I did. . . .

In the fall of 1811, I made a bargain with the man that I was bound to, that if he would give me four months in the winter of each year when the business was dull, I would clothe myself. I therefore went to

Waterbury, and hired myself to Lewis Stebbins, (a singing master of that place,) to work at making the dials of the old fashioned long clock. This kind of business gave me great satisfaction, for I always had a desire to work at clocks. In 1807, when I was fourteen years old, I proposed to my guardian to get me a place with Mr. Eli Terry, of Plymouth, to work at them. Mr. Terry was at that time making more clocks than any other man in the country, about two hundred in a year, which was thought to be a great number.

My guardian, a good old man, told me that there was so many clocks then making, that the country would soon be filled with them, and the business would be good for nothing in two or three years. This opinion of that wise man made me feel very sad. I well remember, when I was about twelve years old, what I heard some old gentleman say, at a training, (all of the good folks in those days were as sure to go to training as to attend church,) they were talking about Mr. Terry; the foolish man they said, had begun to make two hundred clocks; one said, he never would live long enough to finish them; another remarked, that if he did he never would, nor could possibly sell so many, and ridiculed the very idea.

I was a little fellow, but heard and swallowed every word those wise men said, but I did not relish it at all, for I meant some day to make clocks myself, if I lived.

What would those good old men have thought when they were laughing at and ridiculing Mr. Terry, if they had known that the little urchin who was so eagerly listening to their conversation would live to make *Two Hundred Thousand* metal clocks in one year, and *many millions* in his life. They have probably been dead for years, that little boy is now an old man, and during his life has seen these great changes. The clock business has grown to be one of the largest in the country, and almost every kind of American manufactures have improved in much the same ratio, and I cannot now believe that there will ever be in the same space of future time so many improvements and inventions as those of the past half century—one of the most important in the history of the world. Everyday things with us now would have appeared to our forefathers as incredible. But returning to my story—having got myself tolerably well posted about clocks at Waterbury, I hired myself to two men to go into the state of New Jersey, to make the old fashioned seven foot standing clock-case. Messrs. Hotchkiss and Pierpont, of Plymouth, had been selling that kind of a clock without the cases, in the northern part of that State, for about twenty dollars, apiece. The purchasers, had complained to them however, that there was no one in that region that could make the case for them, which prevented many others from buying. These two men whom I went with, told them that they would get some one to go out from Connecticut, to make the case, and thought they could be made for about eighteen or twenty dollars a piece, which would then make the whole clock cost about forty dollars—not so very costly after all; for a clock was then considered the most useful of anything that could be had in a family, for what it cost. I entered into an agreement with these men at once, and a few days after, we three started on the 14th Dec., 1812, in an old lumber wagon, with provisions for the journey, to the far off Jersey. This same trip can now be made in a few hours. We were *many* days. We passed through Watertown, and other villages, and stopped the first night at Bethel. This is the very place where P. T. Barnum was born, and at about this time, of whom I shall speak more particularly hereafter. The next morning we started again on our journey, and not many hours after, arrived in Norwalk, then quite a small village, situated on Long Island Sound; at this place I saw the salt water for the first time in my life, also a small rowboat, and began to feel that I was a great traveler indeed. The following night we stopped at Stamford, which was, as I viewed it, a great place; here I saw a few sloops on the Sound, which I thought was the greatest sight that I had ever seen. This was years before a steamboat had ever passed through the Sound. The next morning we started again for New York, and as we passed along I was more and more astonished at the wonderful things that I saw, and began to think that the world was very extensive. We did not arrive at the city until night, but there being a full moon every thing appeared as pleasant, as in the day-time. We passed down through the Bowery, which was then like a country village, then through Chatham street to Pearl street, and stopped for the night at a house kept by old Mr. Titus. I arose early the next morning and hurried into the street to see how a city looked by day-light. I stood on the corner of Chatham and Pearl for more than an hour, and I must confess that if I was ever astonished in my life, it was at that time. I could not understand why so many people, of every age, description and dress, were hurrying so in every direction. I asked a man what was going on, and what all this excitement meant, but he passed right along without noticing me, which I thought was very uncivil, and I formed a very poor opinion of those city folks. I ate nothing that morning, for I thought I could be in better business for a while at least. I wandered about gazing at the many new sights, and went out as far as the Park; at that time the workmen were finishing the interior of the City Hall. I was greatly puzzled to know how the winding stone stairs could be fixed without any seeming support and yet be perfectly safe. After viewing many sights, all of which were exceedingly interesting to me, I returned to the house where my companions were. They told me that they had just heard that the ship Macedonian, which was taken a few days before from the British by one of our ships, had just been brought into the harbor and lay off down by Burling Slip, or in that region. We went down to see her, and went on board. I was surprised and frightened to see brains and blood scattered about on the deck in every direction. This prize was taken by the gallant Decatur, but a short distance from New York. Hastening back from this sickening scene, we resumed our journey. . . .[1]

A young man from the lower part of New Jersey worked with me all winter. We boarded ourselves in the same building that we worked in, I doing all of the house-work and cooking, none of which was very fine or fancy, our principal food being pork, potatoes and bread, using our work-bench for a table. Hard work gave us good appetite. We would work on an average about fifteen hours a day, the house-work not occupying much of our time. I was then only nineteen years old, and it hardly seems possible that the boys of the present day could pass through such trials and hardships, and live. We worked in this way all winter. When the job was finished, I took my little budget of clothes and started for home. I traveled the first day as far as Elizabethtown, and stopped there all night, but found no conveyance from there to New York. I was told that if I would go down to the Point, I might in the course of the day, get a passage in a sailing vessel to the city. I went down early in the morning and, after waiting till noon, found a chance to go with two men in a small sail boat. I was greatly alarmed at the strange motions of the boat which I thought would upset, and felt greatly relieved when I was again on terra firma.

---

1. Stephen Decatur was a hero of the War of 1812, after his capture of the British ship *Macedonian* in the fall of 1812.

I wandered about the streets of New York all that afternoon, bought a quantity of bread and cheese, and engaged a passage on the Packet Sloop Eliza, for New Haven, of her Captain Zebulon Bradley. I slept on board of her that night at the dock, the next day we set sail for New Haven, about ten o'clock in the forenoon, with a fair wind, and arrived at the long wharf in (that city) about eight o'clock the same day. I stopped at John Howe's Hotel, at the head of the wharf. This was the first time that I was ever in this beautiful city, and I little thought then that I ever should live there, working at my favorite business, with three hundred men in my employ, or that I should ever be its Mayor.—Times change.

Very early the next morning, after looking about a little, I started with my bundle of clothes in one hand, and my bread and cheese in the other, to find the Waterbury turnpike, and after dodging about for a long time, succeeded in finding it, and passed on up through Waterbury to Plymouth, walking the whole distance, and arrived home about three o'clock in the afternoon. This was my first trip abroad, and I really felt that I was a great traveler, one who had seen much of the world! What a great change has taken place in so short space of time.

Soon after I returned from my western trip, there began to be a great excitement throughout the land, about the war. It was proposed by the Governor of Connecticut, John Cotton Smith, of Sharon, to raise one or two regiments of State troops to defend it in case of invasion. One Company of one hundred men, was raised in [the] towns of Waterbury, Watertown, Middlebury, Plymouth and Bethlem, and John Buckingham chosen Captain, who is now living in Waterbury; the other commissioned officers of the company, were Jas. M. L. Scovill, of Waterbury, and Joseph H. Bellamy, of Bethlem. The company being composed of young men, and I being about the right age, had of course to be one of them.

Early in the Summer of 1813, the British fleet ran two of our ships of war up the Thames River, near New London. Their ships being so large could not enter, but lay at its mouth. Their presence so near greatly alarmed the citizens of that city, and in fact, all of the people in the eastern part of the State. Our regiment was ordered to be ready to start for New London by the first of August. The Plymouth company was called together on Sunday, which was the first of August, and exercised on the Green in front of the church, in the fore part of the day. This unusual occurrence of a military display on the Sabbath greatly alarmed the good people of the congregation, but it really was a case of necessity, we were preparing to defend our homes from a foreign foe. . . .

I soon became sick and disgusted with a soldier's life; it seemed to be too lazy and low-lived to suit me, and as near as I could judge, the inhabitants thought us all a low set of fellows. I never have had a desire to live or be anywhere without I could be considered at least as good as the average, which failing I have now as strong as ever. We not having any battles to fight, had no opportunities of showing our bravery, and after guarding the city for forty-five days, were discharged; over which we made a great rejoicing, and returned home by the way of New Haven, which was my second visit to this city. The North and Centre Churches were then building, also, the house now standing at the North-east corner of the Green, owned then by David DeForest; stopping here over night, we passed on home to Plymouth. I had not slept on a bed since I left home, and would have as soon taken the barn floor as a good bed. This ended my first campaign.

After this I went to work at my trade, the Joiners business. I was still an apprentice; would not be twenty-one till the next June. . . .

All of the old people will remember what a great rejoicing there was through the whole country, when peace was declared in February, 1815. I was married about that time to Salome Smith, daughter of Capt. The-ophilus Smith, one of the last of the Puritanical families there was in the town; she made one of the best of wives and mothers. She died on the 6th of March, 1854. We lived together 39 years. A short time after we were married, I moved to the town of Farmington, and hired a house of Mr. Chauncey Deming to live in, and went to work for Capt. Selah Por-ter, for twenty dollars per month. We built a house for Maj. Timothy Cowles, which was then the best one in Farmington. I was not worth at this time fifty dollars in the world.

1815, the year after the war, was, probably the hardest one there has been for the last hundred years, for a young man to begin for him-self. Pork was sold for thirteen dollars per hundred, flour at thirteen dollars per barrel; Molasses was sold for seventy-five cents per gallon, and brown Sugar at thirty-four cents per pound. I remember buying some cotton cloth for a common shirt, for which I paid one dollar a yard, not better than can now be bought for ten cents. I mention these things to let the young men know what a great change has taken place, and what my prospects were at that time. Not liking this place, I moved back to Plymouth. I did not have money enough to pay my rent, which however, was not due until the next May, but Mr. Deming, who by the way, was one of the richest men in the State, was determined that I should not go till I had paid him. I promised him that he should have the money when it was due, if my life was spared, and he finally consented to let me go. When it came due I walked to Farmington, fifteen miles, paid him and walked back the same day, feeling relieved and happy. I obtained the job of finishing the inside of a dwelling house, which gave me great encouragement. The times were awful hard and but little business done at anything. It would almost frighten a man to see a five-dollar bill, they were so very scarce. My work was about two miles from where I lived. My wife was confined about this time with her first babe. I would rise every morning two hours before day-light and prepare my breakfast, and taking my dinner in a little pail, bid my good wife good-bye for the day, and start for my work, not returning till night. About this time the Congregational Society employed a celebrated music teacher to conduct the church singing, and I having always had a desire to sing sacred music, joined his choir and would walk a long distance to attend the singing schools at night after working hard all day. I was chosen chorister after a few weeks, which encouraged me very much in the way of singing, and was afterwards employed as a teacher to some extent, and for a long time led the singing there and at Bristol where I afterwards lived. The next summer was the cold one of 1816, which none of the old people will ever forget, and which many of the young have heard a great deal about. There was ice and snow in every month in the year. I well remember on the seventh of June, while on my way to work, about a mile from home, dressed throughout with thick woolen clothes and an overcoat on, my hands got so cold that I was obliged to lay down my tools and put on a pair of mittens which I had in my pocket. . . .

At the beginning of this book I have said that I would give to the public a history of the American Clock Business. I am now the oldest man living that has had much to do with the manufacturing of clocks, and can, I believe, give a more correct account than any other person. This great business has grown almost from nothing during my remembrance. Nearly all of the clocks used in this country are made or have been made in the small State of Connecticut, and a heavy trade in them is carried on in foreign countries. The business or manufacture of them has become so systemized of late that it has brought the prices exceedingly low, and it has long been the astonishment of the whole world how they could be made so cheap and yet be good. A gentleman called at my factory a few years ago, when I was carrying on the business, who said he lived in London, and had seen my clocks in that city, and declared that he was perfectly astonished at the price of them, and had often remarked that if he ever came to this country he would visit the Factory and see for himself. After I had showed him all the different processes it required to complete a clock, he expressed himself in the strongest terms—he told me he had traveled a great deal in Europe, and had taken a great interest in all kinds of manufactures, but had never seen anything equal to this, and did not believe that there was anything made in the known world that made as much show, and at the same time was as cheap and useful as the brass clock which I was then manufacturing.

The man above all others in his day for the wood clock was Eli Terry. He was born in East Windsor, Conn., in April, 1772, and made a few old fashioned hang-up clocks in his native place before he was twenty-one years of age. He was a young man of great ingenuity and good native talent. He moved to the town of Plymouth, Litchfield County, in 1793, and commenced making a few of the same kind, working alone for several years. About the year 1800, he might have had a boy or one or two young men to help him. They would begin one or two dozen at a time, using no machinery, but cutting the wheels and teeth with a saw and jack-knife. Mr. Terry would make two or three trips a year to the New Country, as it was then called, just across the North River, taking with him three or four clocks, which he would sell for about twenty-five dollars apiece. This was for the movement only. In 1807 he bought an old mill in the southern park of the town, and fitted it up to make his clocks by machinery. About this time a number of men in Waterbury associated themselves together, and made a large contract with him, they furnishing the stock, and he making the movements. With this contract and what he made and sold to other parties, he accumulated quite a little fortune for those times. The first five hundred clocks ever made by machinery in the country were started at one time by Mr. Terry at this old mill in 1808, a larger number than had ever been begun at one time in the world. Previous to this time the wheels and teeth had been cut out by hand; first marked out with square and compasses, and then sawed with a fine saw, a very slow and tedious process. Capt. Riley Blakeslee, of this city, lived with Mr. Terry at the time, and worked on his lot of clocks, cutting the teeth. Talking with Capt. Blakeslee a few days since, he related an incident which happened when he was a boy, sixty years ago, and lived on a farm in Litchfield. One day Mr. Terry came to the house where he lived to sell a clock. The man with whom young Blakeslee lived, left him to plow the field and went to the house to make a bargain for it, which he did, paying Mr. Terry in salt pork, a part of which he carried home in his saddle-bags where he had carried the clock. He was at that time very poor, but twenty-five years after was worth $200,000, all of which he made in the clock business. . . .

In 1818, Joseph Ives invented a metal clock, making the plates of iron and the wheels of brass. The movement was very large, and required a case about five feet long. This style was made for two or three years, but not in large quantities.

In the year 1825, the writer invented a new case, somewhat larger than the Scroll Top, which was called the Bronze Looking-Glass Clock. This was the richest looking and best clock that had ever been made, for the price. They could be got up for one dollar less than the Scroll Top, yet sold for two dollars more.

I must now go back and give a history of myself, from the winter of 1816, to this (1825). As I said before, I went to work for Mr. Terry, making the Patent Shelf Clock in the winter of 1816. Mr. Thomas had been making them for about two years, doing nearly all of the labor on the case by hand. Mr. Terry in the mean time being a great mechanic had made many improvements in the way of making the cases. Under his directions I worked a long time at putting up machinery and benches. We had a circular saw, the first one in the town, and which was considered a great curiosity. In the course of the winter he drew another plan of the Pillar Scroll Top Case with great improvements over the one which Thomas was then making. I made the first one of the new style that was ever produced in that factory, which became so celebrated for making the patent case for more than ten years after.

When my time was out in the spring, I bought some parts of clocks, mahogany, veneers, etc., and commenced in a small shop, business for myself. I made the case, and bought the movements, dials and glass, finishing a few at a time. I found a ready sale for them. I went on in this small way for a few years, feeling greatly animated with my prosperity, occasionally making a payment on my little house. I heard one day of a man in Bristol, who did business in South Carolina, who wanted to buy a few clocks to take to that market with him. I started at once over to see him, and soon made a bargain with him to deliver twelve wood clocks at twelve dollars apiece. I returned home greatly encouraged by the large order, and went right to work on them. I had them finished and boxed ready for shipping in a short time. I had agreed to deliver them on a certain day and was to receive $144 in cash. I hired an old horse and lumber wagon of one of my neighbors, loaded the boxes and took an early start for Bristol. I was thinking all the way there of the large sum that I was to receive, and was fearful that something might happen to disappoint me. I arrived at Bristol early in the forenoon and hurried to the house of my customer, and told him I had brought the clocks as agreed. He said nothing but went into another room with his son. I thought surely that something was wrong and that I should not get the wished-for money, but after a while the old gentleman came back and sat down by the table. "Here," he says, "is your money, and a heap of it, too." It did look to me like a large sum, and took us a long time to count it. This was more than forty years ago, and money was very scarce. I took it with a trembling hand, and securing it safely in my pocket, started immediately for home. This was a larger sum than I had ever had at one time, and I was much alarmed for fear that I should be robbed of my treasure before I got home. I thought perhaps it might be known that I was to receive a large sum for clocks, and that some robbers might be watching in a lonely part of the road and take it from me, but not meeting any, I arrived safely home, feeling greatly encouraged and happy. I told my wife that I would make another payment on our house which I did with a great deal of satisfaction. After this I was so anxious to get along with my work that I did not so much as go out into the street for a week at a time. I would not go out of the gate from the time I returned from church one Sunday till the next. I loved to work as well as I did to eat. I remember once, when at school, of chopping a whole load of wood, for a great lazy boy, for one penny, and I used to chop all the wood I could get from the families in the neighborhood, moonlight nights, for very small sums. The winter after I made this large sale, I took about one dozen of the Pillar Scroll Top Clocks, and went to the town of Wethersfield to sell them. I hired a man to carry me over there with a lumber wagon, who returned home. I would take one of these clocks under each arm and go from house to house and offer them for sale. The people seemed to be well pleased with them, and I sold them for eighteen dollars apiece. This was good luck for me. I sold my last one on Saturday afternoon. There had been a fall of snow the night before of about eight or ten inches which ended in a rain, and made very bad walking. Here I was, twenty-five miles from home, my wife was expecting me, and I felt that I could not stay over Sunday. I was anxious to tell my family of my good luck that we might rejoice together. I started to walk the whole distance, but it proved to be the hardest physical undertaking that I ever experienced. It was bedtime when I reached Farmington, only one-third the distance, wallowing in snow porridge all the way. I did not reach home till near Sunday morning, more dead than alive. I did not go to church that day, which made many wonder what had become of me, for I was always expected to be in the singers' seat on Sunday. I did not recover from the effects of that night-journey for a long time. Soon after this occurrence, I began to increase my little business, and employed my old joiner "boss" and one of his apprentices: bought my mahogany in the plank and sawed my own veneers with a hand-saw. I engaged a man with a one horse wagon to go to New York after a load of mahogany, and went with him to select it. The roads were very muddy, and we were obliged to walk the whole distance home by the side of the wagon. I worked along in this small way until the year 1821, when I sold my house and lot, which I almost worshipped, to Mr. Terry: it was worth six hundred dollars. He paid me one hundred wood clock movements, with the dials, tablets, glass and weights. I went over to Bristol to see a man by the name of George Mitchell, who owned a large two story house, with a barn and seventeen acres of good land in the southern part of the town, which he said he would sell and take his pay in clocks. I asked him how many of the Terry Patent Clocks he would sell it for; he said two hundred and fourteen. I told him I would give it, and closed the bargain at once. I finished up the hundred parts which I had got from Mr. Terry, exchanged cases with him for more, obtained some credit, and in this way made out the quantity for Mitchell. . . .

In the winter and spring of 1822, I built a small shop in Bristol, for making the cases only, as all of the others made the movements. The first circular saw ever used there was put up by myself in 1822, and this was the commencement of making cases by machinery in that town, which has since been so renowned for its clock productions. I went on making cases in a small way for a year or two, sometimes putting in a few movements and selling them, but not making much money. The clocks of Terry and Thomas sold first rate, and it was quite difficult to buy any of the movements, as no others were making the Patent Clock at that time. I was determined to have some movements to case, and went to Chauncey Boardman, who had formerly made the old fashioned hang-up movements, and told him I wanted him to make me two hundred of his kind with such alterations as I should suggest. He said he would make them for me. I had them altered and made so as to take a case about four feet long, which I made out of pine, richly stained and varnished. This made a good clock for time and suited farmers first rate.

In the spring of 1824, I went into company with two men by the name of Peck, from Bristol. We took two hundred of these movements and a few tools in two one horse wagons and started East, intending to stop in the vicinity of Boston. We stopped at a place about fifteen miles from there called East Randolph; after looking about a little, we concluded to start our business there and hired a joiners' shop of John Adams, a cousin of J. Q. Adams. We then went to Boston and bought a load of lumber, and commenced operations. I was the case-maker of our concern, and "pitched into" the pine lumber in good earnest. I began four cases at a time and worked like putting out fire on them. My partners were waiting for some to be finished so that they could go out and sell. In two or three days I had got them finished and they started with them, and I began four more. In a day or two they returned home having sold them at sixteen dollars *each.* This good fortune animated me very much. I worked about fourteen or fifteen hours per day, and could make about four cases and put in the glass, movements and dials. We worked on in this way until we had finished up the two hundred, and sold them at an average of sixteen dollars apiece. We had done well and returned home with joyful hearts in the latter part of June. On arriving home I found my little daughter about five years old quite sick. In a week after she died. I deeply felt the loss of my little daughter, and every 7th of July it comes fresh into my mind.

In the fall of 1824, I formed a company with my brother, Noble Jerome, and Elijah Darrow, for the manufacturing of clocks, and began making a movement that required a case about six or eight inches longer than the Terry Patent. We did very well at this for a year or two, during which time I invented the Bronze Looking Glass Clock, which soon revolutionized the whole business. As I have said before, it could be made for one dollar less and sold for two dollars more than the Patent Case: they were very showy and a little longer. With the introduction of this clock in the year 1825, closed the second chapter of the history of the Yankee Clock business.

With the introduction of the Bronze Looking Glass Clock, the business seemed to revive in all the neighboring towns, but more especially in Plymouth and Bristol. Both Mr. Terry and Mr. Thomas, did and said much in disparagement of my new invention, and tried to discourage the pedlars from buying of me, but they did as men do now-a-days, buy where they can do the best and make the most money. This new clock was liked very much in the southern market. I have heard of some of these being sold in Mississippi and Louisiana as high as one hundred and one hundred and fifteen dollars, and a great many at ninety dollars, which was a good advance on the first cost. . . .

Samuel Terry, a brother of Eli, came to Bristol about this time, and commenced making this kind of clock.

Several others began to make them—Geo. Mitchell and his brother-in-law Rollin Atkins went into it, also Riley Whiting of Winsted. The business increased very rapidly between 1827 and 1837. During these ten years Jeromes and Darrow made more than any other company. The two towns of Plymouth and Bristol grew and improved very rapidly; many new houses were built, and every thing looked prosperous. . . .

About this time, also, Chauncey and Lawson C. Ives, two highly respectable men, built a factory in Bristol for the purpose of making an eight day brass clock. This clock was invented by Joseph Ives, a brother of Chauncey, and sold for about twenty dollars. The manufacture of these was carried on very successfully for a few years by them, but in 1836, their business was closed up, they having made about one hundred thousand dollars. Soon after this, in 1837, came the great panic and break-down of business which extended all over the country. Clock makers and almost every one else stopped business. I should mention that another company made the eight day brass clock previous to 1837,

Erastus and Harvey Case and John Birge. Their clocks were retailed mostly in the southern market. They made perhaps four thousand a year. . . .

In 1835, the southern people were greatly opposed to the Yankee pedlars coming into their states, especially the clock pedlars, and the licenses were raised so high by their Legislatures that it amounted to almost a prohibition. Their laws were that any goods made in their own States could be sold without license. Therefore clocks to be profitable must be made in those states. Chauncey and Noble Jerome started a factory in Richmond, Va., making the cases and parts at Bristol, Connecticut, and packing them with the dials, glass &c. We shipped them to Richmond and took along workmen to put them together. The people were highly pleased with the idea of having clocks all made in their State. The old planters would tell the pedlars they meant to go to Richmond and see the wonderful machinery there must be to produce such articles and would no doubt have thought the tools we had there were sufficient to make a clock. We carried on this kind of business for two or three years and did very well at it, though it was unpleasant. Every one knew it was all a humbug trying to stop the pedlars from coming to their State. We removed from Richmond to Hamburg, S.C. and manufactured in the same way. This was in 1835 and '36.

There was another company doing the same kind of business at Augusta, Geo., by the name Case, Dyer, Wadsworth & Co., and Seth Thomas was making the cases and movements for them. The hard times came down on us and we really thought that clocks would no longer be made. Our firm thought we could make them if any body could, but like the others felt discouraged and disgusted with the whole business as it was then. I am sure that I had lost, from 1821 to this time, more than one hundred thousand *dollars*, and felt very much discouraged in consequence. Our company had a good deal of unsettled business in Virginia and South Carolina, and started in the fall of 1837 for those places. Arriving at Richmond, I had a strong notion of going into the marl business. I had been down into Kent county, the summer before, where I saw great mountains of this white marl composed of shells of clams and oysters white as chalk. I had sent one vessel load of this to New Haven the year before. At Richmond I was looking after our old accounts, settling up, collecting notes and picking up some scattered clocks.

One night I took one of those clocks into my room and placing it on the table, left a light burning near it and went to bed. While thinking over my business troubles and disappointments, I could not help feeling very much depressed. I said to myself I will not give up yet, I know more about the clock business than anything else. That minute I was looking at the wood clock on the table and it came into my mind instantly that there could be a cheap one day brass clock that would take the place of the wood clock. I at once began to figure on it; the case would cost no more, the dials, glass, and weights and other fixtures would be the same, and the size could be reduced. I lay awake nearly all night thinking this new thing over. I knew there was a fortune in it. Many a sensible man has since told me that if I could have secured the sole right for making them for ten years, I could easily have made a million of dollars. The more I looked at this new plan, the better it appeared. My business took me to South Carolina before I could return home. I had now enough to think of day and night; this one day brass clock was constantly on my mind; I was drawing plans and contriving how they could be made best. I traveled most of the way from Richmond by stage. Arriving at Augusta, Geo., I called on the Connecticut men who were finishing wood clocks for the market, and told Mr. Dyer the head man, that I had got up, or could get up something when I got home that would run out all the wood clocks in the country, Thomas's and all; he laughed at me quite heartily. I told him that was all right, and asked him to come to Bristol when he went home and I would show him something that would astonish him. He promised that he would, and during the next summer when he called at my place, I showed him a shelf full of them running, which he acknowledged to be the best he had ever seen.

I arrived home from the south the 28th of January, and told my brother who was a first-rate clock maker what I had been thinking about since I had been gone. He was much pleased with my plan, thought it a first rate idea, and said he would go right to work and get up the movement, which he perfected in a short time so that it was the best clock that had ever been made in this or any other country. There have been more of this same kind manufactured than of any other in the United States. What I originated that night on my bed in Richmond, has given work to thousands of men yearly for more than twenty years, built up the largest manufactories in New England, and put more than a million of dollars into the pockets of the brass makers,—"but there is not one of them that remembers *Joseph.*"

We went on very prosperously making the new clock, and it was admired by every body. In the year 1839, some of my neighbors and a few of my leading workmen had a great desire to get into the same kind of business. We knew competition amongst Yankees was almost sure to kill business and proposed to have them come in with us and have a share of the profits. An arrangement to this effect was made and we went on in this way until the fall of 1840. I found they were much annoyance and bother to me, and so bought them all out, but had to give them one hundred per cent, for the use of their money. Some of them had not paid in anything, but I had to pay them the same profits I did the rest, to get rid of them. One man had put in three thousand dollars for which I paid him six thousand. I also bought out my brother Noble Jerome, who had been in company with me for a long time, and carried on the whole business alone, which seemed to be rapidly improving.

I made in 1841, thirty-five thousand dollars clear profits. Men would come and deposit money with me before their orders were finished. This successful state of things set all of the wood clock makers half crazy, and they went into it one after another as fast as they could, and of course ran down the price very fast—"Yankee-like." I had been thinking for two or three years of introducing my clocks into England, and had availed myself of every opportunity to get posted on that subject; when I met Englishmen in New York and other places, I would try to find out by them what the prospects would be for selling Yankee clocks in their country. I ascertained that there were no cheap metal clocks used or known there, the only cheap timepiece they had was a Dutch hand-up wood clock.

In 1842, I determined to make the venture of sending a consignment of brass clocks to Old England. I made a bargain with Epaphroditus Peck, a very talented young man of Bristol, a son of Hon. Tracy Peck, to take them out, and sent my son Chauncey Jerome, Jr., with him. All of the first cargo consisted of the O.G. one day brass clocks. As soon as it was known by the neighboring clock-makers, they laughed at me, and ridiculed the idea of sending clocks to England where labor was so cheap. They said that they never would interfere with Jerome in that visionary project, but no sooner had I got them well introduced, after spending thousands of dollars to effect it, than they had all forgotten what they said about my folly, and one after another sent over the same goods to compete with me and run down the price. As I have said before, wood clocks could never have been exported to Europe from this country, for many reasons. They would have been laughed at, and looked upon with suspicion as coming from the wooden nutmeg country, and classed as the same. They could not endure a long voyage across the water without swelling the parts and rendering them useless as time-keepers; experience had taught us this, as many wood clocks on a passage to the southern market, had been rendered unfit for use for this very reason. Metal clocks can be sent any where without injury. Millions have been sent to Europe, Asia, South America, Australia, Palestine, and in fact, to every part of the world; and millions of dollars brought into this country by this means, and I think it not unfair to claim the honor of inventing and introducing this low-price time-piece which has given employment to so many of our countrymen, and has also, been so useful to the world at large. No family is so poor but that they can have a time-piece which is both useful and ornamental. They can be found in every civilized portion of the globe. Meeting a sea captain one day, he told me that on landing at the lonely island of St. Helena, the first thing that he noticed on entering a house, was my name on the face of a brass clock. Many years ago a missionary (Mr. Ruggles,) at the Sandwich Islands, told me that he had one of my clocks in his house, the first one that had ever been on the islands. Travelers have mentioned seeing them in the city of Jerusalem, in many parts of Egypt, and in fact, every where, which accounts could not but be interesting and gratifying to me.

It was a long and tedious undertaking to introduce my first cargo in England. Mr. Peck and my son wrote me a great many times the first year, that they never could be sold there, the prejudice against American manufactures was so great that they would not buy them. Although very much discouraged, I kept writing them to "stick to it." They were once turned out of a store in London and threatened if they offered their "Yankee clocks" again to the English people "who made clocks for the world;" "they were good for nothing or they could not be offered so cheap." They were finally introduced in this way; the young men persuaded a merchant to take two into his store for sale. He reluctantly gave his consent, saying he did not believe they would run at all; they set the two running and left the price of them. On calling the next day to see how they were getting along, and what the London merchant thought of them, they were surprised to find them both gone. On asking what had become of them, they were told that two men came in and liked their looks and bought them. The merchant said he did not think any one would ever buy them, but told them they might bring in four more; "I will see" he says, "if I can sell any *more* of your Yankee clocks." They carried them in and calling the next day, found them all gone. The merchant then told them to bring in a dozen. These went off in a short time, and not long after, this same merchant bought two hundred at once, and other merchants began to think they could make some money on these Yankee clocks and the business began to improve very rapidly. There are always men enough who are ready to enter into a business after it is started and looks favorable. A pleasing incident occurred soon after we first started. The Revenue laws of England are (or were, at that time) that the owner of property passing through the Custom-house shall put such a price on his goods as he pleases, knowing that the government officers have a right to take the property by adding ten per cent to the invoiced price.

I had always told my young men over there to put a fair price on the clocks, which they did; but the officers thought they put them altogether too low, so they made up their minds that they would take a lot, and seized one ship-load, thinking we would put the prices of the next cargo at higher rates. They paid the cash for this cargo, which made a good sale for us. A few days after, another invoice arrived which our folks entered at the same prices as before; but they were again taken by the officers paying us cash and ten percent, in addition, which was very satisfactory to us. On the arrival of the third lot, they began to think they had better let the Yankees sell their own goods and passed them through unmolested and came to the conclusion that we could make clocks much better and cheaper than their own people. Their performance has been considered a first-rate joke to say the least. There will, in all probability, be millions of clocks sold in that country, and we are the people who will furnish all Europe with all their common cheap ones as long as time lasts. . . .

In the winter of 1844, I moved to the city of New Haven with the expectation of making my cases there. I had fitted up two large factories in Bristol for making brass movements only the year before, and had spared no pains to have them just right. My factory in New Haven was fitted up expressly for making the cases and boxing the finished clocks; the movements were packed, one hundred in a box, and sent to New

Haven where they were cased and shipped. Business moved on very prosperously for about one year. On the 23rd of April 1845, about the middle of the afternoon one of my factories in Bristol took fire, as it was supposed by some boys playing with matches at the back side of the building, which set fire to some shavings under the floor. It seemed impossible to put it out and it proved to be the most disastrous fire that ever occurred in a country town. There were seven or eight buildings destroyed, together with all the machinery for making clocks, which was very costly and extensive. There were somewhere between fifty and seventy-five thousand brass movements in the works, a large number of them finished, and worth one dollar apiece. The loss was about fifty thousand dollars and the insurance only ten thousand. This was another dark day for me. I had been very sick all winter with the Typhus fever, and from Christmas to April had not been able to go to Bristol. On the same night of the fire, a man came to tell me of the great loss. I was in another part of the house when he arrived with the message, but my wife did not think it prudent to inform me then, but in the latter part of the night she introduced a conversation that was calculated to prepare my mind for the sad news, and in a certain manner informed me. . . .

It was hard indeed to grapple with so much in one year, but I tried to make the best of it and to feel that these trials, troubles and disappointments sent upon us in this world, are blessings in disguise. Oh! if we could really feel this to be so in all of our troubles, it would be well for us in this world and better in the next. I never have seen the real total depravity of the human heart show itself more plainly or clearly than it did when my factories were destroyed by fire. An envious feeling had always been exhibited by others in the same business towards me, and those who had made the most out of my improvements and had injured my reputation by making an inferior article, were the very ones who rejoiced the most then. Not a single man of them ever did or could look me in the face and say that I had ever injured him. This feeling towards me was all because I was in their way and my clocks at that time were preferred before any others. They really thought I never could start again, and many said that Jerome would never make any more clocks. I learned this maxim long ago, that when a man injures another unreasonably, to act out human nature he has got to keep on misrepresenting and abusing him to make himself appear right in the sight of the world. Soon after the fire in Bristol I had gained my strength sufficiently to go ahead again, and commenced to make additions to my case factory in New Haven (to make the movements,) and by the last of June was ready to commence operations on the brass movements. I then brought my men from Bristol—the movement makers—and a noble set of men as ever came to New Haven at one time. Look at John Woodruff; he was a young man then of nineteen. When he first came to work for me at the age of fifteen, I believed that he was destined to be a leading man. He is now in Congress (elected for the second time,) honest, kind, gentlemanly, and respected in Congress and out of Congress. Look at him, young men, and pattern after him, you can see in his case what honesty, industry and perseverance will accomplish.

There was great competition in the business for several years after I moved to New Haven, and a great many poor clocks made. The business of selling greatly increased in New York, and within three or four years after I introduced the one day brass clock, several companies in Bristol and Plymouth commenced making them. Most of them manufactured an inferior article of movement, but found sale for great numbers of them to parties that were casing clocks in New York. This way of managing proved to be a great damage to the Connecticut clock makers. The New York men would buy the poorest movements and put them into cheap O.G. cases and undersell us. Merchants from the country, about this time, began to buy clocks with their other goods. They had heard about Jerome's clocks which had been retailed about the country, and that they were good time-keepers, and would enquire for my clocks. . . .

Since I began to make clocks, the price has gradually been going down. Suppose the cheap time-keeper had been invented thirty years ago, when folks felt as though they could not have a clock because it cost so much, but must get along with a watch which cost ten or fifteen dollars, what would the good people have thought if they could have had a clock for one dollar, or even less? This cheap clock is much better adapted to the many log cabins and cheap dwellings in our country than a watch of any kind, and it is not half so costly or difficult to keep in order. I can think of nothing ever invented that has been so useful to so many. We do not fully appreciate the value of such things. I have often thought, that if all the time-pieces were taken out of the country at once, and every factory stopped making them, the whole community would be brought to see the incalculable value that this Yankee clock making is to them. . . .

After saying so much as I have about my misfortunes in life, I must say a few words about what has happened and what I have been through with during the last four years.

When the Jerome Manufacturing Company failed, every dollar that I had saved out of a long life of toil and labor was not enough to support my family for one year.[2] It was hard indeed for a man sixty-three years old, and my heart sickened at the prospect ahead. Perhaps there never was a man that wanted more than I did to be in business and be somebody by the side of my neighbors. There never was a man more grieved than I was when I had to give up those splendid factories with the great facilities they had over all others in the world for the manufacture of clocks both good and cheap, all of which had been effected through my untiring efforts. NO one but myself can know what my feelings were when I was compelled, through no fault of my own, to leave the splendid cluster of buildings with all its machinery, and its thousands of good customers all over this country and Europe, and in fact the whole world, which in itself was a fortune. And then to leave that beautiful mansion at the head of the New Haven bay, which I had almost worshipped. I say to leave all these things for others, with that spirit and pride that still remained within me, and at my time of life, was almost too much for flesh and blood to bear. What could have been the feelings of my family, and my large circle of friends and acquaintances, to see creditors and officers coming to our house every day with their pockets full of attachments and piles of them on the table every night. If any one can ever begin to know my feelings at this time, they must have passed through the same experience. Yet mortified and abused as I was, I had to put up with it. Thank God, I have never been the means of such trouble for others. . . .

When I first saw this city in 1812, its population was less than five thousand, and it looked to me like a country town. I wandered about the streets early one morning with a bundle of clothes and some bread and cheese in my hands little dreaming that I should live to see so great a change, or that it ever would be my home. I remember seeing the loads of wood and chips for family use lying in the front of the houses, and

---

2. The Jerome Manufacturing Company failed in 1855 after a disastrous merger with its competitor, Terry and Barnum.

acres of land then in cornfields and valued at a small sum, [which] are now covered with fine buildings and stores and factories in about the heart of the city.

When I moved my case making business to New Haven, the project was ridiculed by other clock-makers of getting to a city to manufacture by steam power, and yet it seems to have been the commencement of manufacturers in the country, coming to New Haven to carry on their business. Numbers came to me to get my opinion and learn the advantages it had over manufacturing in the country, which I always informed them in a heavy business was very great, the item of transportation alone over-balancing the difference between water and steam power. The facilities for procuring stock and of shipping, being also an important item. Not one of the good citizens will deny that this great business of clock-making which I first brought to New Haven has been of immense advantage and of great importance to the city. Through its agency millions of money has been brought here, adding materially to the general prosperity and I have been told that there is nothing in the eastern world that attracts the attention of the inhabitants like a Yankee Clock. It has this moment come into my mind of several years ago giving a dozen brass clocks to a missionary in Jerusalem; they were shipped from London to Alexandria in Egypt, from there to Joppa, and thence about forty miles on the backs of Camels to Jerusalem, where they arrived safe to the great joy of the missionary and others interested, and attracted a great deal of attention and admiration. I also sent my clocks to China, and two men to introduce them more than twenty years ago.

I will here say what I truly believe as to the future of this business; there is no place on the earth where it can be started and compete with New Haven, there are no other factories where they can possibly be made so cheap. I have heard men ask the question, "why can't clocks be made in Europe on such a scale, where labor is so cheap?" If a company could in any part of the old world get their labor ten years for nothing. I do not believe they could compete with the Yankees in this business. They can be made in New Haven and sent into any part of the world for more than a hundred years to come for less than one half of what they could be made for in any part of the old world. I was many years in systematizing this business, and these things I know to be facts, though it might appear as strong language. No man has ever lived that has given so much time and attention to this subject as myself. For more than fifty years by day and by night, clocks have been uppermost in my mind. The ticking of a clock is music to me, and although many of my experiences as a business man have been trying and bitter, I have the satisfaction of knowing that I have lived the life of an honest man, and have been of some use to my fellow men.

$\mathcal{A}$LLEN $\mathcal{T}$RIMBLE

$1\ 7\ 8\ 3-1\ 8\ 7\ 0$

$\mathcal{A}$ L L E N Trimble, unlike the other autobiographers, came from a relatively prosperous Virginia family, filled with men who, like Trimble himself, distinguished themselves as judges and legislators. His memoirs were found in his desk by his grandchildren, who had been totally unaware that the memoirs existed. Trimble had begun them at the age of seventy. His early childhood was filled with adventures on the Kentucky frontier, to which his father, a fairly well-off veteran of Lord Dunmore's campaign, had taken his family in 1784. Trimble portrays his mother and father as courageous, resourceful people. When the Treaty of Paris brought peace and independence to the United States, they sought a new home on the Kentucky frontier. Because of the resistance of the Indians to American incursions into the West, the Trimbles joined a party of 500 organized under military-like discipline, with all the adults—including the women—carrying pistols. The story of this discipline, which was accepted by families moving westward at that time, proves fascinating reading.

Trimble's mother is the heroine of several of his most exciting stories, for as he explains, she often demonstrated a presence of mind that "she had beyond most mortals and which never forsook her." Placed in the lead when their party crossed the Clinch River, his mother discovered that her horse was having difficulty in the "boisterous mass of water"; so she let the horse have the rein, bringing her three-year-old son to her lap while she clutched the mane with her right hand and the bystanders wailed, " 'She's lost!' 'Turn back!' 'Oh! Save her!' " "With a firm reliance upon Divine Providence and her noble horse," Trimble concludes in what must have been an oft-told family tale, "she stemmed the billows of the rugged Clinch River and arrived safely with her charge on the opposite bank, amid palpitating hearts."[1]

Once in Kentucky the Trimbles quickly brought twenty acres into cultivation. The incredible fertility of the soil produced bountiful harvests, while their livestock fattened on the natural grasses of the lush range. Soon they and their neighbors were converting their surplus grain—corn, rye, and barley—into Kentucky whiskey, which they sold down the Mississippi in New Orleans, then still a French city. Within ten years of settlement, someone had built a riverboat with planks cut at the elder Trimble's sawmill.

Although the family carried slaves into the Kentucky country, Trimble's father turned against the institution. Despite his wife's opposition, he entered into agreements with his enslaved workers to give them their freedom after five years of service, a promise that Trimble reports "was made in 1798, and fulfilled to the letter in 1803."[2] Trimble's father later decided to move to Ohio because of his distaste for slavery, but died before the plans could be executed.

Meanwhile, Trimble had heard a man regaling a group with stories of having driven pigs long distances for the Continental Army. With pork in Kentucky being "a drug" on the market at two dollars per hundred but fetching ten dollars in the East, Trimble convinced his father to lend him the money for a pig-driving enterprise. With one partner and 500 hogs, Trimble set off on the high adventure of a six-hundred-mile march through the wilderness and cultivated areas that lay between his Kentucky home and Washington, D.C. Although he had not shared his father's aversion to slavery, his sojourn on a Virginia plantation during this trip caused him to think about slavery. As he looks back on that

---

1. Allen Trimble, "Autobiography," in *The Old Northwest Genealogical Quarterly*, 9 (1906), pp. 195–287; 10 (1907), pp. 1–49; p. 207.
2. Trimble, "Autobiography," p. 226.

occasion, he reflects that the institution "had been so frequently discussed by our family that the arguments pro and con came to my mind that evening and I had the truth of some of my father's positions fully demonstrated."[3]

Returning home with his profits from the sale of the hogs proved almost as hazardous as the outbound trip, but having succeeded once, Trimble repeated the venture two more times. After his father's death, Trimble, at twenty-one, took over the family affairs, moving his mother and younger siblings to the Ohio property his father had bought before his death. Soon married, Trimble created a home for his wife and mother. As he explains the family's affairs, his mother had sold her dowry (the possessions she brought to her marriage) with their Kentucky lands; in Ohio her children set off a 240-acre farm for her and divided the remaining 4,500 acres into eight parcels for themselves.

Preparations for the War of 1812 take up much of Trimble's memoirs, for both he and his brothers became involved in the conflict, much of which was fought in the Great Lakes area. The disastrous surrender of Detroit without a fight by General William Hull, for which Hull was court-martialed, gets its share of attention, as do the capture of Trimble's younger brother and his own service under the popular William Henry Harrison.

Elected to the Ohio state legislature in 1816, Trimble served both in the House and the Senate, where he was immediately elected speaker pro tem in 1817, a position he held until elected governor of the state in 1826. Once in executive office, Trimble devoted the lion's share of his attention to canal building and education. His most distressing responsibility, he remembers, was the pardoning power of the governor which led to mob violence when he saved a man about to be executed.[4] Trimble's brother was elected United States senator from Ohio.

---

3. Trimble, "Autobiography," p. 11.
4. Trimble, "Autobiography," pp. 102–6.

$\mathcal{A}$T the request of my family, I have prepared the following account of my ancestors, as derived from the two past generations.

My paternal grandfather, John Trimble, with three brothers, emigrated from the North of Ireland to America, in the early part of the 17th century. Their ancestors were of Scotch descent, disciples of the great reformer, Knox, and deeply imbued with the religious zeal and uncompromising spirit of that extraordinary man, and had witnessed and felt the consequences of the bloody scenes that followed the Reformation. . . .

Although the Indian tribes had retired to the Ohio, and to the country north-west of that river, they claimed that their hunting parties occupied the entire region north-west of the Allegheny, and they made frequent attacks upon the settlements east of the Blue Ridge and in the Valley from Winchester to the James river, and the inhabitants were forced very often to abandon their improvements and protect themselves by erecting Block-houses. Here several families could congregate and together defend themselves against the sudden attacks of the enemy. This state of things continued several years previous to 1760 and afterwards up to 1774. When General Lewis, with his Western Virginians, called Virginia Brigade, in the hard fought and bloody battle at the mouth of the Great Kanawha, defeated the combined forces of the Northwest Indians, under Logan and the Chief called "Corn-stalk," a temporary respite followed. Peace was immediately afterwards made by Governor Dunmore with these tribes at their towns, or more properly called "villages," on the Scioto river at Doit Charlotte, R. Mausais, and also the old town now called Chillicothe (then only an Indian lodge), where they raised their tepees.

Thus were those pioneers of the border of Virginia schooled for the trials they underwent during the Revolution. For as soon as the war commenced between the Colonies and the Mother Country, the savages commenced hostilities anew under the protection of the British Government; and from 1776 to 1784 continued to war against the whites, and were not subdued until defeated by General Anthony Wayne in the memorable battle of the Maumee River, of the Lake [Erie], in 1794.

Governor Dunmore, with the main body of the army, marched from Richmond by Winchester to the mouth of the Little Kanawha, intending to drop down and join Lewis at Point Pleasant. But the Indians, aware of the movement of the army, supposing Lewis to be off his guard and on the Ohio, above the Point, attacked him before the arrival of Dunmore and were defeated, although Dunmore did not come to his rescue.

To continue with the history of our ancestry. My father, James Trimble, was born in 1753, near Staunton, Augusta County, Virginia. He was the only child of John Trimble and his wife, Polly Christian, who had been previously married to John Moffitt. . . .

He married Jane Allen, daughter of James and Margaret Allen, (Margaret was the daughter of the Rev. Anderson), both of Augusta County, Virginia, whose ancestors were among the first settlers of that county. . . .

Immediately after the war of the Revolution, my father visited Kentucky to locate the land warrants which he had obtained for his services during the wars with the Indians and British, and on his return to Virginia, he described the country he had seen to my mother and they determined to remove as soon as arrangements could be made for the purpose. A number of families in Augusta County, from the representations they had heard of Kentucky, concluded to make it their home. William Anderson, an uncle, and William Allen, a brother of my mother, also Robert Trimble and a distant relative by the name of Joseph Colvin, with several others, agreed to write and unite and form an emigrating company. In the autumn of 1784, (October, I think, was the exact month), they commenced the long journey. Notice had been given of the time of starting and also the place of rendezvous, and when they arrived at Beans Station and Holston river, the frontier fort and place of meeting, near five hundred persons, men, women and children, were assembled.

Colonel Knox, of Revolutionary memory and fame, was of the number and chosen by acclamation to take command. After a day's rest and preparation for entering the Wilderness, Clinch Mountain was in view and first to cross by a serpentine trail around craggy peaks, and through narrow defiles where ten Indians could defeat one hundred men. The Colonel appointed a guard of ten men to go in advance and patrol the mountain on both sides of the trail, and when they arrived at Clinch river, which swept the western base of the mountain, if no signs of Indians appeared, to cross the river and take a hasty view of the valley in the west shore, and be prepared to act as circumstances required, while the main body would cross the river. My father was of this guard. A rear guard was also selected. Colonel Knox headed the line, and when near the top of the mountain, several miles from its eastern base, a messenger overtook him, with the information that the pack horses of a certain family were unable to climb the mountain and without assistance would be left and probably massacred by the Indians, who had been discovered on a spur of the mountain, watching the movements of the emigrants.

Colonel Knox turned to my mother, who was with the front guard of the train, and she was exactly in front and very near to him, and requested her to march on to the river, where she would meet the front guard and he would return and bring the distressed family.

When my mother reached the river, the front guard had crossed and were posted on the opposite bank. The ford was a difficult one, running up near the shore, which was rock bound 150 yards, and then forming the segment of a circle, reaching the western bank some distance, say 50 yards higher than the entrance on the east shore. It was called a "horse-shoe" ford. Mother was not aware of its character. The bottom from the foot of the mountain to the ford was narrow and the emigrants in the rear were crowding upon those in front, and the pack-horses rushing in towards the front. Mother's horse became restless and started for the opposite bank and proceeded only a short distance before she was aware that he was far gone into the dangerous quick-sand. She found it impossible to turn her spirited horse, and with a presence of mind, which she had beyond most mortals and which never forsook her, she gave this splendid horse the rein, caught her little son, not three years old, who rode behind her, when her husband was on duty, as he then was, she brought him to her lap, (the little boy), where I, a feeble infant, eleven months old, was reposing; grasping both of us with her left arm, and her horse's mane with her right hand, and thus adjusted for the fearful adventure, amid loud exclaims of "She's lost!" "Turn back!" "Oh! Save her!" With a firm reliance upon Divine Providence and her noble horse, she stemmed the billows of the rugged Clinch River and arrived safely with her precious charge on the opposite bank, amid palpitating hearts. My father, supposing it impossible for any horse to bear himself and rider, over such a boisterous mass of water for three hundred yards, stood upon the other bank, prepared for any emergency.

The wife of William Irwin was next to my mother when she entered the river and followed her until she saw her getting into such deep, dangerous water, when she wheeled her horse suddenly, which threw him, the horse, into deep water that floated from under her. She had two little negro children which she carried in a wallet across her saddle. But for the large bag, which inclosed the little darkies (all but their heads), they would have been drowned. But Mr. Wilson, who was an admirable swimmer, watched the opportunity of recovering the bag and its dark contents, and as it passed a bend in the river, he caught it and brought the little fellows safely to the shore. Mrs. Irwin and her horse were saved and the little army, soon as they saw my mother safe and understood the ford, proceeded and crossed the river without any loss. Then Colonel Knox soon followed with the rear guard, bringing with them the family that had been left on the east side of the mountain. When he had learned what had happened to my mother in consequence of not being informed of the character of the ford, he expressed to her his deep regret that she had been exposed to such fearful danger, but rejoiced that she had proved herself equal to the emergency and had with her precious charge been so miraculously preserved. He said he had not, during his whole life, known of such an exhibition of *female presence of mind,* courage and skill as she had shown and demonstrated on this most wonderful and dangerous occasion, and he added: "That when the noble horse struck the opposite river bank, there was a dead silence at first, that had followed the lamentations of the women when she had started, and then this silence was followed by a shout of joy from both sides of the Clinch River, that drowned, for a moment, the dashing, turbulent waters of that dark stream, and sent its echo far up the gorges of the old mountain and down the valley of the river, 'She's saved! She's saved!' "

By this time the day was far spent and it was determined to encamp for the night on the west side of the river, just below the ford, and Colonel Knox and his associates, for he had a large number of experienced and brave men to rely upon, laid out the encampment in expectation of an attack from the Indians; for Indians had been seen all during the crossing of the mountain by spies the entire day, watching carefully, as an Indian only can do, the movements of the emigrant train.

The river protected one line of the camp, then the horses were all tied in the centre, and the pack saddles were strewed within the upper line from the river bank, back, and also protected by a strong guard. The lower and back lines by the balance of the men. Then the women who were armed, as most of them were with pistols, took positions with their husbands. The balance of the women and children were placed in a position near the river, supposed to be the safest. And thus arranged, watch was kept up during the night by sentinels closely posted on the lines soon after dark (and it was a dismal night and with rain). The Indians were heard in the adjoining woods, howling like wolves and "Hoo! Hoo!-ing" like owls, until midnight, after which an attack was expected. But it was supposed the fires that had been kindled and kept burning some distance outside the three exposed lines, saved them; for Indians seldom expose themselves to the first fire of their foes, as they would have done by placing themselves between the fires and the sentinels—especially, where, as in this case, *all were sentinels.*

The next morning, after allowing their horses an hour or two, both to graze and drink, and wringing the water out of their wet clothes, having been exposed to a severe rain during the night, and taking their breakfast, the line of march was resumed.

The weather continued cloudy, with occasional showers. In addition to music during the night by *owls* and *wolves,* fresh moccasin tracks discovered in the morning gave unmistakable evidence of Indians being on the lookout for an opportunity to obtain scalps or horses, or both.

As it was expected that the "Defeated Camp," as it was called, would be passed on this day's march, great caution was observed, and the dreadful massacre that gave its name to this camp impressed the minds of all with fearful forebodings. And when they arrived at the spot and saw the bodies of some fifteen of their countrymen strewed upon the ground, some hawked and scalped, some stripped naked, and their bodies torn by wild beasts and vultures, exhibiting little of the human frame but bone and sinew, the feeling of fear departed and the feelings of humanity, as by one impulse, banished every other thought, and the men stacked their arms and gathered the fragments of their slaughtered brethren and gave them such burial as in their power, sufficient to protect them from the wolf, the panther, the bear and the vulture. The performance of this sacred duty occasioned such delay as to make it necessary to encamp for the night at or near this "bloody ground," and during this night, the real wolf, panther, bear and bird of ill omen, not willing to be deprived of the bones they had stripped, were more daring than the savage murderers themselves; for they not only approached the encampment, but even entered the lines themselves of an enemy greatly their superior in number and prowess. They even attempted to dive under the frail tents and very few eyes were closed for the night, only the aged and the little children.

A large bear was shot dead whilst furiously and fearlessly entering the encampment and would have furnished a delicious morsel for breakfast but for the fact that no one could think of eating the flesh of an animal that had been fattening upon the flesh and blood of human beings, so his skin was only taken, leaving the flesh for animals that would relish it. . . .

Although late in the day it was thought advisable by their leader, Colonel Knox, to proceed to a more eligible position, some three miles in advance, where they had encamped for the night and an order was forthwith issued: "That if undisturbed by the enemy, breakfast should be taken and the march commenced by sun-rise, in order to make up for the loss of distance the previous day." Nothing occurring to prevent it, the order was obeyed to the letter and a very successful march was made, crossing the Cumberland River and passing through the celebrated "cane-brake," that had been the dread of emigrants, from the time it was first penetrated by Daniel Boone, in 1774.

The progress of the party was not further interrupted or molested by the Indians, and, having met and overcome the difficulties so common to emigrants of that perilous period, they arrived at *Crab Orchard*, on the 20th day from Beans Station, without the loss of an *individual*, man, woman or even a child, or a horse. *Here* they encamped together for the first time and also for the *last* time, each family the next day taking the chosen route to their favorite locality, both north and south of the Kentucky river.

Then Colonel Knox walked round the entire encampment and took an affectionate leave of men, women and children, complimenting them for their fortitude and good conduct, passing upon my mother a very high compliment, as being the heroine of the band, and then receiving in turn from each and all, a hearty "God bless you, Colonel Knox."

Our family, Wm. Anderson's, Wm. Allen's, William Irwin's, and several others took the route to Boonsboro, and Lexington and settled in what was then Fayette County, now called Woodford, and Independence County; and my father, as before mentioned, had purchased this land from William Allen.

It was a heavily timbered tract of land, with much undergrowth of cane, tall and thick as hemp, in a well cultivated field. And the first necessity was a tent to shelter the little family and also their baggage. This was soon constructed. The next was provisions for the family. The horses, ten in number, were doing well on the cane. Flour and corn meal were not to be had, under any considerations, but at Craigs Station, there was corn, but no mill to grind it. Hominy, manufactured in a block by a pestle, with an iron wedge inserted in one end, made an excellent substitute for corn bread and this, with bear meat, venison and wild turkey and also Buffalo steak, of which father furnished a good living, and a rich supply, made in those days (with a cup of coffee on Sundays), what they termed *good living.* But the *"Hominy block,"* though never abandoned, was soon relieved from daily pounding by its universal associate in Pioneer life, the *"Hand Made Mill."*

My father, though not a professed mechanic, was one practically, for he constructed his own plows and other farming utensils, and in addition to tools for operating upon wood, had brought with him from Virginia a stone hammer etc., for working and operating upon stone. He had seen hand mills in operation and very soon constructed one which manufactured corn meal to perfection, as my mother afterwards assured me, equal in *quality* to the celebrated Raccoon Burr stone. Two men upon the mill would grind a peck of corn in half an hour.

A more comfortable home was erected and then all hands pitched into the cane with mattock and grubbing hoes to clear a field for corn. The forest trees were left standing and girded, except only the sugar or maple trees and they were scorched by burning cane piled around them, this being the only method of destroying their vitality the first year. So by the first of the next May, twenty acres were thus prepared for planting corn.

The next difficult part of the preparation was breaking the sod, or plowing, through the tough cane roots; this required a strong team of horses and also a very powerful plow and a skilful plowman, each and all of which were at the command of my father. And my mother said that many persons and neighbors, not having these last two requisites, were under the necessity of digging holes in the ground with hoes and thus planting the corn, without plowing the ground, either before or after planting, but she said the pioneer was richly rewarded for his labor by a good crop in the virgin soil. . . .

In those days it did not require a large crop of corn to support a family and but little was required for stock; work horses, only, required to be fed on grain. The range, for other animals, was rich and abundant. This left a large portion of the corn crop for sale; and the only demand for this surplus was created by the emigrants, and they multiplied so rapidly, and so soon became self-supporting and self-supplying, and even venders, themselves, that really, corn soon became a drug on the market, for at that time we had no ready means, as now, for shipping thousands of carloads to the east and European markets. So in order to use the great surplus of fine corn, *distilling* was resorted to, as a means of converting the surplus grain, corn, rye and barley into Kentucky Whiskey. And indeed, in every neighborhood, and at almost every large farm, might be found a small distillery.

At this period, about 1794, whiskey found a market at New Orleans. The first New Orleans boat from our section of the state was built at General Scott's landing, which was on the Kentucky river, by Elijah Craig, a neighbor of ours; the plank for which was cut at my father's saw-mill, ten miles from the boat yard. The first cargo was made up of flour, whiskey and Irish potatoes. Father sent the next year, by John and James McAfee, two brothers, one hundred barrels of flour to be sold on commission, and received good returns in money. The two McAfee's continued this trade for several years, annually purchasing the surplus products in that region. . . .

The deer, bear and turkey were abundant in the region in which we settled, and required but little effort of such a hunter as my father was, in his rambles through the neighboring woods, searching for and salting his stock, to take a buck or gobbler, and sometimes a bear home with him. In one of these excursions he encountered a bear under rather singular circumstances. At the crossing of a small stream his dogs (two noble curs) looked up the branch, and, after smelling and scenting, seemed anxious to take a run, and they were encouraged to do so and made a dash at half speed. Father rode on across the stream, on a path through the thick cane, some 200 or 300 yards, when he heard his dogs barking, apparently in his rear. So he turned his horse to meet them and had proceeded but a short distance when a tremendous bear came running to meet him, and the path was so narrow, hemmed in with cane on either side, neither he or the bear could turn with safety, and both determined to abide the result of a meeting. My father determined, when sufficiently near, to make his horse leap over the stream and take a position with his dogs, some short distance in the rear; but Bruin was determined to arrest both horse and rider. As the horse raised to make his leap, the bear raised on his hind legs, gripped the horse by the nose and threw his hairy arms around his neck, and held him as if he had been in a vise. And there, like the Lion and the Unicorn (in our old Primers) they stood, the rider holding his horse's mane with the *left hand* and his trusty rifle in his right, but without being able to use it. At this critical moment, the faithful dogs came to the relief of their master. And here was a fine field for the display of their great courage and skill, and they exhibited both in a moment, as you will see. One took his position a few steps in the rear, whilst the other pitched savagely at the bear, snapping at his stern so as to avoid coming into too close contact or quarters. Finding his rear attacked so furiously, the bear released the fine horse to wheel upon the dogs. That moment the horse made a desperate bound forward, cleared the bear, broke the girth of the saddle and left it with the rider, bear and dogs all in a great muss! The bear seemed to fear the dogs more than the rifle, or he felt like having his *revenge* of the two vicious dogs on account of the severe wound he had received in his stern. He therefore pursued the dogs for a short distance and, finding that they would not stand and fight, he turned to face the rifle, but this was a fatal step for my father was an unerring shot with the old long rifle; for a ball was sent by his unerring aim to his brain and there on the identical spot where she had held the horse in durance vile, she met her fate. It was an old she bear and had two little cubs in a hollow tree, at a short distance from where she was shot. So the next day there was a *Bear Hunt,* and several neighbors collected with their dogs and repaired to the battle ground of the previous day. The two pretty little cubs were soon found and captured alive, and the old *he bear,* was, after a long chase and severe fight, killed. We kept the cubs until they were one year old when they became dangerous and were killed.

About this time my mother had an adventure where her courage and skill in the management of her horse was put to a severe trial. She was summoned to the sick bed of a neighbor who was said to be dying (Mrs. Warnick). She hastened to obey the call, and continued with her sick friend during the entire day. In the evening Mrs. Warnick was much better and considered out of danger and mother concluded to return home. Mr. Warnick insisted on seeing her safely home, but she advised otherwise, and started alone. She had proceeded about a mile when, hearing a noise, she looked back and saw a wolf of tremendous size pursuing her at a rapid loap. She saw in a moment from the fierce look of the ravenous animal that her only safety was in the speed of her noble horse. This was the same noble animal that she had ridden from Virginia. Now, she had barely time to tuck up her riding skirt and give her horse an intimation of her wishes when the fierce wolf was at his heels. The road here was narrow, merely a bridle path, hemmed in on either side with the cane-brake. She soon discovered the object of her pursuer was to unhorse her, for several attempts were made to reach the near side of her horse, but the character of the road did not favor his object, so he attempted to *leap* upon the *horse's rump.* The horse was now at full speed and the wolf evidently had the heels of him, and now perceiving this fact, the danger seemed eminent. But it was soon discovered that when the wolf set himself to make a spring the magnificent horse gained and the wolf lost, which rendered his leap, or what they call *spring, fruitless.* And thus they ran for two good miles. Then the last half mile of the road widened and the vicious wolf was able to gain the near side of the horse and even made several attempts to reach the rider but succeeded only in reaching her riding skirt, which was very badly torn by his sharp teeth.

Such was the determined purpose of the hungry animal that he continued the pursuit until the dogs from the homestead, hearing the *Whoop and call* of their mistress, came to her relief. And also father, as soon as he heard mother's "*Whoop!* Hoo! Hoo!" ran rapidly, gun in hand, supposing she was chased by the Indians (as the week before, two of General Scott's sons had been killed and scalped on their own farm, and that was only ten miles from us). It was now dark and the pursuit of the wolf had to be abandoned.

Mother rode up to the cabin door, where the entire little family, both white and black, was assembled, crying, "Mother! Oh, mistress! Oh! Do tell us what was the matter?" The noble animal still panting and also set with sweat, assured them that something very serious had happened. And if additional evidence had been wanting, her riding *skirt,* torn to ribbons, would have furnished that evidence.

Then she dismounted, bade the servant boy to take good care of her fine horse, who had saved her life, took a seat and very deliberately gave us a history of the *race,* and her miraculous escape. She supposed, that having handled *Assafoetida* in the sick room at Mr. Warnick's, some of it had adhered to her clothing and was the cause of the wolf pursuing her so fiercely and scenting her so far off.

The wolf was the last of the wild animals to retreat from civilization and the buffalo the first. The *meat and hides* of those wild cattle were so important to the early emigrants to Kentucky that a buffalo hunt in the autumn, to obtain meat for family use during winter and the hides to be tanned for shoes, was usually provided for. If a man was not a hunter himself he joined a neighbor who was and acted as butcher and pack-horse master. . . .

As the fear of the Indian visitation subsided, the log cabin, with its strong fixtures of slab doors, with strong bars and bolts, port holes, etc., gave place to the heavy log house, stone and brick, according to the taste of the owner, and also according to his ability to afford such luxuries, as they were called in those pioneer days.

Now as I have said before, my father had erected a saw mill and prepared lumber for a frame dwelling, and it was the first of its kind erected in the neighborhood. And raising the frame (two stories high, 32 x 18 feet) was at that time considered a serious undertaking.

The carpenter, John Porter, was an Irishman, and allowed to manage the undertaking and enterprise *alone*. I do not now remember the number of hands but, for that day, they were quite numerous, and they were called from distant neighborhoods with forks and ropes in abundance, for great caution was observed to prevent any accidents, and I am glad to say, none occurred.

The parties of workmen were all sober, for there was nothing to make them otherwise. The frame was raised, without a single accident, nor was anyone hurt in the least. . . .

Having erected a more commodious dwelling, the enlargement of the farm seemed to be the next necessity. The disappearance of the cane, as the country became more thickly settled, suggested to the farmers, who had very much stock, the necessity of making *tame pasture,* and growing more corn, to meet those approaching necessities.

Now my father concluded to increase his labourers, and as slaves at that time were very high in Kentucky, and white labourers scarce, he prepared himself and set out for Virginia for the purpose of purchasing a few negroes. But on his way, he lost his money, but, collecting funds due to him in Virginia, he proceeded to the low countries and made purchases of several slaves.

Whilst travelling through the country in search of such as he desired to purchase, he saw slavery as he had never seen it before, especially as to the effect the system was producing upon society, and the subject so impressed his mind, that in weighing the results of the system upon the moral, intellectual and political interest of the country, the conclusion was that slavery was a great evil, he was lead to believe. He, however, brought those he purchased to his home in Kentucky, but soon after his return to his family, he communicated to my mother some of the incidents which he had witnessed, also giving some thrilling accounts of the immorality of the masters and cruelties of overseers, and the effect the system of slavery was producing upon the rising generation, who were being thus brought up in idleness and acquiring habits that would unfit them for usefulness, both to themselves or their country; and he said, after much reflection upon the subject, that he had come to the conclusion that it would be their duty, as it would also be to their interests, to free themselves from slavery, just as soon as they could do so, thus consistently with their own and the interests of the slaves, themselves.

It was a new subject, and mother was slow, in this one instance, to fall in with my father's views. But, seeing he was so thoroughly convinced of the correctness of his views, and knowing him to be a man of firmness of purpose, she yielded to what she regarded as a necessity.

It was therefore concluded that the slaves should be *set free*, after five years of service. They were accordingly mustered and informed if they would serve their master and mistress *faithfully five years*, they should be set free, and this promise was made in 1798 and fulfilled to the letter in 1803.

When it was settled that our slaves should be set free, a new question was presented: "Shall we remain in Kentucky, or remove to the North-western Territory, where slavery is, by the Ordinance of 1787, prohibited?" Both father and mother differed in their opinions upon this, as they had done upon the question of manumitting their slaves. She objected to again emigrating to a new country on account of the difficulty of giving the younger children a suitable education and also of giving them the benefit of good society, etc. Now, in order to meet the first objection, a teacher was immediately employed to open a school in our own house (as there were none in the neighborhood) and every member of the family of children, both white and black, were placed under the rigid discipline of Robert Elliott, an acceptable and experienced teacher. The result was what might have been expected, we all looked upon it as the last chance we would have to be schooled and made the best possible use of the opportunity afforded us.

Schools had been kept during the winter in our neighborhood, some of them about four miles from our residence, which we attended but you must remember that teachers were hard to procure in those early times; and often very poorly qualified. So of course the pupils were not well taught, still it was better than we even expected at that time to find in the new state of Ohio, at that early day.

Father, about this time, joined one of his neighbors, Alexander Dunlap, in the purchase of lands in the Virginia Military District, north-west of the Ohio river, situate on Scioto and Paint creeks, and purchased one tract on his own account, situate upon *Paint and Clear Creeks.* In the following autumn of the year 1801, taking me with him, we visited these lands. . . .

In the spring I undertook to work on the farm, but could not stand it. I went to the Olympian Springs, in Montgomery County Kentucky, which is a watering place of some celebrity, and spent July and August there without much benefit. In the Autumn of 1802 I again accompanied my father to Ohio, which was a second reconnoisance of our lands, and spent some time in Chillicothe whilst the convention that founded the Constitution of Ohio, were in session, made the acquaintance of several of the members, and returned home late in December, my health still delicate but somewhat improved. One physician, Dr. Brown, advised that I should continue to travel, and it was agreed in the family counsel that I should go to Virginia and spend the winter with some of our numerous relatives. . . .

I was apprehensive that travelling under such circumstances would not improve my health. Then Mr. Davis drew out his bottle of whiskey and, for the first time, I joined him in a hearty "here goes for a better acquaintance."

I was soon in the saddle again and although pretty thoroughly wet did not feel uncomfortable until the spirits from friend Davis' bottle began to die. It was a cold day, but I thought the thermometer had certainly fallen much below the freezing point. After we had finished swimming the rapid little stream, called "Stinking Creek," and before we had reached our lodging place, I was chilled, my teeth in motion, or chattering, my buckskin pantaloons frozen to my legs, and even in many places they were adhering to my saddle, but aided by the kindness of the good landlord, I was soon extricated and seated by a comfortable fire.

Mr. Davis, after having our good horses cared for, came in, and invited me to take some more spirits, but my head was so affected with what I had already taken (for indeed it ached violently), I therefore declined. I requested the landlord to make a strong cup of tea for me. But the landlady said to her husband that she had no tea or coffee, but that she could make me some "yarb" tea. I inquired what kind of "yarb" tea. She said, "Sassa-frax" yarb. I told her to prepare at least a quart cup for me alone and that just as soon as possible. I also saw a string of red pepper pods, suspended from the joist and I recollected that our old Guinea negress who belonged to my father often used red pepper in making "sassa-frax" tea and mixed it with Seneca snake root for colds, which we had found at home very effective. So I inquired of the landlady if she had any snake root. "No, there was none in her house." I then requested our hostess to put a pod of red pepper in the tea, which she was preparing for me. It was done as I had directed, and I have no doubt at all that the highly peppered tea, drank on that occasion, prevented me from taking a deeply seated cold.

I was at a loss to determine how to manage my leather pantaloons; how to dry them whilst I had them on, for I would not be able to take them off. And to take them off and dry them, I would not in any way be able to get them on again. But the landlord, who as most hunters were in those days, was a skin dresser, said to me, if I would take them off, he would dry them and have them ready for me in the morning, just as large and soft as they were before getting wet; and he did so, by drying them slowly and rubbing them with a broad smooth rubbing board, which he used in dressing deer skins.

Mr. Davis and I slept or lay on a straw bed, which was laid on a rough slab of wood, just in front of the fire. Mr. Davis was up very early and had our horses fed, and the madam had for us an early breakfast, which was composed of choice venison, bear meat, and johnny cake, with "Sassa-frax" tea, "to work it down," as she said playfully to him; and we started with friend Davis in the lead. When we reached the "Raccoon" Creek, Mr. Davis said there was no alternative and went plunging through, swimming from bank to bank, and I followed and got very wet, up to my knees. Then we crossed several streams, some of which had fallen so as to be forded by our horses, but sad to relate, our feet and legs were wet all day. That night we had a more comfortable lodging, and the next day a more comfortable ride, crossing the Cumberland river on a boat, with our two horses swimming on each side, and then reached, after crossing the Cumberland Mountain, the beautiful Powell's Valley. . . .

I left Claibourne Court House and arrived at Clinch river at about nine a.m. Here my parents and family, with emigrants from Virginia and North Carolina, in October, 1784, crossed this mountain stream, and it was here that my mother was so miraculously preserved with her two little children, and borne across this frightful chasm of rocks and billows by her noble and spirited horse. I felt that I was a *child of Providence,* and should never, no never, distrust the goodness and great mercy of Almighty God, and the efficacy of a mother's prayer.

And I had afterwards heard, not only my mother, but from others who witnessed the frightful occasion and also the occurrence, but I had formed no correct idea of the actual hazard and the apparent impossibility of any horse (even Beucephalus himself) successfully stemming a torrent of water, upwards of 200 yards broad, rolling and tumbling over and around rocks, some of them towering above the highest water, and bearing his sacred charge of three human beings safely to the opposite shore. And it must have been an exciting scene to those who witnessed it; for the very thought of the reality made the cold chills run over me. I left, reflecting upon the dangers and difficulties encountered by the first emigrants to Kentucky: and felt *proud* that I was a descendant of such a bold and enterprising race of good and honest people.

I reached Beans Station after crossing the river and Clinch mountain, and put up with Mr. Gordon, the Inn keeper. When leaving in the morning Mr. Gordon gave me a particular description of the *place* where the merchant was attacked by the two robbers which I have before referred to. This was one of the coldest days I had ever travelled. I passed the tavern at which the merchant lodged on the night before he was attacked, and I was strongly inclined to call and warm myself. But I did not, and as I passed the fatal spot referred to, I was struck with the suitableness of the situation for a deed of darkness and murder. A thick forest, large pine trees scorched black and the tree behind which the two robbers stood, was in the center of the road.

I reached Rogersville and put up with the proprietor of the town, Mr. Rogers, who was one of the most obliging landlords I have ever met with.

I parted in the morning with my warm hearted Irish host, who invoked a blessing upon the young traveller. As I passed a tavern in the village, I observed a gentleman mounted and about to start, leading a horse with a pack, lashed on a pack-saddle. So I rode up and inquired if he was travelling towards Staunton. He replied that he had to learn the road himself and that he would not be company for me. I saw in a moment that the recent murder of Staley was operating upon his mind and he feared that I might kill him for his money, which he was packing in Spanish coin upon his lead horse.

He remarked to me that he had business *off the road,* and would not be company for me. I saw in a moment that the fact that Staley had been killed by a "traveling companion" was the thing which in fact operated most on his fearful and timid mind. The report had reached his ears and had very much influenced his fears. So I rode on alone and saw no more of the affrighted merchant. . . .

My relatives were taken by surprise, not expecting any of their relatives from Kentucky at that inclement season, and especially one all alone and such a young man as myself. But they were very glad to meet me, for indeed in those early days, a guest was always welcome, if only for company, since news was only carried by the traveller on horseback. . . .

The thirteenth day after leaving Colonel Allen's in Virginia I arrived at my home in Kentucky. I had been absent over four months. It was a joyful meeting. All crowded around me and after the "shaking hands" all around on such occasions was over my mother inquired for the health of her parents and family of relatives in Virginia and having learned that they were in good health she said she hoped I had a pleasant and profitable visit. I answered in the affirmative. . . .

I first drew out some presents from the Virginia friends to mother and my sisters, but they were light articles. I next drew out the surveying instruments before mentioned. The compass was a large and heavy one for those times. I unwrapped it and handed it to father, who examined it, inquiring in the meantime if I had bought it for myself. I said I had, adding that as it was possible I might go to the new country—I concluded I would when I had so favorable an opportunity to get a set of instruments. I discovered that my father was much gratified, and he said that I had acted very wisely. I was very happy to feel that nothing I had done during my absence was a disappointment to my parents, but that they approved. A knowledge of this fact I have often thought strengthened my purposes to so conduct myself as to look for and expect their further approval. Nothing had occurred during my absence to occasion a painful thought. My own health had improved and the family were in usual health upon my return.

Mother had always expressed a wish that I should obtain a good education. She was a reader of good books. When fifteen years of age she had committed the four Gospels to memory, large portions of Milton, Young, Cowper, Thomson, and she was a beautiful letter writer; and she was ambitious for her children, as was father. But as he could not spare both brother William and myself from the farm—there were six sons of us, and two daughters—I being fond of farming and having lived now at ease for so long, work was agreeable, it was decided that William should go to school, and I assist father.

I related to him that I had met in Virginia a Mr. Steinberger who resided on the south branch of the Potomac, an extensive farmer and engaged in feeding, marketing and fattening cattle in Richmond and Baltimore, and perhaps Philadelphia; and that at the suggestion of one of our relations, Mr. Bell, Mr. Steinberger proposed forming a partnership with me, the object of which was to purchase cattle in Kentucky and drive to Virginia. I should make the purchase and drive or cause them to be driven to Virginia, where he would receive and market them and give me a share of the profits, to be agreed upon, etc. I had informed Mr. Steinberger that I was a minor, had no capital, was unacquainted with the business and should not enter into such an agreement without consulting with my father.

Whilst we were in conversation on this subject, Mr. Nicholas Lewis and his wife, who was a sister of my mother paid us a visit during which the Steinberger proposition was mentioned, I had become rather anxious to impress my father favorably in relation to this matter. I told him of the fact that beef and pork had commanded in Virginia ten dollars per hundred, when in Kentucky pork was a "drug" at two dollars and beef only saleable on the hoof at even a lower price. My father's objection was that partnerships were dangerous and required the utmost probity and strictest care, even when the parties were united in the oversight of their business; and separated as Mr. Steinberger and I were—over five hundred miles apart—the dangers and difficulties of such partnership would be too much, that he could not consent to it. This told the whole story—a firm, decisive man my father was.

Mr. Lewis remarked that there was more money to be made by driving hogs to the eastern market, than cattle. We were all surprised at this remark, supposing it was altogether impracticable to drive hogs so great a distance, but Mr. Lewis said that they travelled as fast and carried their flesh better and on less feed than cattle, and as proof of this fact he told us that he was connected with the contractor for the supply of General Anthony Wayne's army in the Indian campaign of 1794–5. And that they were compelled to rely upon hogs in part for the supply of the troops from Cincinnati to Detroit; that the hogs were less trouble, travelled better and although they had a grain to feed them they kept their flesh better than cattle; that a part of those hogs bought in Kentucky, near Lexington, had been driven to Detroit. If Mr. Lewis had not been a man of character his statements would not have been believed.

I at once suggested to father that he loan Mr. Lewis and me the money necessary to purchase a drove and make the experiment of driving hogs from Kentucky to Virginia. Mr. Lewis said yes, he would join me with pleasure. Father hesitated, and said he did not altogether approve my suggestion. Mr. Lewis had been in very affluent circumstances but had failed in business in Frankfort where I had lived and had consequently retired to a small farm given him by his father and the title retained for Mr. Lewis had been extravagant and suspected of gambling. So although he had united with the Presbyterian Church a short time before, father thought he would not be a very safe partner. But after consultation with mother and Aunt Lewis, who, by the way, was a remarkably sensible woman, and a great favorite with our family, father yielded to our importunity, and Mr. Lewis and I commenced engaging hogs to be fully fatted and delivered by the 15th ult. at $2 per hundred lbs. net. This was in July. Having engaged the number he wanted, about four hundred, we made preparation to start by procuring "hands," pack horses and equipments.

Knowing that from the Crab Orchard to Beans Station, one-half the distance to Richmond, we would be in a country almost uninhabited and destitute of provisions for man at least we provided as for a campaign of thirty days—bread, cheese, coffee, sugar and cooking utensils etc. 1803, about the 25th of October, we collected our drove and began a march for Richmond, Va., some 600 miles distant. The subject of driving fat hogs to Virginia was new and produced in the neighborhood quite a sensation, and many were the predictions as to the result of our enterprise. Some of Mr. Lewis' acquaintances who knew his fondness for a game of brag said a certain man would brag A. Trimble out of his hogs before a week and then swap them for a race horse. Others wondered that Captain James Trimble would furnish money for a speculation where there was so little hope of the principal being saved, etc.

Amidst all these unfavorable auguries I started with high hopes of success. Up to the fourth day (during which time was passed through a rich settlement) we obtained corn for our hogs, but on the fifth day we left Crab Orchard and entered the wilderness. That night we camped in the woods for the first time. We had some fears that the hogs would scatter, (as we had no corn for them), but we had travelled through beech and chestnut woods the latter part of the day and so slowly that our pigs had without much delay satisfied their hunger and lay down as contentedly that night as if they had been in their own sty. In East Tennessee and Western Virginia we found oak and beech sufficient to keep the hogs in good condition, but when we left the mountains and entered the pine lands we had to purchase corn, from 75 cents to $1 per bushel, until we reached James River and Carter's Ferry and on to Richmond we paid only 50 cents per bushel.

Mr. Lewis had a relative, a wealthy farmer, residing on the north side of the river and near the road we were travelling, upon whom he said he must call and left us for that purpose. The next morning Mr. Lewis and his uncle, Colonel Curd, met us and the Colonel informed me that he had laid an embargo (a very common and significant word then in old Virginia), upon Mr. Lewis and the drove must be driven to his farm near the river, and that I must bring the boys to his house. It is unnecessary to say the order of the Colonel was obeyed to the letter, the Colonel guiding to where on the farm the drove was to be put up. And then on to his mansion. I soon discovered that Colonel Curd lived in a style indicating not only wealth, but taste and refinement. When dinner was announced we were taken into the parlors by the Colonel and his two sons and introduced to Mrs. Curd and her two daughters and then conducted to the dining room where we partook of an excellent dinner— bacon and cabbage were served as one course.

It was about the 20th of December. I was anxious to get to Richmond (thirty miles off) before Christmas, so I inquired of Mr. Lewis after dinner, in presence of the family, how long he intended to remain with his friends. He said not more than a day. "A day indeed," said the Colonel, "you must stay a week at least." "Oh, yes, yes," said the old lady and her daughters, "cousin Nickey, you may stay until after Christmas anyhow." I remarked that I would go on next day with the drove and Mr. Lewis might remain two days and overtake me at Richmond on the third day. The Colonel said: "Boys, that will not be a wise arrangement. One of you ought to go to Richmond one or two days before the hogs arrive in order to ascertain the state of the market and make arrangements for slaughtering or selling on foot, as may be best." I admitted the Colonel had a sensible view of the subject, but there seemed difficulties in adopting his plan. Thomas Lewis, a brother of Nicholas, who had spent his fortune in early life at cards, etc., had accompanied us. He remarked in his waggish manner, for he was a great wag, that he would arrange the matter so as to accommodate all parties. If Nicholas let him have his horse he, Tom, would go on with the drove to Richmond, make sale of the hogs and return to Col. Curd's, allowing his brother in the meantime to finish his visit. Nicholas laughingly said: "Brother, I fear you might meet some of your old friends in Richmond such as George and Frederick Straws, who would soon relieve you of the drove and the price of it." "There might be some danger," replied Tom, "but would there be more safety for money in your hands than mine? The last time we were in Richmond together old Straws got more money from you two to one than he did from me." Tom's repartee (but for the kind feeling of the family toward these relations), would have produced a hearty laugh at Nicholas' expense. . . .

The occurrences of the evening opened a new chapter for reflections: The question of negro slavery had been so frequently discussed by our family that the arguments pro and con came to my mind that evening and I had the truth of some of my father's positions fully demonstrated. He maintained that great as the wrong of slavery was, the negro was not the only sufferer wherever it existed but that its tendency was to enervate the white race and that it would not only produce idle, dissolute men, but that it would be unfavorable to moral or intellectual progress, and prove a curse wherever it existed, especially to the rising generation. On that evening I had seen and heard young men (my seniors) conversing on various topics, common intellects even of ordinary cultivation, and although some of them were graduates of Colleges they were as ignorant of the extent and the history of the country in which they lived as the aborigines of the West and some of them more so.

And this in Virginia! My native State, the history of whose brave and superior people and their gallant traditions I had learned from nursery tales that made deep and strong impressions upon my youthful mind. The names of Washington, Jefferson, Madison, Monroe, Henry, Lee, Marshall, etc., and their great achievements, had been household words and their memories have been cherished with a feeling for greatness, their characters held up as models of intellectual worth and moral fulfillment. It was not strange that I should have felt the great pride I did in my native State. But the mortification to find in this Old Dominion, among the wealthy and educated, such unmistakable evidences of a decline in mental vigor and aspirations among the youth of this great and renowned commonwealth. I came to the conclusion that slavery made its impress upon the character of the people where it existed, and that the evils of African slavery would be cumulative and keep pace with the progress of the system.

I left there for Richmond, reached there the five-mile house mentioned by Colonel Curd that night, and early the next morning mounted my horse and rode to Major ——'s mansion. Nicholas Lewis admonished me to be on my guard if I called on this gentleman. He said he knew him well and that he was one of the most pompous aristocrats in Virginia. I rode up to his stile ten paces from his dwelling and seeing no one, I dismounted, stepped to the door, and, upon knocking, a black boy came and opened the door. I inquired if Major —— was in. He said he was, but he wasn't yet out of bed. "Tell him," I said, "there is a gentleman here on business." I did not give him time to inquire my name but said I was cold and asked if he had a fire. "Yes sir," he said, "take a seat." He then went to tell the Major. I could hear the conversation between them: "Master, gent in room wants to see you." "Who is he?" "I don't know, sir." "What the devil did you let him in before he told you his name and business? Go and stay in the room until I come." It was fully a half hour before the Major entered, exhibiting one of the most austere, haughty looking Virginians I had ever seen. I rose, bowed slightly, a horse whip and my hat in hand. I said, "You are Major ——, I suppose, I am Allen Trimble, a young drover from Kentucky. I have a fine drove of hogs, and have been directed to inquire of you before going to Richmond. Having understood that you had a large family of negroes and an active overseer, I thought that you might possibly have made some arrangements for slaughtering of hogs at your farm and deliver them dressed in Richmond on better terms than I could get it done in the city."

I kept my eye on his countenance while I made my statement, and I saw that as soon as he comprehended my object his expression changed and before I finished my short address the Colonel had relaxed his features and come down to the attitude of a Virginia gentleman. "Why, sir, take a chair, astonishing! astonishing! Why, yes, sir, I would like very much to have your hogs or a part of them slaughtered or the offall. Tom, go tell the overseer to come here instantly." Mrs. —— then made her appearance. The Colonel gave me a very formal introduction, adding, "my dear, this young gentleman, Mr. Trimble, has a drove of fat hogs from Kentucky that will be here tonight." Mrs. —— had learned the value in the NS. She remarked, "that she hoped the enterprise would be profitable and that the trade would increase and raise the price of pork in Virginia." By this time the overseer was at the outer door with his hat under his arm, to learn the will of the Colonel who inquired of the overseer if he could make arrangements to slaughter a large number of hogs, stating where they were from etc. After a few moments of reflection the overseer said, they would slaughter a portion of them and perhaps all but he would not say positively how many. I told the Colonel I did not wish to make a positive engagement until I went to the city, that I would return that evening and let him know whether it would be most profitable to butcher in the city or country and prepared to leave but Mrs. —— said breakfast was ready and I must stay to breakfast. I did so. I have mentioned these occurrences at Colonel —— as an illustration of the character of a class of Virginia gentlemen as they were called, so opposite to that of Colonel Curd who was much the wealthiest man.

I proceeded to Richmond and found it would be most to our interest to drive our stock there. I concluded, however, that I was under some obligation to Colonel —— for his second thought, hospitality and gentlemanly bearing, and consequently I left a small lot to be slaughtered at his farm.

After selling our pork for $9.00 per head Mr. Lewis left immediately for Kentucky, leaving me to settle and raise the money for our pork, and to follow him at my leisure. Mr. Lewis was sensible of his weak points of character, and to avoid meeting his old companions left Richmond as soon as possible. I remained in Richmond about ten days. During that time I met a Mr. Bell, originally from Augusta County, and an intimate acquaintance of my family. He was a bachelor and engaged in speculations in cattle, etc. He was very polite and kind to me; and called one evening at my lodgings and asked me to walk with him to the Baron as it was called, the terminus of the James River Canal, nearly a mile from our quarters. After strolling around the Baron, and dark approaching, I spoke of returning. He said he wished among the curiosities of the city to show me Geo. Frederick Straws' establishment, after which he would accompany me to my lodging. Not suspecting the character of the house he was about to enter I followed Mr. B—— to a large three-story building. We were admitted at the door by a porter and I followed my friend up two flights of stairs. He rapped at the door which was opened by a second porter or sentinel. Mr. B—— was known and passed me in as his friend. There were probably thirty or forty well dressed men in the room standing round a table at least thirty feet long strewed with cards. There was a superior gentlemanly looking man richly dressed sitting at the head of the table shuffling a pack of cards. I discovered at once the character. That it was Geo. F. Straws' gambling house, the same George referred to by Lewis at Col. Curd's. I felt very uncomfortable. Mr. Bell saw I was disposed to leave but took me aside and said that I need not be alarmed. Mr. Straws was a gentleman and would not allow any improper conduct in his room and said we would not remain late and that he would accompany me to my quarters.

The game, "faro," as I learned, proceeded. Money in larger and larger sums was placed by persons around the table upon cards that had been distributed. Mr. B—— placed one dollar upon a card and won an equal amount. I stood near him. He said to me, "Put a dollar upon this card," pointing to it, and I obeyed him, not knowing whether it was his, Bell's, venture or mine. Straws shuffled his pack of cards and played out the game. One of the gamblers, for there were three of them, walked around the table, taking up from the losing cards the money deposited upon them and won by Straws and adding to the winning cards the amount won by adventurers (as I soon learned) for I did not yet understand the game. My card was winner and a dollar was added to my stake on first venture. Mr. Straws again shuffled his cards and played the second game. The same process of taking up and putting down on losing and winning cards as in the first game, two dollars were added to the stake on my card making four dollars. The game or games continued until the sixth hand had been played, my card doubling each game, producing sixty-four dollars. Mr. B—— seeking a more lucky card, had changed his position at the table and was some distance from me but discovering the pile of dollars on my card, and supposing, which was the fact, that I did not know I was winner, came to me and said you had better take up your money. I inquired of him in a low tone if it was mine. "Certainly," said he, "your card has been —— from the beginning," and deliberately pocketed the specie, stepped back and took a seat. Bell came to me and explained his reason for advising me to lift the money. He said he saw from Straws' eye that he would change my luck and probably the next game would be his when I would have to double the stake and in place of taking up I would have to add sixty-four dollars to the pile. I thanked him for his advice and proposed leaving, for I was satisfied that not only Mr. Straws but the company looked upon me as a "green horn" as I was in such associations. And I felt some uneasiness when I contemplated my situation, surrounded by gamblers with the proceeds of a drove in bank notes buttoned round my body and a total stranger except to Mr. B—— who, I discovered, was using brandy freely and I feared would soon be incapable of taking care of himself. At this moment a great noise below and numerous footsteps ascending the stairs caused a dead silence and the extinguishing of the lights in the room in which Straws and his guests were. Within, everything was as silent as death and dark as a dungeon. The officer with his paper (for it was the police in search of gamblers) tapped at the door which was locked and strongly barred and demanded entrance but no response was given. The owner of the house expostulated with the officers, swearing that Straws and his party were not there, and invited them down to the bar. Then they retired but left us in *durance vile* until the party below got their carousal for the landlord would not allow any quarters to be lighted until the police had retired. I think we had been one hour in the prison (an hour of deep reflection), when lights were brought. I determined to leave and took B—— by the arm and requested him to accompany me. He did so with great reluctance for he had been loser and hoped to regain his losses. We left at eleven o'clock in a darkness which I never witnessed. We had not gone more than a square until he met a patrol who hailed us. We continued in silence. Bell in front. The officers ordered us to halt. A second patrol arrived meeting Bell on the sidewalk, attempted to take hold of him, but missed him, when B—— knocked him down and ran across the street, the other patrol after him. I was in the rear and stepped into an alley, losing sight or sound of B——. I found my way alone to my quarters. I went to bed but sleep had departed from my eyes. A thousand thoughts rushed through my mind. The escape I had made from loss of character (which would have resulted from being caught by the police and locked up as a night rambler in the round house among thieves and robbers), the loss of money which would have ruined Mr. Lewis, my partner, and myself, and last though not least the danger of ruin to soul as well as body by such improper acts and associations. I thought of my family and friends, especially my mother, how they would be pained to know what had occurred that night, and the impression was deeply made on my mind that my mother was praying at the very time I was in the gambling house; praying to the Most High, for my preservation from harm and crime. I was melted into tears and believing as I did, that through her prayers I had been preserved I made a vow that I would never again enter a gambling house, or other immoral establishments, and I can now say that vow has had its influence upon my whole life.

Mr. B—— called to see me the next morning and apologized for his conduct. I told him it was the first adventure of the kind I had made and I had determined it should be the last.

My business affairs were closed that day and I left the next day for Augusta County where I spent a few weeks with my relatives and then travelled to Kentucky in February. The roads were very deep and water high. I had no company. It was a lonely trip and one incident only seems worthy of remark. I rode from Kentucky a very uncommon looking horse, black as a crow, short necked, and cropped or foxed ears. I carried a brace of pistols in holsters on the front of my saddle, under a very black bear skin cover. I was therefore, recognized when I reached the road upon which we travelled our drove as "the little Kentucky drover," and one occurrence on the journey had given me and my horse additional notoriety. A few miles south of Abington, Va., on Holston River, passing a farm house a furious dog sprang out and stopped the drove, seizing one of the hogs and tearing it severely. One of the hands ran up and struck the dog a severe blow, two men who stood in the yard looking on with perfect indifference until the dog was stricken, sallied out with clubs and attacked Lewis. At that moment I rode up, drew a pistol, cocked it and told the foremost man who had his club raised, and my pistol cocked when the three other hands came up with rocks and clubs, the dog and his masters said they were overmatched and retreated, the men pouring out curses and threats of prosecution for threatening to shoot, etc. We gathered up our scattered drove and travelled on without further detention. We understood through travellers who passed us and had heard of the affray that those men followed us to Abington for the purpose of having us arrested but were advised not to attempt it. . . .

It was Sunday. Reflecting as I rode, solitary and alone, upon the occurrence of the morning, the thought struck me that I was breaking the Sabbath and would perhaps suffer additional punishment for the crime. Whilst I was meditating and hunting for an excuse, two men rode at a rapid pace past me, and their appearance and manner increased my apprehensions that the end was not yet. I felt that I had been indiscreet in opening my belt of bank notes in such a place as the Tavern, and thought it not improbable that the men who passed me, had knowledge of the occurrence, and were going ahead of me in order to select a suitable place to rob me. I was so deeply impressed with this idea, that I examined my pistols and prepared for an attack. . . .

Nothing worthy of remarks occurred during the balance of my journey. When I arrived at home, April, 1804, I learned that father had set his slaves free and had gone with a wagon loaded with farm implements and some laborers, to build a house. I remained a few days, during which time he communicated to me fully his purpose, and plans for the settlement of his family in Ohio, and directed me to return to the family and prepare for removal in the fall of the year. The first assigned was to go to Tennessee and sell a tract of land he owned in that state, then employ myself in attending to the family, and preparing the farm stock for sale in the fall, as he designed selling as much stock as would, with the sale of the Tennessee land, pay for the land he had recently purchased from General Calmes, amounting to $3,600, which was to be paid in one year. . . .

Father had left special instructions, that on my return, I should visit him without delay, for the purpose of receiving his instructions for the future. I only rested a few days before I set out for Ohio. I found my father in the midst of a dense forest, encamped on a tract of land, purchased from General Calmes of Kentucky. He had several men at work preparing timber for a house, and clearing a spot for an apple orchard. The trees for planting he had taken out with him. This was among the first orchards planted in Highland County, from which numberless grafts were in a few years furnished to Mr. Murphy, a nurseryman, who supplied the emigrants to Highland County and adjoining counties, with the celebrated Never-fail apples, then called Robinsons, for the man in Kentucky who was celebrated as an orchardist, and first introduced this unsurpassed Winter apple in that State.

Father had for many years before he set his slaves free, refrained from hard work, and exposure. When he went to Ohio to prepare a residence for his family he worked more than he had been accustomed to do, which, with the exposure, brought on an attack of bilious fever, from which he recovered so far as to be able to return to his family in Kentucky. But, alas! had a relapse and died on the — day of September, 1804.

This sad event seemed to derange all our plans for the future. My mother, although a woman of much firmness of purpose, and possessed of a capacity for the performance of all the duties which appertained to her province, had never troubled herself about her husband's affairs; she was therefore unprepared for the position she was then forced to occupy. No will having been made or provision for the payment of the debt to Calmes, it became a serious question, how and from what source this debt could be met.

I was yet a minor, and it was understood that General Calmes desired to administer on the estate; this I determined to prevent. I therefore visited my mother's brother, Wm. Allen, and prevailed upon him to take out letters of Administration, in order to prevent Calmes, pledging myself, so soon as I became twenty-one years of age, to relieve him, and take upon myself, the settlement of the estate. Not anticipating the disaster that had befallen the family by the loss of its head, I had, with my father's consent, engaged with a Mr. Bell, our neighbor, to purchase (with him), a second drove of hogs, for the Richmond market. The purchases were made before father's death. I had made money on the first drove, and felt confident of doing better on the second, and as we were left in a situation to require all the money we could raise, mother and the family united on me, complying with my engagement with Mr. Bell. Brother William, who had been absent at school, returned and remained with the family during the Winter.

About the 20th of October we started our drove, 500 head of fine hogs, for Richmond by the Kanawha route, striking the Ohio River at the mouth of the Big Sandy, then through Lea's Valley, to the mouth of Coal, then up the Kanawha to the mouth of Ganley, where we took the mountains, Ganlo, Albanya, Warm Springs, north and south, via Lewisburg, Staunton, and Charlottsville, to Richmond. I left the drove with Mr. Bell, at Staunton, and proceeded to Richmond, where I met Mr. Wm. Bell, (to whom I have before referred), the brother of my partner, who was of much service in effecting sales. After the arrival of the herd, we were detained only three days in making sale, and on the 4th was on our way homeward. . . .

The removal of our family from Kentucky to Ohio, had always been, until my father's death, of questionable propriety with mother, but after she became a widow, she often said she felt that Divine Providence had punished her for not yielding a hearty assent to the wishes of her husband, upon the subject, and now she felt that it was her duty to carry out his purposes as far as in her power and no inducement could have been offered that would have tempted her to remain in Kentucky.

I had, until the death of my father, entertained the hope that our Kentucky home farm would not be sold, but reserved to retreat to, if Ohio should prove unhealthy, or otherwise unsatisfactory to the family; but after father's death I came to the conclusion that as mother was determined to remove to Ohio, it would be to our interest to preserve our Ohio lands, sell out in Kentucky, and leave nothing to fall back upon. And that in this view of the matter, it would be my duty to accompany the family, to the new home prepared for us, in Ohio and remain with our mother as long as she desired we should. In this sentiment the entire family concurred. As soon, therefore, as the contract was made with Mr. Calmes, we went to the work of preparation, and by the — of October, 1805, were on our way to Ohio. (Brother William and James remained in Kentucky at School.) . . .

After arranging matters for the comfort of the family during the winter, I left to close and settle a land transaction, between my father and Jas. McNair of Tennessee. On my return through Kentucky I concluded to attend to another matter that I had for some time contemplated; and in January, 1806, I married Margaret McDowell, daughter of Gen. Joseph McDowell, of North Carolina, deceased, whose widow and family then resided in Kentucky. We arrived at our Highland home in January, and

I continued to live with my mother, who received and treated her daughter-in-law, as a valuable accession to her household.

We lived together as one family, having a common interest, and we lived happily. The want of Society such as we had enjoyed in Kentucky was the greatest privation we had to endure. Mother would frequently say: "Have patience, dear children, we have the Bible, let us improve the blessings we have, and the Lord will send us such other aids as we may stand in need of." Not long after this conversation took place, James Hoge (now Dr. Hoge), a young clergyman, the son of a schoolmate, and dear friend, of my mother, (a Miss Rose), came to see us. . . .

When the call was made for Ohio Volunteers, in 1812, two full companies were raised in Highland County. I then commanded a battalion of militia, and I had determined to turn out as a private, in order to encourage others to volunteer. A company of fifty (50) men was raised. Before it was organized I was prevailed upon by my brother, Wm. A. Trimble, to allow him to take my place. He insisted that as I had the care not only of my own but our mother's family, and he a young man, that it was more proper he should go into the army for me.[1] . . .

Gen. Hull did not arrive at Dayton, the place of rendezvous, for several days after those volunteers met and organized.

As before remarked I accompanied the Highland companies to Dayton, and remained until William A. Trimble and James Denny were elected Majors, and McArthur, Colonel of the Regiment. Then I returned to Highland to collect blankets, of which there was a very limited supply among the soldiers. I again arrived at Dayton with the blankets, I had collected a horse load. (I do not remember the exact number).

The next day Gen. Hull arrived, with his son, a young man, say twenty-five years of age; and also Major Morrow, of Gen. Cass' Red's, with a small Company of mounted officers, met, and escorted the General to his quarters. The contrast between the General and his aid-de-camp, upon their New England ponies, and also Morrow's Guard, in their parade dress, and elegantly mounted, was too striking not to be observed.

A general order was issued for a review of the Army on the day

---

1. In 1809 his wife had died, leaving him two sons. Remarrying two years later, Trimble had set up housekeeping with his mother and younger brothers.

following. The General took lodging at Mr. Reid's, the principal hotel, and had been waited upon by the officers, and a few distinguished citizens, such as Judge Burnett, Gen. Gano, Col. Davis, Major Oliver, etc., from Cincinnati, and others of like character.

The soldiers, and the citizens of Dayton, and the surrounding country, who had not seen Gen. Hull, learning there was to be a grand review, determined to embrace the opportunity it would afford, to see the far famed General. As I quartered at the same hotel, and belonged to Gen. McArthur's Mess, I had been introduced to Gen. Hull and his son, and on the morning of the review was invited to their room, where I found McArthur, Capt. Finley, Gano, and Judge Burnett. Judge Burnett was soliciting the appointment of aid-de-camp for his brother-in-law, Captain Wallace, and he succeeded in obtaining the desired appointment. I was a listener to the conversation, which was general but pointing to the object of the campaign, and its probable results. We are apt on the first sight of distinguished men, to form some opinion of their character. In the first place I was disappointed in the appearance of Gen. Hull, for he was a short, corpulent, good natured old gent; bore the marks of good eating and drinking, but none of the marks of a chief, according to my notions of a great general. In a word, he did not strike me "as a man born to command." . . .

The drums announced the hour for parade, and the Colonels left to take charge of their respective commands, leaving the General and his aids, his son, and Col. Wallace, to prepare for the review.

I walked with Mr. McArthur, with whom I was on intimate terms, to his room. He asked me what I thought of Gen. Hull. I replied: "It would be treason to give expression to my thoughts." He smiled. I then asked him if he would dare to give his opinion. "Not publicly," said he, "but I say to you, he won't do. He is not the kind of man we want, and I fear the result of our campaign; 'twill be disastrous. But as you say, it would be regarded as treason for me to express this opinion publicly."

The Regiments were soon paraded in line, on the beautiful common north-east of the town. The want of uniform was visible among the officers, many of them being in citizen's dress, but they all looked as if they would fight, if need be; Col. Cass was in full uniform and wore the highest plume of an officer in the Army, but Major Munson of his right, was the observed of all observers: six feet, two inches high, straight as an arrow, trim and well proportioned, the best horseman and upon the finest horse in the army. But it was admitted on all hands that McArthur looked more like a go-a-head soldier than any of his brother officers.

The line being formed and the officers formed and posted, Gen. Hull and his Aids commenced their review. The General and his son were in old state or style. They rode what was called New England ponies: short jointed, compact, trotting horses, about fourteen and one-half hands high. Wallace was richly equipped with epaulettes, etc., mounted on a fine, splendid gelding.

They commenced the review at a walk, but the musick, drum and fife seemed to give life, even to the General's ponies, fatigued as they were, from the long journey they had just made from New England; but Wallace's horse pranced and snorted like an old buck. As they passed the head of the Second Regiment, the display of the colors and the roar of the drums frightened Wallace's horse, and he ran at half speed in a wrong direction. The horse of Captain Hull dashed off at a rapid trot after Captain Wallace's. The General's pony followed his aids, and he was a hard trotter, throwing his rider up, until you could see daylight between his seat and the saddle. Well balanced as they all were for a review, with splendid swords, at their sides, they were not so well adapted to a race, especially at a trot. The consequence was, that the General's feet lost the stirrups, he lost his balance, his hat flew off, and to save himself he seized the horses mane. The frightened animal going at the rate of a mile in four minutes, at a hard trot. By this time the yells of the spectators and some of the wild volunteers, rendered the scene one of the most amusing I ever witnessed at a military review. The General and his aids, having fallen in with a cavalcade of citizens on horseback who occupied a position at some distance as lookers-on, were unable to learn the true cause of all this peculiar commotion.

After a parley of some fifteen minutes whether true or not, it was a subject of merriment among the soldiers, that Captains Wallace, and Hass planned the only Mad Review, before their youthful aid-de-camps could take him up. So they concluded not to attempt again to pass the army in review, but to take a position and require the army to pass them, then in the usual military style. This order was announced, (I think), by Gen. Cass, and executed with a good deal of life, a non-commissioned officer holding Gen. Hull's horse the while, to keep him from bolting. After the review, the army was brought into close column by command, and formed a hollow square. The General and his Staff, and field officers, took position in the center, and the commander-in-chief made a speech to the first army of Ohio. It was well made, delivered, and atoned in some measure for the failure at the review.

After aiding brother William in an outfit for the campaign, I returned to Hillsboro. The subject of war with England was the engrossing topic all over the United States, and particularly in the West, where a long line of frontier was exposed to Indian depredations; and as a large majority of the citizens of Ohio was in favor of the Government declaring War, and the State was called upon to furnish the first regiment of volunteers, it was natural that our people should feel deep solicitude for the success of Hull's army, as it was called. The public ear was quick to catch everything like suspicion. That General Hull was not the man for the occasion; those suspicions soon assumed the form of opinions, and nothing occurred on the March from Dayton to Detroit, to weaken those conclusions; but the surrender of the army to the British General, Brock, at Detroit, removed all doubt as to the correctness of the opinion, that Gen. Hull was totally unfit for the command assigned him by the President of the United States.

When the army arrived at Detroit, Michigan, the General issued a proclamation, calling upon the Canadians to capitulate for their safety, and pledge themselves not to take up arms against the United States, threatening in case of refusal, to invade the country and the overthrow of the government, etc. If he had in pursuance of his declared purpose, crossed the river at once, and attacked Malden, the garrison, a small one, would have surrendered, or been captured, and with it, upper Canada, with her host of Indians would have been subjected to the control of the United States army; but he waited until Gen. Brock, the British General, entered, and in the meantime, showed such a lack or want of Generalship, as to encourage Brock, to demand the surrender of Detroit.

Gen. Hull was charged with treason, and acquitted by a courtmartial. Brother William was a witness on the trial. I know his opinion and have reason to believe his opinion was correct. He often told me he had no confidence in Gen. Hull's judgment or integrity on military subjects. If he ever had talents upon any subject (which he doubted), they had become weakened by age, and beclouded by free living, eating and drinking. That however brave he had proved himself to be in early life, (as it was said he did), his conduct at Detroit exhibited unmeasurable evidence of timidity, and a total want of confidence in himself or his army. "In a word, he proved himself destitute of those great qualities that fit a man to command: a sound judgment, large intelligence, true courage, and self-reliance, that would gain the respect and obedience of the soldier."

When the news came to Hillsboro, that Hull's army had been surrendered, its truth was doubted. Joseph, Jasper Hand and myself determined to know as soon as possible, whether the report was well founded, and immediately mounted our horses and set out for Urbana, 67 miles distant. Here we found several persons who had left the northern settlements and fled to Urbana for safety from Indian depredations. They confirmed the report of the surrender of Hull's army. We learned that the northern Indians were preparing to let loose their combined forces upon the frontier settlements of Ohio, Indiana and Illinois, and that the British Canadians and Indians of Upper Canada were preparing to strike at the northern settlements of Ohio.

After hearing those rumors Dr. Hand and I concluded that the Governor of Ohio would probably make a requisition of militia to defend the frontier, and that our services might be required at home, so we returned. Governor Meigs took immediate steps to protect the frontier. General Winchester was ordered to Ohio to take command of the regulars and militia, raised and to be raised in Ohio.

The disastrous result of Hull's campaign was all attributed to the General's want of courage, or patriotism. To sustain the latter charge it was alleged that the army, instead of being at once actively employed against the enemy, as threatened in the proclamations, remained idle for weeks, the General sending out small detachments to reconnoiter the enemy's position, and ascertain their strength, giving time to collect and concentrate their forces, and subjecting those small parties to loss of confidence in their commander; and the further fact that McArthur and captains, and regiments, the strength of their army, were a day's march on the road to Browns-Town, the River Ra[i]sin, to meet an escort of prisoners from Ohio.[2]

The surrender of the garrison at Detroit, including all the absent detachments, gave colour to the idea that it had been under contempla-

---

2. After General Hull's surrender of the army at Detroit, Trimble joined a regiment organized to take the place of the captured army, which included his now-paroled brother.

tion; the General knowing full well that McArthur and Cass would not consent to a surrender without a fight, was evidence of what would have been the opinion and action of those two officers, had they been in the fort when its surrender was demanded. When they were overtaken by a messenger from General Hull, with an order to return to Detroit, as prisoners of war, a counsel was held by the officers of those two regiments, to determine whether they would return to Detroit and surrender or fight their way to Ohio. . . .

It was not strange that the people of the North-west, particularly those of Ohio, after the failure of General Hull, should look with fearful apprehension to danger in the future, from committing the command of the North-west army to inexperienced or incompetent hands. Gen. Winchester, accomplished as he was admitted to be, as an officer and general, was unknown to our people. He was not one of us, and there were murmurs and complaints. That Eastern men were sent to lead our armies, who knew nothing of the Indian mode of warfare, and but little of western character; that we had men in the West, pioneers, possessed of more physical and mental power and more perfect knowledge of the theater of the war to be carried on upon our border, than any specimen of an Eastern General that had been sent to us from beyond the Alleghenies.

ℋ𝒶ʀʀɪᴇᴛ ℬ. Cooᴋᴇ

1 7 8 6 – p o s t - 1 8 5 8

 ℋ A R R I E T Cooke was one of a handful of women who both led remarkable lives and recorded their experiences in memoirs. The opening line of her autobiography forcefully conveys the spirit of the woman: "I never was a *child.*" At the age of sixteen, Cooke became a schoolteacher, a vocation that opened up to more and more young men and women in the early years of the nineteenth century. Although the campaigns for publicly funded education and compulsory attendance lay in the future, in the 1790s the actual numbers of elementary schools greatly increased with the return of prosperity and as more and more communities established local districts to pay for the maintenance of schools and teachers. Usually in session for but ten or twelve weeks in the summer and winter, the schools hoped to teach the district children the "three R's"—reading, [w]riting, and [a]rithmetic.

More a stepping-stone than a lifetime career, school teaching was particularly attractive to teenagers who wanted to get out on their own. Poorly paid, they at least won freedom from the drudgery of farmwork and at best a measure of independence. Most women who taught school stopped when they got married; most men found more remunerative careers because of their educational attainments. Harriet Cooke was no exception to this rule; she married when she was twenty-one. Her husband went into trade with her brother, and she began a family. But after seven years as a homemaker, she returned to the schoolroom because of her husband's financial reverses. Her husband went to debtors' prison briefly after the failure of his business venture, and Cooke taught during the summers while he sought new work.

Just as Julia Tevis had looked up to Emma Willard, the famous founder of the Troy Academy for Women, so Cooke discovered a model in Isabella Marshall Graham. A Scotswoman, Graham had settled in 1789 in New York, where she ran a school and promoted the earliest relief societies for widows and orphans. Such role models were particularly important to able and strong-willed women like Tevis and Cooke, because so much of the literature of the early nineteenth century stressed the importance of women's staying within the domestic realm and making their mark on society through their influence as wives and mothers. Deeply religious and acutely conscious of defying authority, both Tevis and Cooke needed the precedence of other independent women.

While staying home was an option for Tevis, Cooke had no choice but to return to work, for her husband died of yellow fever in 1820. Left a widow with four children in Augusta, Georgia, where her husband had gone to recoup his losses, Cooke kept a boardinghouse for three years after his death. It was during this period when she was struggling to support her family that, according to her memoirs, "The example of Mrs. Graham, of sainted memory, often inspired me with courage when heart and flesh seemed failing, who, when sitting down to her frugal meal of *potatoes and salt* could say, 'I delight to do Thy will, O my God.' . . . Her experience and submission did serve greatly to encourage and strengthen mine." Cooke learned about Graham through a biography at a time when American inspirational literature was becoming abundant.[1] Despite the difficulty of this time in her life, Cooke has left a charming account of her conversations with the twelve boarders who shared her home, several of whom delighted in teasing her about the strictness of her religious practices.

After three years keeping boarders, Cooke calculated her finances

---

1. Harriet Cooke, *Memoirs of My Life Work: The Autobiography of Mrs. Harriet B. Cooke* (New York: Robert Carter, 1858), p. 66.

and learned that her expenses were larger than her returns. She therefore decided to return to Middlebury, Vermont, where her mother was living, raising the money for the trip by selling all her furniture at auction. Her departure from Charleston was not without incident, for she prevented the captain of the vessel from taking advantage of fair wind by her refusal to depart on the Sabbath. "As I steadfastly refused compliance with his wishes," Cooke writes, "he left me, declaring that 'he knew that I was a *Yankee,* because I was so determined to have my own way.' "[2] The keeping of the Christian Sabbath was a contentious issue in the early nineteenth century. Many states had laws proscribing any business activity on the Sabbath. In the 1820s groups organized to oppose even the movement of the mails on Sunday, while anti-Sabbatarians protested this intrusion of religious precepts into the realm of government.

Once back in New England, she started a school in Vergennes, Vermont, a small town of 999 people and two school districts. Cooke was then thirty-seven years old, and she continued to teach for another thirty years. Because her autobiography is the only record we have of Cooke, her date of death can only be guessed from the fact that she lived long enough to see her memoirs published in 1858.

I N E V E R was a *child.* Trained by an ambitious father, and an industrious and intellectual mother, my earliest recollections find me at the age of four, seated in my little chair, beside my mother, learning "to make papa's shirts," and committing to memory from her lips, interesting passages from "Thomson's Seasons," and other favorite authors. She was fond of poetry, and from her I soon learned to love the early writers of her ancestral home. Indeed so far as reading was concerned, it was these or nothing. Moore, Byron, and Bulwer had not cast their blighting influence over the youthful mind, nor had the teeming press disgorged its "millions of yellow trash," to pollute and destroy the intellect and the heart.

---

2. Cooke, *Memoirs,* p. 78.

True, there were romances in rich abundance, but so extravagant were they in their exhibition of character, and in their developement of life scenes, that a reflecting mind could hardly fail to become satiated and disgusted in their perusal. Such was my experience as I turned from them to the study of History and the English classics.

My early religious education was confined to a strict observance of rites and ceremonies; but although I read the Bible occasionally, of its precious truth and doctrines, I was entirely ignorant. Proud, vain, and self-conceited, it was my boast that "my *heart* was good;" my motto, "the *generous*, love and hate with all their heart," and well did I honor this motto.

At the early age of twelve, I was deprived of the care and protection of a father, whom I almost idolized. I well remember with what pride I looked upon his manly form and noble bearing. In my view he was no common man. With the enthusiastic ardor of youth and the generous confidence of a sailor's daughter, I regarded my father as a being, far above his kind—my beau ideal of perfection. I never dared to disobey him, and yet there was no terror mingled with my affection. Even now I can almost hear his voice in song, or the soft tones of his flute, as they melted the soul to tenderness and love.

Never shall I forget the morning of that day which brought the sad intelligence, that my mother was a widow,—that I was fatherless. He died far from home, from friends and sympathy, and his body was committed to ocean's waves to rest amid its waters, 'till the morning of the resurrection:

> "With white upturned brow,
> He lies where pearls lie deep;
> And the wild winds rave, and ocean waves
> Sing requiems o'er his sleep."

No tidings respecting his illness—no last words, or messages of affection, ever reached our ears;—they were all buried with him in the deep. The circumstances attending and succeeding his death were such as for a long time to occasion peculiar emotions, amounting sometimes almost to the hope that we might yet possibly see his face again. A passing barque that had spoken his ship, was greeted with the intelligence of the death of its captain, but the ship itself was never heard of more. Undoubtedly it foundered at sea, and none survived to tell the story of his death or of their own calamity, yet often afterwards, in the stillness of the night would the thought find indulgence that the passing greeting of the two vessels might have been misunderstood, and that he might yet be restored to us.

O what trials then came over my young heart; what blighting of bright prospects, what crushed affections, what disappointed hopes and dark days followed. Wonderful was the mercy of God, in those seasons of trial and poverty. My poor mother was strengthened for her trying duties. The widow's God was near to help her, and through His blessing on her unwearied efforts, her children were educated for respectability and usefulness. Thanks be to God for such a mother: her children do, indeed, call her blessed, and they praise the Lord that she was spared to them and to the Church of Christ. "The righteous shall be in everlasting remembrance." "The memory of the just is blessed." They rest in heaven.

Just fifty years after the death of my father, I unexpectedly came across a letter which he had written to me, when I was but ten years of age. With what mingled emotions did I look upon the sacred relic, and in its expressions of earnest affection recall the oft repeated admonition, "My dear H. love and obey your mother; imitate her example; I ask no greater boon for my child."

Much responsibility rested on me, as the eldest of four children, and the dependence of my mother on me for comfort, companionship, and assistance in training her young charges, gave, perhaps, a maturity to my character, that did me good service in after life. Possessing a bold, ardent and independent mind, I was generally the leader in every daring enterprise. Once I remember being in imminent danger of drowning, through one of my youthful impulses. A few of us—school girls—had wandered along the banks of the Connecticut, in search of recreation. Seeing a boat most invitingly empty, we agreed to take possession of it, and have a sail. I volunteered to loosen the rope, and push it from the shore. I succeeded admirably in this attempt, but losing my balance, I was compelled to spring into the water. The assistance of a kind sailor saved me from being swept away by the current, and probably from being drowned.

At the age of sixteen I commenced my pedagogical career. Allured by the glowing representations of interested seekers for teachers, then not so easily obtained as now, and by a desire to "see the world," I was induced, in the year 1802, to exile myself from my early home and take up my residence in the Green Mountain State. . . .

My removal to Middlebury, in 1805, to join my mother, who had previously removed from Connecticut, and thus once more to complete the family circle, was an important era in my life. Here I found a general interest awakened in the minds of the people on the great subject of the soul's salvation, an interest so new and strange to me that I resolved to keep aloof from every effort to affect my feelings. Up to this time I had never attended an evening meeting, unless on some *great saint's* day, when, though there was much to please the eye and the ear, there was little, under the *presiding administration,* to touch the heart. I say this with no sectarian feeling, for if I know my own heart, I believe I can truly say, "I love the church of God in all its branches."

A few friends had been for a long time in the practice of collecting at my mother's, to spend the Sabbath evening, as we said, in *rational conversation.* As the religious interest in town increased, the question arose among the female portion of our party, "is it right for us to spend our Sabbath evenings in visiting, when there are those collected for prayer who would rejoice to see us with them?" Influenced by the urgent invitation of a friend who had herself been benefited by these meetings, we resolved henceforth to spend the Sabbath evening in a manner more befitting holy time, and promised to accompany her to the house of prayer. Our friend Catharine met us at the appointed hour, and we went like *strangers* going to a *strange* place. Half way there, we espied the little company of our male friends, who had formed a part of our Sabbath evening circle, as we thought, approaching us, and not having sufficient independence to invite them to accompany us, or perhaps fearing that they would persuade us to a walk, we turned from the public road, and passed unnoticed to the place of meeting.

We were scarcely seated before those same friends whom we had sought to avoid, entered the room. Had Van Amburgh let loose half his menagerie upon us, it could scarcely have created a greater sensation. Looks of gratified surprise, passed from eye to eye, and the beaming countenance of Dr. A., who was then acting as our pastor, spoke his delight. With the affectionate solicitude of a father did his earnest gaze rest on the youthful band, while all his energies seemed aroused and concentrated on this one point—to attract our attention and to effect our hearts. The words chosen as the basis of his remarks accorded well with my feelings. Had he placed before me the threatenings of the law against sinners—had he dwelt on the misery of the lost, I should have listened calm and unmoved. I had been *baptized* and *confirmed,* and in accordance with my early instructions I was prepared for the Kingdom of heaven; but when the man of God arose and repeated, with deep feeling and solemnity, "God is love,"—when he spread out before us the exhibition of that love in the forbearance and patience manifested towards us—His watchful providence guiding our wayward and inexperienced steps—guarding us from dangers—supplying our wants, and, above all, giving his only Son to suffer and to die for us, and freely offering salvation to all who would accept of this Saviour—when he contrasted this exhibition of his love with our forgetfulness of Him—our ingratitude, rebellion, and rejection of his Son, my heart was touched; I felt that I was *the one* to whom the words of this ministry had been sent. From that moment a fire was kindled in my soul that was not quenched till the blood of Jesus extinguished it forever. . . .

Two years after the public consecration of myself to the service of my Saviour, I made in my Journal the following record. "A new era has commenced in my life. I have exchanged a single for a married state; have left that home, in the bosom of which I have enjoyed many happy hours, for a situation most responsible. For the goodness of God in granting me a companion, who, I have reason to hope, has sought and obtained the pearl of great price,—an interest in the Saviour, with whom I can journey through life, in one mind, one faith, and one Lord, I hope I am not wholly insensible." He was one of the little company of friends who so singularly met, early in the revival of 1805, in that "place where prayer was wont to be made," and who dated from that evening their first serious impressions.

How necessary is it that a woman placed in the responsible situation of a head of a family, should possess firm and correct principles: a heart warm with love to God and to her fellow creatures. Actuated by that benevolence which seeketh not her own, but the good of those around her, she will strive to imitate her Divine Master. Continuing, fervent in spirit, and faithful in the discharge of duty, she will fully prove that "the price of a virtuous woman is far above rubies." "The heart of her husband will safely trust in her, she will do him good and not evil, all the days of her life. Her children shall rise up and call her blessed; her husband also, and he praiseth her.". . .

In the winter of 1813, my husband was persuaded to enter into mercantile business, and formed a partnership in trade, with my brother. Many reasons were urged, in favor of such a change. The place first chosen as a residence, was peculiarly unpleasant, from the fact that the church was in such a state of dissension and declension, that we could not enjoy the stated preaching of the gospel. We therefore removed to Middlebury, and were for a time most happy in the society of early friends. Business prospered at first, but an unfortunate contract, made by my brother, previous to his connection with my husband, to furnish supplies for the fleet, on Lake Champlain, during the last war with England, for which, owing to governmental difficulties, he was never compensated, brought disaster and failure. As my husband had endorsed my brother's notes, he was involved in the common ruin, and our family was thus at once reduced to comparative poverty.

Of the trials of that season, none can conceive, who have not been placed in similar circumstances; it proved a fitting discipline for the severer chastisements that were soon to succeed. My brother sought a home in a southern city, hoping there to retrieve his shattered fortunes, but my husband remained for the purpose of effecting, if possible, a compromise with their creditors. After occupying several months, in a vain attempt to accomplish this object—at the close of a week spent in most agitating conflicts of feeling—there seemed no alternative, but that the doors of a prison were to close upon him. The trial came at last. An unfeeling creditor would make no compromise, and late one evening, having spent a day of agonizing forebodings, my husband returned home, to tell me that *that* night he must sleep in the debtor's room. Oh, the distress of that hour! it seemed as though my heart would surely burst; "the *wormwood* and the *gall,* my soul hath them still in remembrance.". . .

Soon after this our family circle was again broken. My husband journeyed to one of the Southern states in quest of business; and I, with my children, took board in my mother's family till we should be summoned to join the absent one in the land of strangers. Wearisome days and months were those, and yet much mercy was mingled with the trials of our temporary separation. My time was spent in instructing my children, visiting the sick, and comforting the afflicted.

In the summer I taught school and thus was able, by my own efforts, to remove from my husband during his absence the burden of supporting his family from his slender means. . . .

We embarked on board the Levant, and after a stormy passage of eight days, reached Savannah in safety. Here I left the friend who had thus far taken charge of me and mine, and proceeding to Augusta, the place of our final destination, arrived there on the morning of December 25, 1819, in season to partake of a Christmas dinner with my beloved husband. How did my heart bound to meet him from whom I had been so long separated. I hope I was thankful—I am certain I was rejoiced.

That winter passed happily away, in the society of of my best earthly friend, and in efforts to train our children for God. Many are the mournful records in my Journal, of my forgetfulness of recorded vows; of my worldliness and unfaithfulness in my Master's service. I prayed to be delivered from this worldliness, that my soul might no more cleave to the dust. My heavenly Father heard my prayer, and answered it by blighting all my earthly prospects. The "desire of my eyes," was removed by a stroke,—my "house was left unto me desolate,"—"widow and orphans," was written against me and my bereaved children. What a change did a few short days effect in my situation. At one moment, I was blessed with the affection of a worthy and beloved husband, whose smiles brightened the dear domestic fireside—the next, solitary and sad, I was a stranger, in a strange land—destitute—desolate—afflicted.

During the summer, the fevers to which northern constitutions are generally susceptible, laid many a strong man low; and besides the care of our little family, and the performance of my husband's duties as an instructor of youth, we found our time fully occupied in ministering to the sick, who, like ourselves, strangers from home, had none to care for them in the hour of trial. Some we took into our dwelling, and little did I imagine, while watching beside their beds, how soon I must perform the same painful task, for a far dearer friend.

But the trying hour drew near, and this friend, who had never known what it was to be laid aside from active duties, since my acquaintance with him, was also visited by the fatal pestilence. Of *his* exposure to sickness, I never dreamed; but I often thought of the probability that to myself or to my children, the change of climate might prove fatal.

This fear in my husband, turned all his solicitude from himself, and he watched over us with the tenderest anxiety.

How often did this beloved one speak of his present happiness, and dwell upon the prospects opening for future domestic comfort. A few evenings previous to his illness, he said to me:

"We want nothing to add to our enjoyment but the society of our northern friends."

He then made a calculation of the time it would require to liquidate the heavy debt, with which he was now wholly burdened, by the death of my brother, but which he was fast diminishing, by frequent payments from a generous salary.

"In four years," he said, "I think it can be accomplished, and then we shall be free from this pecuniary trouble, and we may be reunited to those whom we love."

"O do not deceive yourself," I replied, "with hopes that may never be realized. I feel, that with us, every thing future is most uncertain."

"But you know, there can be no great danger in *planning,* if we never execute. It is pleasant even *to talk* of meeting friends again."

Never shall I forget the deep emotions excited in my breast, on the evening of the succeeding Sabbath, as seated with him in our chamber, surrounded by our little family group, enjoying a delightful moonlight scene, we sang at his request the hymn—

> "Come we that love the Lord
> And let our joys be known."

We conversed on the blessedness of those, who behold the glories of Immanuel, and never, never sin. Our souls were raised above the world, and I believe that we enjoyed an elevation of feeling, a solemnity of spirit, that was peculiarly calculated to prepare us for the approaching trial.

On the next day, Mr. C. complained of feeling very unwell, and consulted a physician. Doctor S. seemed anxious, and bade him attend carefully to his prescriptions. As I urged him to eat some food that I had specially prepared for him, for which he had no appetite, I laughingly said: "O you *must* eat; I shall not suffer *you* to be sick," the physician, with a look and manner that struck to my heart, and which has since convinced me that he was aware of the danger that threatened him, said to me, "my dear friend, you are not Omnipotent!"

For three days, my husband was able to walk about the room, but complained much of his head. Some circumstances, since recalled to mind, have led me to believe that *he* was aware of his danger, though he carefully concealed it from me. He was unwilling that I should leave his room, even for a short time, and when I urged the claims of the family, his reply was,

"Let them manage for themselves now, I can not spare you, I want your society.". . .

We did each commence a *new life* indeed. He, I trust, entered into glory—and I was left a widow.

When our friends had gone, Mr. C. complained of great exhaustion, gave his pet, as Maria called herself, a kiss, and fell asleep. I took my seat beside him, resolving to improve the first hours of his awaking. He did awake, but he knew me not—he knew me no more, unless he recognized me in delirium, and never again were the lips of my husband opened to address me, in the language of affection. Though the delirium continued, I entertained no apprehensions of the result of that crisis on the morrow to which I was looking with so much assurance that it would prove favorable.

Though many kind friends offered their services, I preferred to be his only watcher through the hours of that solitary night. As with the point of a diamond, are the sensations of that watch graven on my soul. No creature was near me, save a young servant, and my children, who were all in a sound slumber, unconscious of my distress. Every noise reverberated through the large building in which we dwelt, and as my husband's delirium increased, the loud howling of the watch dog, and the low moaning of the wind, seemed to excite in him a distressing terror. It was a night never to be forgotten; yet it seems strange to me *now*, that through all those dismal hours, I never revolved in my mind the probability of the greater trial that awaited me; nor even when I collected my family in the morning, around the bed of the dear unconscious sufferer, to beg for a blessing on the means employed for his recovery, did I entreat for peculiar support under peculiar trials.

I have since thought, that God in mercy prevented my suspicion of his danger, knowing that exhausted nature would sink under the fatigues of incessant watchings and distress of mind. He continued insensible to the anxiety of friends, and unconscious of the presence of the

the "new life" of the widow

beloved ones, who gathered around his bed until twelve o'clock. At that time, a friend who had just entered, first conveyed to my mind the idea of danger, and just at the moment that the spirit was forsaking its earthly tenement, did I first learn that I was about to be bereaved. Stunned by the blow, I made no resistance to those who led me from the room to my chamber, and there, on my knees, I awaited, what even then, I hoped would be a favorable issue to this terrible crisis. But when the words of Doctor S. sunk into my heart,—

"All human help has failed," I *then* felt in all its bitterness that I was indeed *a widow.*

I was, literally, *alone,* with no female friend to comfort me in this time of trial, though surrounded by many who knew and respected the departed, and who would fain have sympathized with me, in the desolation which spread over my soul. Truly at such a time "the heart knoweth its own bitterness, and a stranger intermeddleth not with it." I was stricken to the dust, but not forsaken; cast down, but not in despair. Though the shock I received, from the suddenness of the blow, nearly dethroned reason, I was not left comfortless. Heaven was now brought near to earth; only a narrow passage—and it seemed *very narrow*—separated me from the friend and companion of my youth and riper years, whom I expected soon to meet in our Father's home. . . .

For four weeks was I prostrated by extreme suffering. I was often deprived of my reason or was in a state of entire insensibility, but when conscious of my situation I fully expected to be summoned to join the loved ones who had preceded me to their heavenly home. Through the whole of this distressing sickness my blessed Father did not forsake me. His comforts and promises refreshed my soul, and before He brought me back to the activities of the world, He made me willing *to live, to suffer,* or *to die,* as He should direct. . . .

With returning health, the question presented itself, what shall I do?—in what business engage, in order to support myself and my children? After much prayer and consultation with friends, I determined to open a boarding-house, and in October, with my pecuniary resources reduced to *nine dollars,* my health still feeble from my severe and protracted illness, I commenced my new life of widowhood and responsibility.

The trustees of the Academy had kindly paid my husband's salary to the close of the term, but this was exhausted by the necessary funeral

much formative guided by scripture

expenses, and by my illness; and they also granted me the privilege of educating my sons in the Institution, free of expense.

Now was the time to feel in its full force, the extent of my loss. Daily was I reminded by my ignorance of business, and my exposure to imposition of every kind, of the affection of that dear husband, who would never suffer me to be burdened by providing for the family when he was near. The wants of a large family of boarders to be supplied, and that liberally and satisfactorily—my children, too young to appreciate their loss, or their mother's care or anxiety on their account,—without resources, and in feeble health, my faith, and hope, and spirits, would at times all sink, and I could only cry out in my distress, "O that it were with me as in months that are past!" Often did I, in the agony of my spirit and the rebellion of my heart, desire that God would prepare my children and take us all to Himself. . . .

Many were the trials I experienced, on account of my children, and from anxiety, lest my sons should be corrupted by intercourse with irreligious and immoral companions; many the difficulties I passed through, in providing for my large family, but I think that after this reproof in the sanctuary I never suffered myself to sink so low in despondency. "Leave thy fatherless children and I will preserve them, and let thy widows trust in me," was a promise on which I rested in confidence.

Often, in a wonderful manner, did my Father, who beheld all my need, graciously supply my wants. Accustomed to carry every burden and lay it at the foot of the cross; to go and tell Jesus my every necessity and every trial, I was never sent from the mercy-seat without some token of His love, while supplies would sometimes be granted in a way so unexpected that it seemed as though the windows of heaven were opened for my relief.

The two succeeding years were marked by events of thrilling interest. They will ever live in remembrance, to awaken humility and gratitude; they were preeminently years of preparation for my subsequent career. I suffered much from pecuniary embarrassments, and often was so straitened for means that I could scarcely maintain abroad an appearance of respectability, and yet the fact was not suspected, as economy and close calculation, aided by my mourning garb, did me good service. My children had little idea of the sacrifices and privations to which their mother submitted that they might enjoy the advantages of good society, and the privileges of a good education.

The example of Mrs. Graham, of sainted memory, often inspired me with courage when heart and flesh seemed failing, who, when sitting down to her frugal meal of *"potatoes and salt"* could say, "I delight to do thy will, O my God."

"Peace with God," says her biographer, "and a contented mind, supplied the lack of worldly prosperity, and she adverted to this, her humble fare, in after life, to comfort the hearts of suffering sisters." Her experience and submission did serve greatly to encourage and strengthen mine.

Among the varied trials to which I was subject, was one of no ordinary character. Most of the boarders who resided with me during the winter, were accustomed to spend their summer months in traveling, or at their northern homes. Only two of the inmates of my dwelling professed to love the Saviour, and they kindly led in our family devotions, and asked the blessing of God upon our daily meals. On the evening previous to their departure, I was conversing with a Quaker gentleman, who was also a member of my family, and proposed that he should perform the latter service for us, as he did not hesitate to call himself a Christian.

"Well, Harriet," said he, "I will see what I can do for thee, the Spirit may not move me. I will see."

"May I then call on you to perform this kind office, and will you promise to oblige me?"

With one of his arch smiles, he nodded, as I thought, his assent, and left me.

When summoned to dinner, we were all seated before he made his appearance, and as he passed to his seat, which was always directly opposite to me, I cast upon him an appealing look, which was answered by an expressive bow, which quite assured me that he would not refuse my request.

"Mr. L.," I said, "will you ask a blessing for us?" With a most amusing smile, he fixed his eyes steadily upon me, and replied,

"Thee will do it thyself, Harriet."

No levity marked the group that surrounded my table, and no discomposure of spirit prevented me from performing the duty thus suddenly imposed upon me. God strengthened me for it, and I had no foolish fears in attempting it.

In the evening I was again summoned to take up the cross. As I was about to commend my family to the care of our heavenly Father for the night, I was interrupted by the entrance of several of my boarders; of course I did not suppose that duty required such a sacrifice of feeling as would be involved in leading our family devotions before such a household. The Bible lay on the table beside me. "Well, Mrs. C.," said a young German, "who is to pray for us to-night?" I was startled by the question: "I think, Mr. D.," was the agitated reply, "that we must do our own praying."

"And why should not *you* do it for us?" said another, who was from my own New England. "I never could see why the head of a family, if she is a widow, should not take the lead in family worship; I boarded," he continued, "for some time with a widow lady who never omitted the duty, and her boarders all respected her for her consistent Christian conduct."

The approval of this course was unanimous, "and now, Mrs. C.," persisted the German youth, "I do not see but you must do our praying for us."

"I certainly can read the Bible," I said, with the feeling that I could proceed no farther. I selected the most devotional of the Psalms, and as I closed the sacred volume, with a feeling that I could not—that I dare not—resist, I kneeled in prayer in the midst of these impenitent young men who had taught me my duty, and again was I strengthened and assisted in the accomplishment of that which at first seemed wholly impossible.

There are those who may be disposed to cavil and object to a female assuming such a responsibility; to convince such of its propriety, I have only to wish that a necessity as *morally imperious* may be laid upon them. The path of duty would be plain to them then. . . .

After a trial of nearly three years, finding that if I continued to seek a support from keeping boarders I should only become more and more deeply involved in debt, I resolved to change my plans of life. The circumstances leading to this change were mortifying and distressing. Here again was exhibited the evidence of a Father's care. I found that my expenses exceeded my income. As my boarders were mostly northern men, they generally spent the summer months at home, thus materially reducing my receipts while the expense of house rent and servants' wages continued through the entire year. The cotton market was not

stationary, and unfortunately, in the autumn of 1822, just as I was settled, as I supposed, in one of the best locations in the city, I found on
the return of business men that I had entirely misjudged. The market
was removed to a distant point, and thither went those who would otherwise have formed a part of my family. Twelve boarders were all that
were left to me, and when at the expiration of the first quarter the rent
was demanded, I had not wherewith to answer the demand. What was
to be done? Boarders were all located elsewhere. In what other business
could I engage? The prospect was appalling. In the deep agony of my
spirit I called upon the Lord, "when my heart is overwhelmed within
me, lead me to the rock that is higher than I. I cried unto the Lord and
He heard my prayer.". . .

During the remainder of the winter I taught a small school, and was
thus enabled to furnish a scanty support for myself and my children. On
the marriage of my mother, in the spring, I was urged to return to my
northern home, and the wish to educate my children in their fatherland
led me seriously to consider the practicability of such a removal. My
eldest son had been sent to Middlebury a year before, and was preparing
to enter college. My wish to return was very great, but I had not the
means of defraying my expenses. I had incurred heavy debts while en-
deavoring to support a boarding establishment, and there seemed no
probability that I should ever again see my friends in the home of my
youth.

I finally agreed to allow a test proposed by a few friends, to decide
the question. My furniture was sold at auction, and a dividend was made
of its proceeds among my creditors. By almost all of them, it was gener-
ously returned to me, so that abundant means were thus supplied to
defray the expenses of my journey to the north, and I determined to
depart.

In the month of May, 1823, I took passage for Charleston, S. C., with
my children and a small party of friends, who were returning home. . . .

A circumstance occurred in connection with this voyage, which, as
it is the second of the kind that has come to my knowledge, I record for
the encouragement of those who reverence the Sabbath. I had engaged
and paid for my passage to New York, with the understanding that the
vessel would sail on the following Monday. Early on the morning of
the Sabbath, word came from the captain—himself professedly a pious
man,—that a favorable wind had sprung up, and that all the passengers

refuse to sail on Sabbath

with the exception of our party were on board, and we were urged to hasten our departure. I decidedly refused compliance with the request; referred to the agreement respecting the *time* of sailing, and desired that if any change was made my passage money should be returned. The captain in great perplexity came to see me. He pleaded his cause earnestly; the passengers were clamorous to depart; a favorable wind promised a speedy passage; a rival vessel, the "President," had hoisted her sails and would reach the great city before them, and finally he begged that I would be less scrupulous and depart with him. I appealed to his religious principles, and to the command to "keep the Sabbath," and asked,

"Why is it, Captain B., that more vessels go out of port on the Lord's day than on any other?"

"Why," said he, with a smile, "it is a *good day,* because there are more Christians praying for us on this day."

"Those prayers," I replied, "are not offered for the mariner's *continuance* in sin, but that he may repent and turn unto the Lord."

As I steadfastly refused compliance with his wishes, he left me, declaring that "he knew that I was a *Yankee,* because I was so determined to have my own way."

While I was at the tea-table he again made his appearance.

"Now, Mrs. C., I have given you a *whole day* to attend church, the President is on her way, out of sight, and the passengers declare that they will be detained no longer."

"Captain, I sincerely regret to be an annoyance to you or your passengers, but with my present views of duty I *can not* comply with your request."

"But some on board are so enraged that they are actually swearing about you."

"That is an additional reason," I said, smiling, "why I should fear to trust myself with them while conscious of doing what I believe to be wrong. I might meet the fate of the prophet of Nineveh. Now, Captain, *Jonah!* no persuasion that you can use will affect my decision. If you feel that you must sail to-day, you go without me and my friends, for they all approve of this decision. If you choose to wait, you shall see us with the early dawn on board your vessel."

"Well," said the Captain, with a long sigh, "I do not intend to lose this company, so I will take up my anchors and pretend that I am about to set sail, but I shall only get my vessel out into the stream, and wait till morning."

Many angry glances greeted us as we ascended the vessel's side on the bright morning of Monday, but the addition to our company of a clergyman and his family, in consequence of the delay, quite restored the Captain's good humor and *we* secured a pleasant party of pious friends.

For six days no cloud obscured our sky; no unpleasant circumstance occurred to disturb our passage; bright moonlight nights and a calm sea, gave us the opportunity every evening, of collecting for the worship of God, and when Saturday night arrived we retired to rest full of bright hopes of anchoring in the harbor of New York on the following morning, in season to attend upon the worship of God in the sanctuary. We were about entering the Narrows, and the beautiful island of Manhattan was looming up in the distance, when a violent gale drove us back to sea, and our Sabbath proved a severely sick and turbulent day. Early on Monday as with renewed hopes and with joyful looks, we were again approaching the city, the Captain summoned me on deck, and pointing to a vessel in the distance that had just risen above the horizon, exclaimed,

"There, Mrs. C., comes the President, still plodding her weary way along, while *we* are about to cast anchor in the harbor."

"Now, Captain, what do you think of *trusting God,* and obeying his commandments?"

"Ah," said he, "I see that it is the best way. I'll remember this."

At this discovery, a shout went up from the passengers and crew for the triumph achieved over the tardy vessel. We afterwards ascertained that contrary winds, on the day of their departure from Charleston, had driven them far to the south, and thus they were disappointed in their expected victory over us. . . .

My mind had become more and more impressed with the belief, that it was my duty to teach, and as circumstances all seemed to point to this as my future employment, most willingly, though with much fear and trembling, I assumed new responsibilities, and in 1825, commenced a school in the city of Vergennes. Here I found many kind friends—and *trials* in abundance. For four years I toiled in the midst of cares, and labors and sorrows of no trifling kind. My eldest son, then a student in college, had been entered there with the express assurance, that the expenses of his education should be defrayed by a friend who had voluntarily agreed to assume the responsibility, but by the removal of that friend from the post that he occupied, R. was cast upon me for support. This unexpected increase of expense continually weighed me down, so that at times it seemed as though I must sink under my difficulties. Anxiety lest his extreme youth should expose him thoughtless as he was, to the temptations that I knew surrounded him, added to my distress, and without Divine support I could never have sustained the burden. My health yielded to the demands made upon my strength to such a degree, that I passed day after day in such bodily anguish, that death seemed the only relief. But my heavenly Father did not forsake me—light was scattered in my pathway. . . .

While in New York I was urgently and repeatedly solicited by a friend to undertake the editorship of a magazine designed expressly for the improvement of young ladies. Several of my friends were of opinion that the experience I had acquired in my years of teaching, aided by the multiplicity of facts that I had collected during those years, peculiarly qualified me for such a work. After much deliberation and prayer I came to the conclusion that God had not then called me to engage in such an undertaking.

I was also invited to become a missionary teacher in Illinois, but having been satisfied that the compensation offered could not meet necessary expenses, and having no capital of my own on which I could fall back in trying emergencies, I was compelled to give the negative to this plan. When I left Woodstock the promise had been made to me that I should be assisted to establish a school in New York in the spring; the spring opened, but for reasons that I never fully understood, and cared not to fathom, the promise was not fulfilled.

While preparing to visit my children in Virginia, I received an invitation to spend a day or two in Bloomfield, N. J., to ascertain the practicability of opening a Seminary in that place.[1] After complying with the request, I concluded to make the experiment, and in July, 1836, once more found myself a stranger in the midst of strangers.

My first term of three months passed rapidly by, and at its close I received an "unanimous call," to make a permanent settlement among that people. I accepted the propositions that were made and passed the month of October, with my children. I proposed to my eldest son to unite

---

1. Considering the limited range of employment open to women, the various opportunities presented to her are impressive.

with me in what I felt would be an arduous undertaking. He desired time for consideration and here for the time being the matter rested. . . .

My son, having concluded to accept my proposition to unite with me in the establishment of a boarding-school, in Bloomfield, I was joined by my children in the spring of 1837, and we commenced our joint labors in May with twenty boarders.

In the arrangements and instructions of the school a similar course was pursued to that adopted in Middlebury, and as we now had the control of the family, a short season was set apart, morning and evening, for private devotion. This season the pupils were *required* to spend alone in their rooms, in the hope that while it was gratefully improved by those who loved to pray, such a retirement, even for a few moments, might lead the minds of the thoughtless to God. . . .

Much has been said and many treatises written, to impress on the mind of woman the extent of her influence on society, and especially on the little circle gathered around her in her own beloved home. That such enforcements are called for, in this age of fashion and worldliness, no one can deny, or too deeply deplore. We need but to take a view of a modern school-room to fathom the trials to which many a conscientious teacher is subjected, to understand fully that we have reached the times portrayed with so much feeling by the Prophet, "The child shall behave himself proudly against the ancient." "As for my people, children are their oppressors, and women rule over them. O, my people, they which lead thee cause thee to err.". . .

Mothers of the present day! I fearlessly appeal to your hearts and consciences—is not this the general training of thousands of our children who are rapidly growing up to take your places in the community?

Forgetting, or perhaps ignorant of the fact that the impress of the first few years stamps the future character of the candidate for eternity, the training process is deferred till the child, as the parent hopes, shall have attained an age when it will yield to reason and to moral suasion. Thus the parent becomes the subject of the *"Young Dominion,"* and the juvenile lord reigns triumphant in the domestic castle.

Thus prepared to assert his or her rights in all circumstances, our "young patriarchs" are transferred to the supervision of teachers, who are expected to transform their youthful charges into models of propriety, gentility, and scholarship. Would the parents encourage the disheartened instructors, by their co-operation in the great work committed to their trust, there might arise some hope of success, but alas! such co-operations are "few and far between." Memory reveals a case of years departed. A mother—a lovely Christian mother—placed in my care two interesting children. "They have many faults, Mrs. C.," she said, "but you need never fear to make me acquainted with them. Correct them when they go astray, and you will always find that you have my confidence and co-operation," and she always sustained me in my efforts to train these children for God's service. Our covenant God brought them both, as we trusted, into the family of His disciples. . . .

"Probably in no enlightened country on the globe are children more anxious to be esteemed, or earlier permitted to become men and women than in our own; it has been with much truth remarked, that in the United States there is no such period as youth; we jump at once from childhood to fancied maturity. In female education is this evil most apparent and most serious in its consequences. As soon as a young lady has attained that age when she begins to appreciate the advantages of a well-stored mind, and the influence that it will secure for her in society—when she is prepared to profit most, by instruction—the usages of society, perhaps the mistaken eagerness of parents themselves, call her away from her studies to assume her position in society, soon, it may be, herself to become the head of a family, destined to train other immortal minds, while as yet her own is only just dawning into maturity. The idea that young ladies who have reached this point will perfect their education by the aid of private tutors or by personal application, after they have given up the duties and the tasks of the school-room, is a delusion that deceives at first, but is soon abandoned. The consequence of this is that the general standard of female education with us is low compared with that of England, and perhaps most of the countries of Europe. But while these various obstacles are well calculated to discourage conscientious teachers, and to excite the heart-sickening inquiry, 'who hath believed our report?' many bright oases are sprinkled over the desert, and upon their 'tent in the wilderness' many bright sunbeams shed their cheering warmth to gladden the heart that would otherwise sink in despondency. Not unfrequently the affection of grateful hearts is permanently secured, and the seed sown in years gone by, springs up to be replanted in other soil, perhaps to furnish fruit in the juvenile vineyard of the youthful mother."

$\mathcal{A}$LFRED $\mathcal{M}$. $\mathcal{L}$ORRAIN

$1790-1860$

$\mathcal{A}$ L F R E D Lorrain entitled his memoirs *The Helm, the Sword, and the Cross* to indicate that in his life he had been successively a sailor, a soldier, and a clergyman. More important, he was a splendid writer with wonderful stories to tell. Born in Maryland, Lorrain grew up in Petersburg, Virginia, where his father was one of the town's first merchants. Of his boyhood, he remembers the horse races spring and fall, the "gander-pulling and cock-fighting," and the fact that the arrival of the Methodists brought about a decline of these sports.

He also recalls that his hometown was "in the heart of slavery." Indeed, he confides to his autobiography a particularly grisly tale of an enslaved man being tortured. Lorrain, who became ardently opposed to slavery, nonetheless felt that his childhood play with African Americans gave him greater sympathy to them than Northerners possessed. "Parents in the South can not lay their fences so high as to separate entirely the children of the two classes," Lorrain maintains, adding that the children often hunted and fished together.[1]

Having witnessed the sale of an enslaved woman who was forced to leave her family to go to her new master in South Carolina, Lorrain reflects that "Many of our citizens used to feel deeply on such occasions, but they seemed to consider them as necessary outrages connected with an institution that appeared to be as firmly settled as the pillars of

---

1. Alfred Lorrain, *The Helm, the Sword, and the Cross* (Cincinnati, 1862), pp. 41–42.

heaven." He remembers, too, the fears and rumors at the time of the Gabriel Prosser scare, when a terrible storm in Richmond frustrated the plans of Prosser and his rebels.[2]

Entering the merchant marine as a teenager, Lorrain embarked on a seafaring life that took him to Europe and the Mediterranean. In England he was surprised to discover interracial courting. Indeed, when fights broke out between white Americans and blacks on the docks, Cockneys would crowd around, Lorrain recalls, shouting: " 'Give it to him, my African! Let him have it! You are not in America now. You are in the land of freedom—the land of liberty, my boy.' " Although he does not describe this as particularly galling to him, Lorrain's patriotism is vividly displayed throughout the memoir in remarks such as this: "The Cockneys take sovereign pleasure in putting strangers out of the way, and laying a stumbling-block in the way of the blind. Happy are the lost if they meet an American sailor, even if he is two sheets in the wind, and the third shivering, he will put you in the right road, if he is half-lost himself."[3] Likewise, Lorrain the patriot describes common English people as speaking "barbarous" English and being very superstitious.

Having plied the Atlantic during the years when the English and French were carrying on a deadly war, Lorrain can recall lively and perilous voyages when the seemingly placid ocean suddenly erupted with volleys from privateers or British men-of-war. After several years at sea, Lorrain sailed with a New England crew and captain, which gave him an opportunity to compare the mores of the North and South. "There is more familiarity between the officers and men on board our Northern ships than would be tolerated South," he notes. Surprisingly, he believes that Southern sailors were "citizens of the world, with few local attachments" whereas the "Yankee crew is often an association of neighbors, having abiding habitations on the land, and sympathies clinging around institutions on shore; and their voyages are more like speculative enterprises than an unconditional lifetime business." Lorrain adds that North-

---

2. Lorrain, *The Helm, the Sword, and the Cross*, p. 44.
3. Lorrain, *The Helm, the Sword, and the Cross*, pp. 64–66.

ern sailors "will talk about deacons and sextons, and never forget thanks-giving day, but distinguish it by large batches of sweetcake, and plenty of codfish."[4]

Returning home, Lorrain got swept up in the military excitement and joined a volunteer brigade organized in Petersburg at the outbreak of the War of 1812. Marching west to join General William Henry Harrison, their unit deliberately went through Charlottesville so that they could pay their respects to Thomas Jefferson. The recently retired president appeared to him as a "very homely old man, dressed in plain Virginia cloth, his head uncovered, and his venerable locks flowing in the wind."

Hull's ignominious capitulation at Detroit, which Trimble discusses, is detailed in Lorrain's memoirs as well. Lorrain was with Harrison when the general landed on the shores of Canada. Harrison forbade the soldiers to touch or destroy Canadian property, he remembers, and his battalion of volunteers, after suffering the privations of the wilderness for twelve months, marched under peach trees bending with fruit. "As these would rattle against our helmets, we endured temptations; but a proud national glory swelled our bosoms, under the magnificence of the scene."[5] The story hardly seems credible, but it at least reflects the intense national pride Lorrain felt when he wrote his autobiography in the years just prior to the Civil War.

After the war and a momentous religious conversion which began with the preaching of the charismatic Methodist preacher Lorenzo Dow, Lorrain became a devout Christian. He was appointed to the land office in New Orleans, where he also taught school. A younger brother in New Orleans was killed in a duel, which caused Lorrain to describe the dueling fever in the South. During the 1820s and 1830s, he wrote frequently for newspapers and journals, including the *Ladies' Repository,* which he thought more men should have supported. After becoming an itinerant Methodist clergyman, Lorrain spent the rest of his life riding circuits in Virginia, Kentucky, and Ohio.

---

4. Lorrain, *The Helm, the Sword, and the Cross,* p. 89.
5. Lorrain, *The Helm, the Sword, and the Cross,* pp. 101, 96.

⁓ & ⁓

ONE can not lightly pass over the period of childhood in reviewing his life. An inconsiderable impediment near the fountain may give direction to the sweeping river. Early childhood! Some say this is the happiest part of human life. This, we think, is questionable. There are some things vastly pleasant to our memory in overhauling the events and circumstances of childhood—the tender care of our parents, the social circle of the family, the absence of anxious care in regard to our provision and defense, and a thousand nameless comforts with that state inseparable—that will be sacredly imbedded in our memory forever. But we easily dismiss from our minds the trials and afflictions, mental, spiritual, and physical, that followed us almost from the cradle; the disappointed hopes, and rudely-crushed toys, which gave us keener anguish at the time than the loss of a ship would give a merchant. We have forgotten the impatience of wholesome restraint, the incessant longing for manhood and liberty, which appeared to be ages distant—and, not the least, the drudgery of the schools, and study, of which we could not comprehend the end—"creeping like snails unwillingly to school." Still the state of childhood is interesting. The Lord has made it so. . . .

My father moved his family from Maryland while I was an infant, and settled in Petersburg, in Virginia. I loved Petersburg in childhood—I love it still. Sweet in my memory are my morning walks on the banks of the meandering Appomattox. I loved to sit on the rocky cliffs, where honeysuckles creep and woodbines flaunt, listening to the murmurings of the falls—music that might lull to sleep, even the head that wears a crown. I have traveled far and near, on field and flood, but never saw any population so beautiful—male and female—as the natives of that town, as then impressed on my heart. About the breaking out of the Southern rebellion I read in a paper, that a professed minister of God undertook to rail against the Union in a congregation in that town, when some of the elders retired; this made him more furious, when the congregation began to move, and as some passed out, they paused on the threshold, and looking indignantly back, said, "Treason! treason!" I laid the paper down and wept, and thought, "O, Petersburg! patriotic Petersburg, surely it will take an iron cable to drag thee from the Union!" My father was among the first merchants who opened stores—wholesale and retail—in that town, and many of the country merchants of North

Carolina were his customers; his business was fair and flourishing, and we were a happy family. We learned by tradition that Petersburg had been a wicked place, but was getting better.

In my remembrance it had several special attractions. 1. The Spring and Fall races. All respectable ladies, who were not religious, attended in their chariots, often making a procession about a mile in length; and they engaged in all the jockey-talk and excitement of the turf—betting on the black gelding or Wilkin's gray. 2. Periodical balls through the Winter were occasions of great social glee, and considered indispensable to health, although some of the old doctors occasionally whispered that they cost annually two or three human sacrifices. 3. Gander-pulling and cock-fighting were precious amusements of the gentlemen—between meals. 4. Feasting on maple biscuit and wine at funerals. This was a custom that could not be dispensed with without drawing down heavy reflections on the mourners.

The Methodist preacher came along, and he doubtless felt as Paul did when he first came to Athens. He began with the funerals. After winding up their feelings to extreme tension, he would turn his eyes to the sideboard, and begin to descant on the decanter and cake, showing how inappropriate they were to the house of mourning, and he would beg them, if they saw fit to honor him with the solemn duty of preaching over their friends, that they would abandon the revolting practice. This sore was soon healed. He was a doctor of the healing, and not of the dissecting practice.

As for the ball, the race, and other iniquitous frolics, the Methodist preacher, in succession, considered them as anvils on which the drum-sticks ecclesiastical might play perpetually. The attendance on the races declined annually, till a decent woman could not be found on the ground. The ladies anchored their attractions at home, and their lords were kept to their moorings, and they found it profitable for this life at least. The balls became few and far between, and the gander-pulling sunk into oblivion with a hiss; as for the cock-fighting, it fell into the hands of the negroes. It was not unusual to see a darkey, on Sabbath morn, passing with hasty strides through the streets, with something wrapped up in a striped cotton handkerchief, under his arm. On drawing nigh might be seen two little bright eyes, under a splendid comb, sticking out at one end, and shining spurs at the other; and Sambo's face would be illuminated with an arch smile, as much as to say, "You all know it is a rooster, and white folks may come if they will behave." This reformation was accorded to evangelical preaching in the pulpit, and right-living in the Church, imperceptibly and gradually affecting public opinion. . . .

It is necessary to this work that its readers should see my early surroundings. My home was in the heart of slavery; and this, I suppose, has given me a tender feeling for the African race; and this feeling abides with those in the free States who have been raised in the South. The African knows this, and when he comes among us to raise money to buy a wife or child, he knows where to go. This can not be otherwise. Parents in the South can not lay their fences so high as to separate entirely the children of the two classes. We went chincapin hunting together, fishing together, in some branch which was dry for one-half of the year, and if we got three or four nibbles, we would fish till sundown. When we got tired at noon, we would lie down on the bank, packed away like a layer of herrings. It is no wonder we caught their brogue. . . . But now let me say, that there was very little said about the institution, especially before children; yet, whether it was by intuition, or inspiration, or what not, I was, while a white-haired boy, bitterly opposed to slavery. In the large towns, their condition is—comparatively—comfortable. The slaves wear, in their turn, the clothes of their owners, and sometimes scarcely soiled. This is often economical, and the masters escape the charge of their garments being motheaten. In a common family, there could be little saved by putting servants under a different regimen; so they eat the same food, tastefully culled, of course, but with this advantage—"The nearer the bone, the sweeter the meat." Dainties are excepted. In some kitchens they occasionally live better than they do in the great house, because they sometimes add a 'possum, or fresh fish, or other rarities, that are overlooked by white folks. We used sometimes to have high life below stairs. It was there that I first realized how a drunkard felt, by getting quite boosy on egg-nog, scalding hot. Still, as Sterne says, "Disguise thyself as thou wilt, O slavery, still thou art a bitter draught!" Even in our town, we had occasional exhibitions of its ugliness. While a little boy, in passing by a lot that was highly fenced with boards, I heard an unusual groaning within. My curiosity led me to hunt a hole, that I might see what was going on within. I saw a negro hoisted up, so that his feet swung clear of the ground, by a rope fastened to his wrists, and passing over a kind of gallows. This was held by a fellow-servant, while a white man was peeling his back with a cowhide. The skin would sometimes be stripped off like ribbons. The tyrant would threaten to lay on in proportion to the noise he made, and continued the cruel chastisement till entirely exhausted. He then took down his victim, and by the forced assistance of the other slave, stretched him on the tail of a dray, with his face down, and brought from the kitchen a tin-cup of melted tallow and poured it on his wounds. This seemed to be the most excruciating part of the whole process. My young bosom was filled with indignation and wrath, supreme. In after years, while reading about Moses, when he saw an Egyptian smiting an Israelite, and where it is said, "And he looked this way and that way, and when he saw that there was no man, he slew the Egyptian, and hid him in the sand," I thought I understood how Moses felt. When I saw this act of cruelty, I felt if I could secretly dispose of that scoundrel without exposing myself to the law, I would be doing God an acceptable service.

But I might mention a case that came much nearer home than this. My father, for about fifteen or twenty years, hired almost a whole family of slaves. They were of sterling integrity, and some of them religious. Aunt Milly, the matron of this colored family, was a dark mulatto, and a very pious Baptist. She had two sons besides her children in our family, who were blacksmiths. One of them came in one day apparently in great anguish, and told his mother that his wife's master had sold her and the children to a Georgia negro-buyer, and that they would pass in the afternoon by our big gate, which was on the Carolina road. When I heard this I became deeply moved, and resolved in my mind to be there. When I arrived, I found Aunt Milly and her son already there. They looked with painful suspense for some time down the road. Presently the sorrowful band was seen advancing with unwilling tread. Several men were handcuffed—two and two. The women and children were not bound. As they came up, Will and his wife rushed into the last sad embrace. The little children grasped his pantaloons. The grandmother's eyes flashed like diamonds, from earth to heaven, from heaven to earth. Only two or three ox drops ran down her cheeks—it was agony beyond tears. I alone was allowed this luxury, and I almost doubled myself down to the earth, and wept as if my little heart would burst. Many of our white acquaintances who knew the worth and sensibility of that colored family, sympathized with them. The negro-trader checked his horse awhile, and seemed to respect this scene of hopeless sorrow, but after a while drove them on. The wife and children cast many a longing look behind. The husband stood like a marble monument of woe, till a turn in the road separated husband and wife, parent and children forever. Many of our citizens used to feel deeply on such occasions, but they seemed to consider them as necessary outrages connected with an institution that appeared to be as firmly settled as the pillars of heaven.

We never felt a sense of comfortable security while living in that beautiful town. Sometimes reports of intended insurrections would send a thrill of fear through every family. One time a boy came up where we were playing near the school, with dismayed visage, and said, "Boys, as I was coming to school, a negro looked at me and said, 'Ah, my lad, you look white and rosy now, but in a few days your face will be as black as my hand.' " Then we gathered up our playthings, and entering into serious squads, began to rehearse all the latest symptoms of an outbreak that we could drum up in our memory. When the school broke the intelligence was carried to every home. . . .

My father, having dissolved partnership with a firm in Philadelphia, was advised by some of his best friends to form a connection with two French gentlemen, who were in a large grocery business. These gentlemen were brothers, and were as distinct in their characters as any two men could be. Alexander, the elder, was very plain, and of an unusually-serious cast. He had emigrated with his father to the western wilds; and one morning, when he was seated at the breakfast-table, an Indian chief stepped behind his father, and drove a tomahawk into his skull. Alexander fled, and with much difficulty made his escape; but it was said he never smiled again. Francis had been brought up in the fashions and amusements of France. He was light and frivolous, a dandy who ran into the most ridiculous extreme of fashion. The business of the house was very promising. They sent a valuable cargo to France, and were looking for a rich return of merchandise. Francis was sent out as supercargo, and was charged to insure the goods. This he did not do—giving, afterward, the simple apology, that, as he was coming back in the ship, he thought if the ship was lost he would be lost, and all would go together. This, however, was not the case. The ship Neptune, returning, as it was said, with the richest cargo which had left that season, sprung a bad leak. With all hands employed at the pumps it still gained on them. When all hope had nearly fled, a sail hove in sight, but cruelly passed, and left her with all her signals of distress flying. Now they sank down in despair; the Protestants broke out in prayer, the Roman Catholic ladies began to count their beads, kiss their crosses, and to call on the blessed Mary. There were many passengers. Just then another sail appeared; hope revived; the pumps were again manned. Those who came to the rescue had barely time to transfer the crew and passengers, without baggage, when the old Neptune went down. I well remember the announcement of this misfortune to my mother. Late one afternoon, Aunt Milly, whom we have already introduced as the matron of the kitchen, stood in the door, with shawl and bonnet on, and said:

"Mistiss, I thought I would step in and ask you if you had heard any thing about this bad news."

"What bad news, Milly? O, do tell me! speak quick! Is my husband dead?"

"O no, mistiss!"

"What then—is my son Edwin?"

He was from home.

"O no, mistiss, it is nothing like that. I thought I would tell you how, as I was coming up from town, I met Mr. Tucker's boy, and he asked me if I had heard of master's bad luck—"

"O, Milly, is he dangerously hurt?"

"No, ma'am. But he said the ship that was fetching all his goods across the sea is gone to the bottom—and it's printed in the papers."

"O, Milly! is that all—is that all? O, I am so relieved! I have my husband and my children yet, thank God! Is that all?"

"Indeed, ma'am, I thought that was enough; the ship and all dem fine goods gone to de bottom!"

In the evening my father approached the house with slow and measured steps. My mother was watching at the door, and with a smiling face said, "Come on; I have heard all. We are all here. We have resources within ourselves, and God will help us." And she so cheered him up, that he could give a deliberate account of the shipwreck, and all that had transpired. But this was only the beginning of the calamity. The brothers agreed to turn over to him the stock on hand, and an interest which they could command in Norfolk, to the amount of several thousand dollars, if he would take upon him the outstanding credits and debts. He felt he could at least weather the point on such terms. The elder brother left at once the country where he had drank so deeply of sorrow. Francis went down to Norfolk to carry out the contract, but was heard of no more. My father buffeted the adverse tide awhile, but finally broke—honorably broke—giving up all, without mental or pecuniary reservation. Many who were his friends in prosperity stood by the family to the last. My oldest brother completed his study of the law, under Mr. Wirt; and my decision was the sea, with an intention to become a sea-captain. This was common in that section of the country. There were few families who had not a representative on the seas. I laid by all other studies, and betook myself to the acquisition of navigation. I soon possessed a good understanding of it theoretically. The gentleman under whom I agreed to sail did not require indentures, but said he did not wish to retain me a moment after I might become dissatisfied. It was my intention not to make use of names in this work, unless absolutely necessary. I think it is wrong in an autobiography. Although many with whom my early history is connected are no more, yet they may have relations and connections still living, and they might not wish to see their names bandied about. Capt. C., or rather ex-Capt. C. was my temporary master. He had made a fortune on the seas, and now owned the beautiful ship "Sheffield.". . .

Having rigged myself off, with jacket and trowsers, I proceeded down to the ship, about twelve miles distant, accompanied by a servant who was to bring the horses back. Arriving at the brink of a high hill overlooking the shipping, I suddenly stopped in amazement. I had never seen such a wide-spread sheet of water as the James River presented at that point. It was a sprinkling and windy day, and the water was considerably ruffled. Here I felt my faith giving way; but then I thought, if you falter at this, what will you do in the swellings of the ocean? Ambition came to my aid, and I went on board. The men were glad that a boy had dropped among them, because he would do many small jobs that they were glad to get rid of; so I became a great favorite.

After we had passed the Capes, I can not describe with what extreme anxiety I watched the dim continent, till the last streak of land disappeared. The sheep and pigs that had been placed under my province were stowed away in the long-boat, amidships, with the pinnace capsized over them for a shelter, and all strongly lashed. I saw the sheep putting out their heads between the boats, and ranging with their eyes the horizon, as though to catch the sight of one more verdant hill, or flowery valley; and then they would bleat most piteously. My whole mind was at once in partnership and sympathy with their sorrow, and I said within myself, "What a strange and unnatural perversion of things!". . .

The captain seemed much pleased when he found I had studied navigation; and as he had a spare quadrant on board, he made me take the sun every day and keep a journal. I would sometimes be greatly annoyed by an antic sailor, who would stand partly concealed by the foremast so that the officers could not see him, while he could be seen by myself; and he would raise the jaw-bone of a hog to his eye, and twist himself about with the motions of the ship, and carry on his mockery, while I would be operating. The sailors did not seem to like it so well when they found I was getting qualified for the cabin. One, who was generally called growler, said, "I expect he will be a bully captain some of these days, and kick and cuff the poor sailors about." And then, instead of looking on me and weeping, as the prophet did before Hazael, he talked himself into a fury, grit his teeth, and clinched his fist, and cursed and swore what he would do with me if he ever fell under my jurisdiction. And so he battled against his man of straw. But I laughed and said, "No, Bill, you are wrong; I am going to be a very good captain to the sailors; I mean to give them their allowance of grog every day, besides splicing the main brace after every storm, and watch and watch, blow high or blow low." And thus I would talk till I got him into a good humor again. . . .

When we made the white cliffs of Old England I was entranced. It was on a clear, sunshining morning; but every thing had to me a diminutive appearance. The farms seemed to be gardens with large beds, the shrub-fences—walks. Seeing a house near the shore, it appeared of the size of our dog-house on board. Here I first learned the relation of sight to distance. I said to an old sailor, "What are they doing with so many dog-houses ashore? Look at that little white dog-house on the beach!"

"Dog-house, indeed! I am acquainted with this part of the coast. That is one of the largest taverns on this part of England. How far do you think you are from land?"

"About a mile or a mile and a half."

"You barber's clerk, you! we are about eight miles off."

As soon as I understood the distance every thing appeared right. We are not going to afflict our readers with a regular log-book, but intend to take a running and general view of our sea-life. We made three voyages to London, and became better acquainted with the points and reaches of the Thames than with those of our own James River.

There is no small perplexity and fun in ascending the last five miles. Here the comers and goers became so thick often, that we had to drift up by the force of the tide, with very little sail, and sometimes get locked in with a raft of vessels of all sizes and nations. In that day American ships were highly ornamented and neat in their rigging. Our ship had a handsome figure-head, and a group of images as large as life reclining around her stern. There was a class of vessels called colliers, commanded by rough North-of-England men, with crews more uncouth and outlandish than themselves. It was one of their peculiar delights to smash a Yankee. They would rush into an American vessel, crying out in their rude brogue, "Take care of your gingerbread works there!" and away would fly an arm or leg from our stern-figures. Onward we would move amid thumping sides and snapping spars. The crews would sometimes get exasperated, and billets of wood and belaying pins would fly through the air. In the general row, if a negro should put his head up a scuttle, a general cry would rise, "Who dat? who dat?" This would be followed by a universal laugh, and the poor darkey would have to dodge back. We labored hard, but without success, to learn the origin of this. One thing is certain, it was not because they had any prejudice against Africans. Their currency in England is undisputed. It is no uncommon thing, in the atmosphere of shipping, to see fair ladies locked arm with the Africans, going to church, and their *beaux* carrying their Morocco prayer-books. Some of our officers got acquainted with a rich tobacconist. When the ship returned to London the young men of the family invited the mates to come and take tea with them, observing that their sister had got married, during their absence, to a Virginia gentleman. When the officers arrived they were invited into a splendid parlor, and introduced to the brother-in-law—a tall, double-jointed negro.

Sometimes our white men would get into a fight, on shore, with some of the colored cooks and stewards. Then the Cockneys would crowd around—"Give it to him, my African! Let him have it! You are not in America now. You are in the land of freedom—the land of liberty, my boy; plank it into him!". . .

If any one gets lost in London, let him ask the first genteel-looking person the way. He will stop, and looking very wise, will say, "Find it out by your learning, as I did." Then turn next to a plain working-man, whose tanned skin appears impervious to mischief, and ask him the direction to London bridge; he will say, "With pleasure sir. Take that street, and go one mile, you will come to an open square, turn to the right and that will lead you *right down to the bridge.*" This will put you two miles more out of the way. The Cockneys take sovereign pleasure in putting strangers out of the way, and laying a stumbling-block in the way of the blind. Happy are the lost if they meet an American sailor, even if he is two sheets in the wind, and the third shivering, he will put you in the right road, if he is half-lost himself. The Londoners speak barbarous English. Well may their literati hail with transports Webster's unabridged. Indeed, their orators ought to finish their English studies in Philadelphia.

They—the common people—are, moreover, very superstitious—full of fearful traditions, which they hold next to Scripture. We might give one example: "The time is coming when a blind man shall hold the horses of three kings at the foot of London bridge, while England shall be lost and won three times in one day." Every one is disappointed in London at first sight. Its principal prestige is its overgrown qualities. The houses are generally made of brick, which are the color of ours before they are burned. This dingy hue, noways improved by smoke and the almost continual moisture of the atmosphere, has any thing but a pleasant appearance. The city is disgusting in comparison with New York, Baltimore, or Boston. . . .

There was a beer-house, not far from the Tower, called the "Beehive," which had been so long patronized by the Yankees, that the American flag waved over it perpetually. At that time there was an unusual number of Portuguese in port, and they came suddenly and unexpectedly upon the Americans, drove them out, and pulled down the flag. The next week the Americans mustered a considerable army, and undertook to dislodge the enemy. The battle was severe. In the midst of the fray, the Irish got to hear of it in their quarters, and they came pouring down like a hurricane. Some one hailed the leader, and asked him where he was rushing:

"There's a fight on hand, me darling! and we mean to have a finger in the pie."

"Which side will you take?"

"American, sure; for they say there is a little Ireland in America."

And they pitched in, knocking down, and dragging out. The fight became so serious that they had to order troops from the Tower to quell it; and several loads of the wounded were carried to the hospital.

The Bee-hive, however, was retaken, and the American flag, for aught we know, may be flying there to the present day. . . .

One of the most interesting voyages I ever made was up the North Sea. As it was in the days of the "Rambouillet decree," our ship joined a fleet of merchantmen of about seventy sail, under the convoy of a large English sloop-of-war, and a government vessel of inferior metal. When the weather is fine, with a tolerable breeze and smooth sea, there can be no scene more pleasant than a fleet under convoy. It always brings to the mind the idea of a hen with her numerous brood. The fleet was made up of vessels of different nations, order, and speed. Ships, brigs, schooners, sloops, and galliots composed the motley mixture. So various were they in respect to speed especially, that, while some were leisurely careering along under close-reefed top-sails, and sometimes one of them aback, others were groaning under a crowd of sail, top-gallant sails, studding sails, and all the canvas that they could show. Sometimes they seemed to lie almost gunwales under, and yet appeared to be stationary on the waves. Ours was a first-rate Virginia merchantman, and her speed had tried many a British frigate in the time of the Chesapeake commotion. Consequently, we walked among them at our pleasure; and, backing and filing through the fleet, we enjoyed the luxury of conversing freely with persons from almost every part of the world. This was vastly pleasant. We had heretofore made long and lonesome voyages across the Atlantic, and we enjoyed but seldom the felicity of speaking a ship at sea. Under such circumstances, the cheering cry of "Sail ho! sail ho!" springs a flash of joy in every bosom, from the captain to the cabin-boy. The strange sail appears at first like a dark speck in the distant horizon. Presently we see her hovering like a dark bird in our wake. We look again, and she is gone. We rush on to our respective destinies; but with renewed impressions of the shortness of the voyage of life, and the rapid flight of time. The Bible student almost involuntarily exclaims, with Job, *"They pass away like the fast-sailing ships."* But on the North Sea we found ourselves in the midst of a floating, fugitive city, and the solitude of ocean seemed to be driven away. One night we were suddenly alarmed by a torrent of blue flame, pouring over the stern of a distant bark. This was the signal of an enemy close aboard. It was at this particular time that the analogy between the fleet and a brood of chickens struck most forcibly. Immediately the man-of-war made signal lights for us to consolidate. The vessels in advance hove to, or shortened sail; while those which were laboring astern, and had been straining a perpetual race from the beginning, crowded more. We soon huddled together like frightened chickens, while the sloop-of-war, wheeling round as an angry hen would do to face the hawk, left us in charge of her consort, and crowded all sail in chase of the privateer. . . .

We have been sometimes asked if we were ever shipwrecked. We never were, but we have encountered many dangerous and stripping storms. Once on the midway ocean we encountered a gale that continued for several days with increasing violence. It came on gradually, so that we could shorten sail as it increased. This we did continually, till we were under bare poles, hoping that this would suffice. But still the gale increased, so that we had to send down our top-sail yards, and even house the topmasts. But it raged on till we had to lower down our lower yards, and then it became a perfect hurricane. The seas broke over our decks, sweeping fore and aft, and we were apprehensive we would have to cut away our lower masts. The heavy thumps of conflicting surges so opened her seams as to cause profuse leaking, and we were under constant apprehension of the ship swamping under us. For several days we had no regular meals, and when we did eat it was raw provision; for it was impossible to cook. . . .

After we had been out more than a month, the discontent of the crew was increased by their tobacco falling short. Those of liberal build, who had not been accustomed to chew their morsel alone, first began to feel the pressure. The foreign sailors, whose standing-rule was to take care of No. 1, held out longer, and speculated some on the necessities of their shipmates; but as the prospect became more dreary, they closed up their stocks against love or money. When we were called to dinner, some would hide their quids in the most secret places they could find; but one peculiar quality of starvation is the sharpening of sight, and others would find these "old soldiers," as they called them, and transfer them to a warmer berth. At last all was gone, and the crew, generally, substituted oakum, or rope-yarn, for the precious weed.

But after a while our provisions began to fail, and short allowance was proclaimed. Our water was not so much reduced; but as it was uncertain how long we might be detained, we were allowed a quart per day. This we thought would do; but we had not taken into consideration that a day was twenty-four hours, and that we would require as much drink in our long watches on deck at night as in the day-time. Well, as for our water, we would generally drink it all off before sunset, and then be tormented with a burning thirst till the next day at noon, when our rations would be distributed.

Our meat allowance was still more spare. At dinner-time the meat was taken into the forecastle. Some just salt was appointed to cut it up into twelve equal pieces. This was spread out on a board. One of the apprentices was sent upon deck, the lid of the scuttle was drawn over, and the carver putting his knife on a piece, would say, "Who shall have this?" the boy above would answer, "Long Jack."

"And who shall have this?"

"Tom—hog-face Tom."

And so they would go on to the end of the mess; and happy was he who got the fattest gob; for the share of one man, for twenty-four hours, was not larger than his thumb.

After being out three months from the Land's End of England, we made the coast of America off Savannah. As soon as the rope was thrown to the pilot-boat, the crew, as with the voice of one man, said, "Have you any tobacco?" "Plenty—plenty," said the pilot, and he soon handed up about a pound of nigger-heads, as they were called in those days. Then the pump was put into the water-cask, the kid well filled, the bread-bag replenished, and the songs and laughter of merry-hearted men were heard in the fore peak. So, we may imagine, felt the poor prodigal, after he had abandoned the hog-trough, and found himself seated with his parents and sisters around the fatted calf, while the old homestead shook with music and gladness. And happier—yea, almost infinitely—feels the poor sinner, when, redeemed from the husks and vanities of the world, he first tastes the celestial riches of redeeming grace and dying love.

Thank God, there is no need of short allowance in the old Ship of Zion; for she is laden with the bread and water of life, and the great Captain says, "Eat, O my friends, and drink abundantly, O my beloved! In my presence is fullness of joy, and at my right hand there are pleasures forever more.". . .

Having spent several years in acquiring a knowledge of seamanship, under promising circumstances I went out second mate of a brig owned in Boston. The captain and the crew, with the exception of myself, were all New England men. I soon saw a great difference between them and Southern sailors. The sailors employed in the South are generally citizens of the world, with few local attachments—their home, if they have any, upon the sea. The Yankee crew is often an association of neighbors, having abiding habitations on the land, and sympathies clinging around institutions on shore; and their voyages are more like speculative enterprises than an unconditional lifetime business. They will talk about deacons and sextons, and never forget thanks-giving day, but distinguish it by large batches of sweetcake, and plenty of codfish. Each man must have a suit of long clothes to go ashore in. The Southern sailor glories in his sea-rigging. There is more familiarity between the officers and men on board our Northern ships than would be tolerated South. . . .

When we returned, we found that our Government had passed the non-intercourse law, interdicting commerce with both England and France. Still some of our merchantmen would clear out, and manage by spurious papers to evade the law. One of our merchants sent for me, and proposed my taking the command of one of his vessels. I told him plainly that I would undertake nothing that involved perjury, let consequences be what they might. Immediately the war followed. There I was like a fish out of water. I can not convey to the reader, unless he has experienced it, the sickening ennui that takes possession of the sailor after he has been a few weeks on shore. It is this which principally continues the supply and unbroken succession. After dreadful disasters at sea, it is amusing to hear the unalterable resolves of the forecastle. One will say, "Bloody end to me, if I am ever caught on sea again, if ever I put my foot on land. Why should I be knocked about all my days, living a dog's life, and no thanks for it? Why, look at the farmer! if it storms, he can get under shelter with his wife and cubs, and can look out of his cabin and laugh at old Boreas—'blustering railer!' What a happy life!"

"Farmer!" says another, "he's a gentleman, I can tell you; and it's because we are his lackeys to carry his produce at the expense of life and limb. I would rather be his servant, and carry guts to a bear, than to live this dog-life."

And thus they will growl on, and resolve and re-resolve—the whole crew, going home—to dip their feet in salt water no more. But, after they have been ashore four weeks, the prettiest farm in the country could not hold them, as a general thing. "Come, boys—who's for blue water?"

I felt this longing for the sea again. Life seemed stripped of all its charms. I could not, just then, get a place in the navy that could meet my aspirations, or do justice to the feelings of my family connections. Then came in the well-timed temptation, to seek a prize-master's berth in a privateer. I saw plainly—with my religious education it could not be otherwise—that it was, morally speaking, a dirty business; and I shall ever adore a merciful Providence that so strangely and mercifully opened up for me a way of escape. While waiting in a seaport, expecting a very successful privateer to come in from her cruise, with the prospect of getting a prize-master's office, I received a letter from home, stating that all my young friends were forming a volunteer company, and were urgent for me to join them. This touched a nobler chord in my heart; so I stuck a cockade in my hat, and returned home.

Have not Christian nations, at least, arrived at that point of moral science and international honesty, that should induce them to abandon the practice of authorizing the shameful enterprise of privateering during war—a mode of reprisal that brings neither profit nor glory to any government; but affliction, and ofttimes ruin, to thousands of private citizens, who have no more share in the injuries perpetrated by their nation than the birds that fly over their heads.

Privateering is robbery.[1] No government can issue any kind of letters or parchments that can divest it of this character in the view of high Heaven.

When a privateer takes a prize, the captives, generally, are exposed to as much insult and outrage as is generally inflicted by a pirate; with the lone exception of being made to walk the plank—a thing which no civilized people would tolerate.

The victors generally strip their prisoners of their personal baggage, their change, their watches, their clothes, down to their shirts and pantaloons, and even if these strike their fancy, they will take them in exchange for some of their cast-off duds, if that may be called *"exchange,"* where one party is bound to submission without any alternative.

It may be said, what can you expect of such unprincipled buccaneers

---

1. Privateering refers to the governmental practice in time of war of issuing letters of marque to ship captains that authorized them to prey on enemy shipping.

as commonly man a privateer? But the whole responsibility does not rest with them. With all their natural and acquired taste for plunder and carnage, they would be comparatively harmless, but for the impulse of those who have fitted them out, and who claim the heft of the plunder. And who are they? Most frequently merchants, who embrace this opportunity of meanly robbing on the high seas, those with whom they formerly stood in friendly and commercial relations, with whom they have for a series of years carried on an honest and lucrative trade. They make no other apologies for their infamous robberies than that the Government has legalized them, and then they laugh heartily at the fogy fanatics who mumble about a higher law.

While privateering inflicts much suffering on the unoffending citizens of the enemy, it has a very disastrous reaction on the nation that institutes and supports it.

It lessens the dignity of a government. What civilized nation in this day would tolerate the practice of its army prosecuting the indiscriminate plunder of the citizens of a country through which they might be marching in triumph? When General Harrison landed on the shores of Canada, he issued general orders forbidding his soldiers to touch or destroy the property of the inhabitants.[2] The battalion of volunteers to which we belonged, although they had been nearly twelve months in a wilderness, under great privations, marched every now and then under trees bending down with the most delicious peaches. As these would rattle against our helmets, we endured temptation; but a proud national glory swelled our bosoms, under the magnificence of the scene. But what right have we to plunder on the seas, more than on the land?

Patriotism is the most diminutive motive lurking in the bosom of a privateersman. He fights for himself, and not for his country. Indeed, he chooses not to fight at all, provided that unarmed and defenseless game can be found; and it is only when by fog or mishap he falls in with an armed enemy, that he is compelled to show his teeth, and *then* no longer than he can devise a way of escape. . . .

When the news of Hull's surrender reached the patriotic town of Petersburg, in Virginia, it overwhelmed the whole population with indignation and sorrow. Some of the most popular young men, with martial

2. Lorrain is here looking forward to the time when he became a soldier during the War of 1812.

music, and the American ensign, paraded the streets, and with impassioned appeals called on their youthful associates to march to the rescue. The scene that followed was soul-thrilling to the patriot. Promising young men sprung their counters, and fell into the ranks. Students of medicine and law shoved aside their volumes, sufficiently uninteresting before, but now made absolutely irksome by the ceaseless din of war, and rushed to the standard. The mechanic threw the uplifted hammer from his hand to swell the train. The placid farmer rode to town to behold the madness of the people, but took the epidemic, and fell in. And in a few days a company of one hundred and four, richly uniformed, offered themselves to the Government to serve twelve months under the banner of the brave Harrison. No married man was admitted into their ranks. There is no incident of merely a terrene nature that ever so swelled our bosom, as did our departure from that lovely town—the bright scene of all our juvenile joys.

At an early hour in the day the company marched to "Center Hill," which overlooked the town. There they were met by a procession of women; while two elect ladies, bearing a stand of colors, richly and tastefully ornamented, presented them to the company, with an appropriate address. Being now all ready, with our knapsacks on our backs, and all accoutered for the perilous campaign, we marched down through the town, to the plaintive tune of

"The girls we've left behind us."

The doors, windows, and side-walks were crowded with our friends, our parents, and our weeping sisters. . . .

We took up our line of march and pressed on. The rumor of our coming, and the knowledge of our daily progress, enabled the people to spread their hospitalities in our way; so that, as far as eating was concerned, we frequently had nothing to do but march up to the rural board and partake of the smoking barbecue. Thus we "sat down to eat, and rose up to play." The report of our history, as it rolled on before, became highly fabulous. "Here comes the flower of Old Virginia! every man splendidly equipped at his own expense! They find their own baggage-wagons, bear their own expense, and there is n't a man among them with less than five hundred dollars—pin-money! Hurrah for Petersburg! Old Virginia never tire!" The people flattered us, and cheered us, till we became as proud as Lucifer. . . .

Monticello lay in our route, or rather we made it so lie, that we might have a sight of Virginia's favorite sage. We drew up, in military array, at the base of the hill on which the great house was erected. About half way down the hill stood a very homely old man, dressed in plain Virginia cloth, his head uncovered, and his venerable locks flowing in the wind. Some of our quizzical clique at once marked him as a fit subject of fun. "I wonder," said one, "what old codger that is, with his hair blowing nine ways for Easter Monday." "Why, of course," said another, "it is the overseer, and he seems to be scared out of a year's growth. I suspect he never saw gentlemen volunteers before." But how were we astonished when he advanced to our officers and introduced himself as THOMAS JEFFERSON! The officers were invited in to a collation, while we were marched off to the town, where more abundant provision had been made.

The most interesting prospect we had was when we first came in view of the Blue Ridge. It appeared, in the distance, like a dark wall stretched along the horizon, and piled to the heavens. We could not but admire the scene; yet our pleasure in beholding it was considerably abated when we contemplated the Herculean task of scaling it on the morrow. At that distance it presented a uniform surface, and seemed to forebode an almost perpendicular ascent. Since that period we have been better qualified to estimate the value of the old proverb, "Do not climb the mountain till you get to it." When we arrived at its base our road wound up a dark ravine. True, when we would look ahead, an insurmountable barrier seemed to stretch athwart our way; but when arrived at the apparent difficulty our tortuous pathway presented a gentle ascent, sometimes a comfortable level, and occasionally a little valley. And when we supposed our troubles were merely beginning, we received the happy announcement that we had surmounted all, and were wending our way down into the valley of the West. So it is in our journey through life. How often does the pilgrim fret about troubles ahead, which loom higher than the Blue Ridge. . . .

Except when passing places of notoriety, the company proceeded in an informal march. On such occasions all the blunders and improprieties of the preceding day and night were canvassed in catechetical form. One, for instance, would cry out with a loud voice, "Who tried to kiss that girl last night, and was shoved over into the wash-tub?" The whole line would respond, "T. C." "Who shot the old sow, and said it was a bear?" "Why, C. W." From such popular decisions there was no appeal.

But the report, "They are coming! they are coming!" climbed the mountains, and rolled on before us; and the hospitality of our countrymen was prodigious. Pressing on by the way of the Springs, down the Kanawha, and crossing the Ohio at Mt. Pleasant, we at last arrived at Chillicothe. Here the Legislature, which was then in session, gave us a splendid dinner, which was quickly followed by one from the citizens. Here the festivals of Virginia were thrown entirely in the shade; for we had not only the substantials, the bacon and cabbage of the Old Dominion, but fowls and turkeys, pies, tarts, custards, and sweetmeats, and floating-islands, and all the luxurious variety that the generous daughters of the Buckeye State could devise. Surely, we thought, there was nothing like the glory and honor of war. But, alas! it was the luscious finale of all our military glory! It is true, we had fed, and feasted, and frolicked for a few short weeks, and our march thus far had been like a triumphal procession. But O, how short our triumph! how vulgar our happiness!

> "We ate—drank—slept. What then?
> We ate, and drank, and slept again."

And this was the total amount of all our joy; and O, how dearly bought!

Our "Indian Summer" was now gone—our "paw-wah" days were over. As we left Chillicothe the bleak North-Wester began to blow, the rains descended, and the snows drove till the face of the whole country was clothed with the white, cold mantle of Winter. Through mud, and ice, and storms, and swollen streams we forced our way to Franklinton, which was then the head-quarters of the army. For the twelve succeeding months our tender volunteers, most of whom had not passed their twentieth year, and in their fathers' houses "had never waked but to a joyful morning," were exposed to labors, dangers, deprivations, afflictions, and deaths, of which their youthful minds had never conceived. . . .

The reaching of Hull's road was a grand desideratum. It is true we had never heard it spoken of, by those who had seen it, except in terms of unqualified execration; but still it was a *road,* and there was a kind of redeeming sound in the phrase that struck pleasantly on the drum of our ear. At last a triumphant peal in the van announced its appearance. We were not slow in rushing to the point of observation. But, O! the burst of indignation that followed! Sure enough the *Hull* was there, and an occasional patch of corduroy, and there had evidently been an opening made through the dense forest; but the road, if there ever had been any, had been mostly washed away before our time. . . .

We were writing something about Hull's road. It was certainly an extraordinary structure. Here and there we found a fragment of railroad, not of the modern, but Gothic order. But for the most of the way the rails had been routed in disorder by the swales, and scattered in every direction and various forms, angular and triangular, vertical and horizontal, visible and invisible, so that our ankles at times appeared to be extremely loth to acknowledge our footsteps. At other times we were scraped, and snagged, and railed. And then we would get our temper up and rail back again; and it was railing against railing. Then old General Hull came in for his share of blessings, and Winchester was not forgotten. But our only hope was in progress; and after a forced march, which could find no prototype—as we believed—in the American Revolution, we joined the army on the banks of the Portage. As we marched in every man was presented with a small glass of *"high wine."* When I drank my allowance, it produced an indescribable titillation, reaching to the ends of my toes and fingers, and appeared to spread a new world upon my vision. I have for many years been a strenuous advocate of the temperance cause; but whenever I hear a lecturer say that spirits have never done good under any circumstances, I deliberately enroll the dogma with clairvoyance, witchcraft, and similar delusions. It is true that strong drink has seldom done good. And of all the drams that moistened my lips, before I embraced religion, that alone can I remember with complacency, because it was Scripturally administered—*"to him who was ready to perish."*. . .

Our distressing march had closed; and for several subsequent weeks we tasted the labors and fatigues of a soldier's life. The troops were employed daily in digging trenches, felling trees, splitting logs, setting up picketing, raising block-houses, and doing every kind of work that was necessary to fortify our post, which embraced nine acres, and which, when finished, was called *"Fort Meigs."* This season of fatigue was replete with hardships, especially as it was in the depth of Winter, and accompanied with many privations. However, our bodies and minds were actively employed, which rendered our condition far preferable to that which immediately followed; for having finished the public and private work which was necessary to make our quarters tolerable, if not comfortable, a state of indolence and inactivity succeeded that was highly deleterious to the army. The Winter was unusually severe, even on the frontiers. One unfortunate sentinel froze at his post in less than two hours. We here had an opportunity of testing the mistaken policy of some fond parents, who think that they have accomplished a stroke of generalship, when they hide their children from the contagious disorders which occasionally visit their neighborhood. Numbers were swept off by the mumps, measles, hooping-cough, and other distempers, which came upon them at this unpropitious time and place, where there was little remedy and less medical skill, and where the soft hand of the warm-hearted mother, and the sleepless solicitude of the affectionate sister could not reach them. They died daily. The mournful air of "Roslin Castle" became the prevailing music of the day, while the sharp rifle-cracks of the platoon told how many were borne to their long home. A deadly homesickness overwhelmed our troops, and we believe a repentance of war was kindled in every bosom, from the highest to the lowest.

Some stirring incident would occasionally occur, as a kind of ennui-breaker, and rouse us from our torpor. At one time our spies brought intelligence that a party of about seven hundred Indians were diverting themselves with a war-dance on the ice, near the mouth of the river. In the dusk of the evening, General Harrison, at the head of fifteen hundred troops, started for the party, although not particularly invited. At a late hour in the night the blazing fires of the enemy appeared on the bank of the river. We were now wide awake. The day of battle, about which so much had been said, was now right before us. The detachment, thrown into a crescent, with the artillery in the center, cautiously approached. We found the fires burning bright with recent fuel; but the Indians had fled. This disappointment was probably owing to our imprudence in marching on the river. It is said that an Indian, by laying his ear flat on the ice, can discover the approach of a large force five miles distant. . . .

The next day, after laying out the dead as decently as circumstances would admit, we committed them to the earth. Then all the cannon around the fort were fired in slow and solemn succession, while the wild and unpeopled banks of the Maumee echoed and reëchoed the funeral honors to the distant lake.

Our army was now restrained from further operations by the War

Department, till the contemplated battle on the Lake. As Perry stood in need of men, there was another beat for volunteers in the fort. This matter was not without its temptations. But I rigidly declined. . . .

Soon after this the fort was broken up, or reduced to an inconsiderable post, and the army was concentrated at Camp Seneca. Here a poor deserter was brought in. He was a young man of agreeable appearance. The court-martial condemned him to be shot. The sad day arrived. The whole army was paraded and formed into a semi-square. The executive platoon was marched out. The unhappy culprit was blindfolded and seated with his back against a stump. A deadly silence pervaded the whole host. Harrison, in full uniform, towered in the midst. I was near enough to the condemned to observe that he trembled like an aspen, and writhed in all the bitterness of hopeless death. The thrilling word was given, "Make ready! take aim!" Here the General waved his hand to the officer, and announced to the trembling deserter that his sin was forgiven. He then solemnly raised his right hand to heaven, and pledged himself, before the Lord of hosts, and God of the armies of heaven, that the next deserter who should be condemned by a court-martial should die. Harrison was always beloved by his men, but never did he appear more majestic or more lovely than he did on that occasion. The poor young man seemed for a while petrified, and utterly incapable of comprehending the sum of benevolence; but when restored to his quarters he gave loose to the most unbounded joy. The next day he was employed on fatigue, in driving an ox cart. As he went, he leaped, and danced, and sung, and squealed, and seemed to be seeking, in every member, every faculty, every sense, for some vital testimony that he was alive, and not dead. . . .

After our discharge we were landed in Cleveland, and left at perfect liberty to follow our own course. The citizens of Cleveland and vicinity showed us no little kindness the few days we rested among them. We diverted ourselves much with one little circumstance; and that was, the citizens, from the lordly dome to the log-cabin, were mostly either generals, or colonels, or majors, or captains, or—squires, any how. We could scarce find a man without some kind of handle to his name. Here I stood on the shore of the lake, high and dry, and said in my heart, "One woe is passed! I shall no more travel that ugly, muddy road from Chillicothe to Columbus! I shall no more flounder over the snow-drifted plains of

Crawford! I shall no more shiver on the bleak banks of the Sandusky! I will hie me home to my own sunny Appomattox, and perhaps live and die on its verdant banks." But there is a book, a blessed but mystic book, which says, *"It is not in man to direct his steps."* Little did I then think that, in less than twelve years, it would be my allotted duty to stand in the city of Columbus, and preach to listening congregations the Gospel of the Son of God. . . .

Our company being broke up at Cleveland, we scattered in little social bands, in different routes, to seek our homes. I traveled in company with three of my most intimate friends. Our reception, or treatment, on the way, was various, according to the religious and political views of the people. One of our company became lame at the commencement of the journey, which retarded us considerably. In this dilemma we saw a very starch-looking Quaker overtaking us with a led horse. At this sight our comrade's limping evidently increased, and his pain became almost insupportable. We each made a very low and handsome bow to the stranger as he approached; but no response did we receive. We, however, surrounded him, and with the most moving eloquence that we could command, began to intercede for our lame friend. He very roughly refused us, declaring that he had nothing to do with war or any who were concerned in it. This exasperated our invalid, and he began to be abusive. I told him this was wrong. Perhaps the Quaker was conscientious in this matter. No doubt he thought he would be doing the devil service by giving him a seat in the vacant saddle. This was like throwing oil on the flame. "Conscientious, indeed! What, too conscientious to give a lift to a poor lame soldier, who has been fighting the battles of his country?" "Yes, it is even so, and you may just as well coil down, and take the world as it is, and not as it ought to be." O, give us forever that religion

"Which hates the sin, but still the sinner loves"—

which hates war, but is ever ready to mitigate the evils and heal the wounds which war has made!

We sometimes met with those who were politically opposed to the war. They also answered us roughly. At other times we had to do with real patriots—true blues. Among these were women, not a few, who, with moistened eyes, blessed us, as we passed, in the name of the Lord. . . .

At last we arrived at Richmond. Here, at the commencement of our career, every door was open to us. But now the returning soldier passed along unheeded, unrecognized. At last a poor man—I believe a pious man—invited us to his home, to take *pot-luck*. And this he did, not through ostentation or vainglory, but sheer benevolence. We found that girding on the armor was one thing, and taking it off was another; and we were well convinced that a young man of fruitful imagination might reap all the honor and glory of war in the domestic muster-field, without suffering any of its evils. Here our little platoon scattered again. I had twenty-five miles to go to reach home. This distance was measured leisurely, soberly, thoughtfully, with an intention to make my return after nightfall. In all my returns home, by land or water, I loved to come in under the cover of night. About dusk I crossed the Appomattox, on Pocahontas bridge—trod lightly over Sandy beach—entered Boling-brooke-street. It was now dark. I was closely scrutinized by every passenger, but had drawn my helmet down. I can not describe my feelings as the familiar scenes of my bright boyhood came up in quick succession. At last I stood, with almost breathless agitation, at my home's door. A few faint raps—raised the latch, and stood in the presence of my mother. She lifted her eyes, gave one shrill scream, and exclaimed, "O Alfred! Alfred! my son Alfred!". . .

One day my mother told me that she and some Methodist ladies were very anxious to go to a camp meeting that was to be held soon; but they could not go without some male person to assist them. I had never been to a camp meeting, and cheerfully consented to take the supervision of things. I intended not to remit my private religious exercises. On the day appointed, we started in the wagon, with our tent and baggage. When we drew nigh to the encampment, and made a sudden turn in the way, a large portion of the camp broke upon our vision. The tents were made mostly of the old bleached sails of sloops and schooners, and sheets and coverlets, and contrasted beautifully with the dark-green pine forest in which they were pitched. When this scene suddenly broke upon us, this idea flashed upon my mind, "How goodly are thy tents, O Jacob! and thy tabernacles, O Israel! Let me die the death of the righteous, and let my last end be like his." This almost overwhelmed me. After we had established ourselves, I walked about the encampment, attended on the services, and did not forget my own religious arrangements.

One dark, rainy night, our young stationed preacher held a prayer meeting in a tent, and after exhorting invited those who were seeking religion to kneel at some chairs that were set out. I went with the rest. Straw was strewed over the floor, and although the tent did not leak much, yet the water, unperceived, had run under it, so that when we kneeled our knees plunged down in the straw and mud, and before midnight it became somewhat of an annoyance; but still I thought I gave myself up, altogether, to God, for time and eternity. Still the meeting broke without affording any comfort. The next day brought no relief. In the afternoon, while lying alone in our tent, bemoaning my state, with tears in my eyes, a beautiful girl, about twelve or thirteen, a daughter of one of our Methodist neighbors, came in, and scornfully turning up her nose, said, "Ar'n't you ashamed, seeking religion? If you do n't quit this, I will never have you in the world," and with indignation burning on her cheeks, she left. This was the first that I knew that such a thought had ever mingled with the whimseys of the little innocent. This was a personification of the gay world—the scorn and contempt that awaited me. Still I thought, if I can only have salvation, I can surely afford that loss.

The next morning, feeling cold and somewhat indisposed, I saw Charles, a mulatto that my father had raised, and who was now a hackman. He was much attached to me, for I had taught him to read. He beckoned me to his hack, and said in a confiding whisper, "I have brought a little spirit along with me, and I think a little dram might do you some good." Well, I truly believed with Charles that it would do me good, physically. I had been in the habit of meeting with other young men, when we would go to market for our mothers, in the dram-shop of a widow, where we would treat each other, and we did not apprehend any danger; but I had found out, before the camp meeting, that I had got so as to have no appetite for my breakfast till I had taken my mint sling; and I had abandoned the practice. It seemed to me that it would amount to a serious sin to take a dram in my present state. I refused, and opened my mind freely to Charles. It was not long before he got to see things in the same light, and became a pious Baptist minister, and finally a citizen of Liberia. I mention these small things to show to what mean shifts the enemy will resort, through his various agencies, to turn aside one who is learning to do right. I wandered about the camp, and was almost driven to infidelity. The argument in my mind was, the Lord had said, "Whosoever cometh unto me, I will in no wise cast out.". . .

I now lived a life of faith. My peace was like a river. I had full confidence in the Church, and esteemed all the brethren better than myself. I looked upon the female members as sisters in all purity; I can not express the celestial chastity with which I regarded them—so diverse from all I had experienced before. Here let me ask, has any soul ever walked in the light and power of their first love for forty or fifty years without wavering? I do not ask if it can be done. The Bible, to me, is clear on this point: "The path of the just is as the shining light, that shineth more and more unto the perfect day." This is God's provision, but who realizes it? Well may we say, "What troubles have we seen, what trials have we passed!" The preacher, having prepared to attend Conference, proposed for me to lead his class in the middle of the week. From this I shrunk back dismayed. But he urged it so vehemently that I got alarmed at my own obstinacy, and finally consented. As the day advanced, the cross loomed up heavier and heavier. I made it a matter of prayer, telling the Lord that he knew I was not sufficient for that work, and that I hoped no one would come. At the appointed time I attended, and found the sexton brushing the benches. We waited there a long time, and, although it was a beautiful day, not one member came. This filled me with gratitude; for I verily believed my prayer was heard—and I think so still. Many a colt has been spoiled by premature harnessing.

I had now to look around for something to do. I had been in a great measure weaned from the sea, and determined to abandon it. No business presented itself where I was. My oldest brother, who was a counselor at law, in New Orleans, invited me to come there; and I concluded to go. Brother Potts, who received me into the Church, told my mother he was sorry I had made that decision. He did not see how a young Christian could stand the seductions of New Orleans. He wished I could continue on the sea. He thought that the power of God, as displayed on the great deep, was calculated to cherish religious emotions in a soul already under the influence of Divine grace. His views influenced me considerably; so that, while on my way to Norfolk to embark for New Orleans, I became undecided and distressed. As soon as I arrived at the hotel, some of my young sea-friends crowded around, and one said in a loud voice, "Why, L., we have heard that you have been converted, and have joined the Methodists; is it so?" I answered in a dignified tone, but as loud, "What you have heard is certainly true."

"Well, that is curious, for a sailor to join the Methodists!"

This gave me an opportunity to "show cause;" and in a little while they began to slip away. The gentlemen around looked at me as a curiosity, smiling—some, as I thought, with scorn—some, with approbation. I was still undecided in my course. I attended the Methodist Church in the evening. The introductory hymn was,

> "God moves in a mysterious way,
>   His wonders to perform."

As they were singing,

> "Ye fearful souls, fresh courage take,
>   The clouds ye so much dread
> Are big with mercy, and shall break
>   In blessings on your head,"

light, joy, and comfort came down, and my pathway to New Orleans shone bright. An intelligent and genteel young man, who belonged to the same volunteer company that I did during the war, took passage with me. I soon made known to him my views and determinations; and although we sometimes disputed on doctrine, yet he always treated me with great respect and consideration; and, as we had the cabin to ourselves, we had an agreeable voyage. When we arrived at the city, and looked around, it seemed to be given up, to a great extent, to idolatry. The holy Sabbath was generally unheeded, or made a day of merriment; and, so far from being drawn into the vortex, my soul shrunk back from the gulf of immorality. I first got a place under my brother, who had been appointed naval-officer of the port. As he still attended to his law business, he made me his deputy in the revenue business, and the principal weight of that concern rested upon me. This at once brought me into business acquaintance with the merchants—French and English—of that city; and happily, as I thought, this was mostly the principal social connection of that people. . . .

I had been two or three months in Orleans, before I discovered a Methodist in the place. It was announced one Sunday that a Baptist missionary would preach in the afternoon. He seemed to be a plain, pious man, but only a slender preacher. After dismissal I spoke to him, and he invited me to take tea with him. The gentleman with whom he stopped earnestly backed the invitation, and it was accepted. In the course of the evening it appeared that this gentleman was also a Baptist. I was acquainted with him in business transactions, but did not know that he was a professor of religion. He informed me that he knew two very worthy Methodists in the city, and directed me where to find them. I lost no time in hunting them up. These were old brother Nabb and his wife. Brother Nabb and myself had often passed and repassed each other, with mutual suspicious glances, but neither had courage to challenge. He was a plain German, had been there fourteen years before me, and had been twice put in the calaboose for exhorting the negroes on the levee to turn from the wrath to come. By the means of this couple I found out another Methodist. Now we began to muster our forces. There were four Methodists, three or four Baptists, and a few Presbyterians. We agreed to establish a prayer meeting on one night in the week, and to labor to gather up any religious persons who might visit the city from time to time. This prayer meeting was very singular, wavering with the seasons and commerce. Sometimes the large room was nearly filled; at other times we were reduced to our original number. Presently we had an addition to the Methodists—brother Hyde, of New York, and Captain Pray, of Brooklyn, and their families. We now made a class, and appointed Captain Pray leader. And the brethren of other Churches attended; for, in the absence of all preachers, we were firmly united. . . .

As I was so favorably situated at New Orleans, both as it regarded my spiritual and temporal interests, it might be proper to say something about the circumstances that led to my removal. My oldest brother, the only one of us who was married, in returning from a visit to Virginia, brought a sister along with him as far as Lexington, in Kentucky, when finding the Ohio River so low that he was obliged to take to a skiff, he left her there. When he got home, it was determined that I should go up for her, hoping that before my arrival the river would be up. The steamboat on which I embarked could get no higher than the mouth of the Ohio, and I was under the necessity of walking up to Louisville, in order to take the stage for Lexington.

It was a very singular Fall. The woods in Kentucky, Virginia, and as far as we could hear from, were all on fire. Although Indian Summer, the sun was not seen for several weeks. In traveling through the forests, we would often have fire on both sides of the road, and sometimes we had to wait till a tree, nearly severed by fire, had fallen. At other times, after nice calculation, we would venture to run past, just in time to hear the crash behind. Sometimes we would get out of the fiery, stifling region, but be waked up in the night by the cry of "Turn out to fight the fire!" And here it would be coming like a mighty army, crackling, roaring, and spitting, as it were, tongues of fire, far ahead. In some parts it enveloped fences, barns, stacks, and even dwelling-houses. . . .

Toward the Spring of the year, as I was coming out of the meeting-house, brother Bascom took me aside, and asked me if I had left any brothers in New Orleans.

"Yes, three."

"Because," said he, "I saw, in a paper, to-day, that a gentleman of your name—I have forgotten his first name—fell lately in a duel."

This went like a dagger to my heart. I requested him to get fuller information, and, hunting up my sister, we passed on rapidly to our home—for it seemed to me that I would drop before we could reach it. As soon as we entered the door, I informed my sister of the awful tidings, and we were plunged into grief inexpressible. The extreme anguish that possessed us is, even in this day, a mystery to me. Brother Overstreet and his kind family bent over us with all the sympathy of close relations. Brother Bascom took a fraternal interest in our sufferings.

The tide of affliction was abundantly swelled by hearing that my youngest brother, John, had fallen, and that my oldest brother died immediately after, with a natural disease. The practice of dueling had kept me uneasy all the time I was in New Orleans. Public opinion there, in that day, was such that no man, unless he was a member of some Church, could refuse a challenge—or, if manifestly insulted, omit to give one—without ruining all his temporal prospects. On this account I often conversed with my brothers on this subject, and tried to inspire them with a proper abhorrence of the practice. But they contended that it was easy enough for me to talk, as every body knew my profession bound my hands. But hardly any official or political man there had escaped being called into the field. The case, as far as I could learn, was this: It was my oldest brother who first became involved in the affair. My youngest brother insisted on taking his place, as he had left his family in Virginia for a while; and he was, moreover, the principal stay of our widowed mother and her family. My oldest brother would not consent to this; but John so managed it as to get in between him and his antagonist, and fell. My brother Thomas was called out into the same field, at the same time, but the seconds brought about a reconciliation. This brother I had saved from a duel before I left New Orleans. . . .

Now our family in Orleans was broken up, and when these sad tidings reached my mother, they almost killed her. We concluded to return to old Virginia in the first place; and we could only do so on horseback. As we were about to start, I was fearful my board would nearly strap me, as they say in these times; but when I asked brother Overstreet for the bill, he pleasantly answered, "Not a cent. I never intended to charge you from the beginning." And he pressed me to move my mother's family out. When we thought of the love and kindness of this family, we departed in tears. When we arrived home, I concluded that, after all that had passed, I never could reconcile it to my feelings to live again in New Orleans. I sent my resignation to Washington, sold one of my horses, and departed on the other for the West, with an intention to seek a living in some place where I might move my mother's family, and live at less expense. In all subsequent years occasional doubts would arise in my mind of having done the best, by yielding so far to my feelings, as to abandon that place—Orleans. My temporal prospects were very fair; fields of usefulness were opening before me. I preached, visited the hospitals, carrying them the Holy Bible, besides distributing it to all the ends of the earth, prayed with those who were dying with the yellow fever, and I enjoyed a Savior's love; but now I see the hand of Providence in giving me a timely removal from the great evil that was coming—before my hands were stained with the institution, or my tongue steeped in rebellion toward God and man.